THE IRISH IN
WORLD METHODISM
1760–1900

Norman W. Taggart

THE IRISH IN WORLD METHODISM 1760-1900

EPWORTH PRESS

British Library Cataloguing in Publication Data

Taggart, Norman W.
The Irish in world Methodism: 1760–1900.
1. Methodist Church——History——18th
century   2. Methodist Church——History——
19th century   3. Irish——Religious life
I. Title
287'.0899162   BX8231

ISBN 0–7162–0423–1

First published 1986
by Epworth Press
Room 195, 1 Central Buildings,
Westminster, London SW 1

Typeset by Gloucester Typesetting Services
and printed in Great Britain by
Oxford University Press

To Margaret
whose understanding, support and encouragement
were essential for the writing of this book
and for so much else.

CONTENTS

Preface   Slender, Struggling . . . yet Fruitful   ix

Acknowledgements   xv

Abbreviations   xvii

1   The Irish and Methodism's World Outreach   1

2   The Missionary Society – Helping or Hindering
   Mission?   19

3   Emigration – Losses and Gains   36

4   The Laity, Primary Agents of Mission   50

5   Canadian Case Study   67

6   Adam Clarke and William Arthur – The Theology
   of Mission   87

7   James Lynch, Reluctant Leader   104

8   John McKenny, Pioneer on Three Continents   128

9   John Barry, Controversialist   146

10 John Barry, Opponent of Slavery   154

11 William Butler, Founder of Two Missions   168

12 Mission Yesterday and Today   181

Appendix   Irish-born Methodist Ministers and
        Probationers in Canada   194

Bibliography and Sources   202

Notes   203

Index   215

PREFACE
Slender, Struggling ... yet Fruitful

This book is a study of Methodism as a missionary movement. Historians have devoted much attention to aspects of Wesleyan theology, tracing the development in Wesley's thought and indicating changes in Methodist doctrine, polity and influence in the generations following his death. Little has been published in recent years, however, on how Methodism spread from the British Isles. This is surprising since Methodism has always had a missionary potential, and mission, at first at home and later beyond these shores, has been an abiding concern.

More precisely, this is a study which examines the part which Irish people have played in Methodism's world outreach up to the end of the nineteenth century. It is a story not previously told, at least with this degree of detail. In the telling of it, having researched the subject, I shall be obliged to challenge previous accounts, to correct inaccuracies, and to expose false assumptions.

Material is presented in biographical and thematic form. Both approaches are important, complementing each other. Most people find that biography enlivens history, yet if characters are not placed in the context of the broader trends and developments which were current in their day, the accounts of their lives and contribution may lack objectivity and be little understood.

Sometimes, especially in the chapters on John McKenny and John Barry, we shall be seeing characters for the first time against their working environment. This enables a fuller, fairer and more accurate portrait to emerge. If McKenny is viewed solely from the standpoint of his abortive mission in Cape Colony, as has happened again in the recent *History of the Methodist Church in Great Britain*,[1] he can be dismissed as a weak person lacking staying power and leadership quality. This, however, does him a great injustice. Barry appears cantankerous and entirely devoid of objectivity when judged only in the light of his last stormy years in Canada and the Caribbean. A different picture emerges, however, when we appreciate his earlier outstanding work in Jamaica and take into account the extent to which ill-health frustrated his ministry. Without excusing his excesses of bad temper, to know more is at least to understand better.

Long before Schumacher made the literate world familiar with the concept of small being beautiful, William Arthur – notable nineteenth-century Wesleyan preacher, author and missionary statesman who will feature prominently in these pages – had said much the same thing about Irish Methodism, describing it as 'a lovely vine of slender stem, struggling in un-friendly soil, yet a fruitful vine, whose branches run over the wall'.[2] Arthur also said of Irish Methodism that whilst it had not been successful in growing timber, it 'had done much in growing fruit'.[3]

No better words could be used to describe Methodism in Ireland than Arthur's – 'slender', 'struggling' and 'fruitful.' There is no denying the *slenderness* of the church. In statistical terms alone it never fulfilled the high hopes entertained on its behalf, having always to *struggle* in an indifferent, and at times even hostile, ecclesiastical environment. Arriving late on the 'church scene', it did not present a serious challenge to the dominance of others. It shared too in the struggles of the other churches arising from the inhospitable social and economic environment in which they were all placed. Poverty, community disorder and endemic emigration imposed great strains on the Irish churches, as indeed they did upon many other institutions.

Yet, against all the odds, Irish Methodism took root and bore *fruit*, influencing churches and individuals inside Ireland and far beyond its borders. There have of course been periods in the church's life – some would argue that it is going through one now – when its very smallness has led it to adopt negative and defensive postures in the mistaken notion that this was a sure way of guaranteeing its survival. Petty jealousies, in-fighting, secrecy, and lack of vision (this last, potentially the bane of all small organizations) are not unknown to Irish Methodism! But when it has been at its best it has responded positively to the challenge of being a small religious minority. At such times it has wisely opted out of ecclesiastical and other power games, refused to become preoccupied with its own identity, and welcomed the freedom of being, in Jesus' words, simply a small lamp on a lampstand or a little leaven in a much larger lump.

In this study we shall be examining only one aspect of Irish Methodism's influence – the extent to which the Irish have been involved in the spread of Methodism throughout the world up to the end of the nineteenth century. It should of course be freely acknowledged that there are difficulties in isolating the role and contribution of the Irish overseas, since they seldom operated separately from people born elsewhere and indeed some of those who feature in the account thought of themselves more readily as 'British' than as 'Irish'. But Ireland is an identifiable geographical area, and Methodism within Ireland, with its own Conference since 1752, has had a distinct history despite its close association with Methodism in Britain. It is therefore a matter of regret that little serious research has hitherto been done on the church in Ireland, and it is to be hoped that more will follow so that the movement can become better known and understood, and more light can be thrown on its significance.

Normally only the contribution of those people actually born in Ireland is noted, and material already readily available on such comparatively well-known figures as Barbara Heck and Philip Embury is not reproduced unless for purposes of re-evaluation or reinterpretation in the light of research.

In the use of quotations preference is given to unpublished material and to material which, though previously published, remains largely unknown. Special care has been taken, especially in the biographical chapters, to enable people from the past to speak to us today in their own words.

It is especially appropriate that the book be published now since the 1980s bring a reminder of certain important events of which the bicentenaries are being observed in different parts of the world. These include the publication in 1783 of Thomas Coke's *Plan of the Society for the Establishment of Missions among the Heathens* (pre-dating William Carey's better known *Enquiry into the Obligations of Christians to use Means for the Conversion of the Heathens*, which did not appear until 1792); the organizing of the large and influential Methodist Episcopal Church in America, at the Christmas Conference in Baltimore, also in 1784; and the acceptance by the Methodist Conference of responsibility for overseas missions in 1786, and the departure from Britain of the first Methodist missionaries to the West Indies in the same year. The Irish played a considerable part in such early developments, a fact which has not always been recognized.

It is hoped that this examination of Ireland's involvement in world Methodism will be seen as more than a recital of historical facts. By rediscovering our past, we can find pointers towards more effective serving and witnessing in our own day. In this sense the Pastoral Address to Irish Methodists in 1898 sounded exactly the right note, even if its backward look was much less critical than ours.

> We have a noble heritage and inspiring traditions, but herein lies a danger . . . We must not live in the past. It will be an evil day for us when we glory in the heroic spirit of our fathers, and yet fail to discern our own present duty and apply ourselves to it with their zeal and enthusiasm.[4]

Many people have helped in the preparation of this book. The following deserve special mention. The Rev. John Stacey encouraged me to re-write my doctoral thesis[5] for possible publication, and arranged for it to be considered by the Editorial Committee of the Epworth Press.

Mrs Shelagh Livingstone and my wife, Margaret, had the unenviable task of reading my first poor efforts. This gave them enormous scope for making suggestions on grammar, modes of expression and content. To their credit, their comments were always kind as well as clear. Remaining blemishes in the text are my responsibility, not theirs.

The Rev. Cyril Davey, Dr David Hempton and Professor Andrew Walls read the typescript at a later stage, and offered extremely valuable advice arising from their areas of interest and expertise. The Rev. Professor Finlay Holmes had supervised the earlier postgraduate research.

As with the thesis, Mrs Rosemary Seton, the Archivist at the School of Oriental and African Studies (where the Methodist overseas archives are housed), and the Rev. Glenn Lucas, the Archivist of the United Church of Canada, went out of their way in providing specialist support.

A subsidy from the Methodist Church Overseas Division (Methodist Missionary Society), facilitated publication.

Finally, my Secretary at the Belfast Central Mission, Miss Esther Fyffe, achieved the apparently impossible, typing the material at each stage without allowing the rest of her work to suffer. This was only possible by working long hours. I am particularly grateful to her.

Belfast 1985   Norman Taggart

ACKNOWLEDGMENTS

The author gratefully acknowledges permission to quote copyright material from the following sources:

Richard Carwardine, *Transatlantic Revivalism*, Greenwood Press, Westport, Connecticut, 1978

The World Council of Churches, *Mission and Evangelism, an Ecumenical Affirmation*, Geneva, 1982

ABBREVIATIONS

JMA	Juvenile Missionary Association
MEC	Methodist Episcopal Church
MMS	Methodist Missionary Society
WMMS	Wesleyan Methodist Missionary Society

The Irish and Methodism's World Outreach

=

Methodism's Missionary Roots

Methodism, when true to itself, is essentially a missionary movement with a concern for the whole world and for life in its entirety. It could not have been otherwise given its origins, beliefs and pragmatism.

John Wesley's grandfather considered serving overseas, first in Surinam and later in Maryland. The background to this was in part the opposition he encountered in his Dorset parish. His son Samuel, John's father, drew up a scheme which he presented to the Archbishop of York, whereby he hoped the British East India Company would aid the spread of Christianity in Asia. It contained three elements, each relating to different groups of people: English people overseas, people belonging to other Christian churches (including the Roman Catholic), and non-Christians. Samuel Wesley envisaged that the work, which he himself was prepared to undertake, would first involve visits to several countries (Abyssinia, India and China were mentioned) to ascertain basic facts such as the number of Christians, ministers working among them, and their moral state. He would then endeavour to revive the spirit of Christianity by such means as the distribution of Christian literature and correspondence. If he reached India he would seek to learn 'the Hindostan language' so that he would be in a position to lead Hindus to the Christian faith. It 'would be well worth dying'[1] to be involved in such work, he wrote. Like his father before him, however, Samuel did not go overseas.

Samuel Wesley was an enthusiastic supporter of General Oglethorpe's scheme in Georgia. Writing to him in 1734 he declared:

> I had always so dear a love of your colony that if it had been but ten years ago, I would gladly have devoted the remainder of my life and labours to that place and think I might before this time have conquered the language without which little can be done among the natives.[2]

This interest in Georgia was passed on to his family, and within twelve months of his death his two youngest sons journeyed to the colony, Charles in the position of secretary to the Governor and John with the ambition of being a missionary to the American Indians.

Samuel Wesley's hymn on redemption anticipated the contrast between the universal and the particular, the all and the one, which became such a pronounced emphasis within Methodism and was so prominently featured in Charles Wesley's hymns, arising from the controversy with Calvinism. As the first two verses indicate, the divine drama is enacted against a universal background.

> Behold the Saviour of mankind
>   Nailed to the shameful tree!
> How vast the love that Him inclined
>   To bleed and die for thee!
>
> Hark, how He groans! while nature shakes,
>   And earth's strong pillars bend;
> The temple's veil in sunder breaks,
>   The solid marbles rend.

Samuel Wesley's wife, Susannah, who exerted such a great influence on the family, also played an important part in making her children aware of the challenge of Christian service in other parts of the world. In 1712 she was herself deeply moved by reading an account of the work of the German missionaries, Ziegenbalg and Plütschau, in Tranquebar in south India. For several days she could think or speak of little else, and this strengthened her resolve to give regular spiritual instruction to her children. It was entirely in character that when John consulted her about his plans to go to Georgia, she declared that if she had twenty sons she would rejoice if they all acted similarly, even if it meant she did not see them again.

Another major influence on John and Charles Wesley, before and after their evangelical awakening in 1738, was that of the Moravians. After their reorganization at Herrnhut in Germany in 1722, the Moravians played a considerable part in overseas missions, often working as a leaven in larger Christian bodies. The Wesleys were deeply impressed by the faith and courage of the Moravians whom they met on the journey to Georgia and also during their stay there. On their return to England in 1738 they benefited greatly from conversations with Peter Böhler and others, gaining a deeper understanding of vital aspects of the Christian faith, including conversion, the nature of saving faith itself, and the fruits of such faith, including missionary zeal.

The Wesleys had gone to Georgia under a strong sense of priestly obligation. John's chief motive was the hope of saving his own soul. 'I hope to learn the true sense of the gospel of Christ by preaching it to the heathen',[3] he wrote. He then intended passing on to others, particularly to the American Indians, 'a saving knowledge of the gospel of Christ'.[4] These hopes were soon disappointed, however. Charles proved a failure as a secretary, and when his health broke down John had increasingly to take over his work. Official correspondence, sorting out the difficulties inevitable in a new colony, and attending to the pastoral needs of the settler communities took an enormous toll of his time and frustrated his efforts to engage in the Indian mission which was his ultimate purpose in going to Georgia. After only two years he returned to England, broken and dispirited, having failed either to evangelize the Indians or to minister effectively to the English settlers. 'I went to America to convert the Indians; but oh, who shall convert me?', he asked.[5]

Painful though the period in Georgia had been, it was far from being disastrous. It became a crucial turning point in the spiritual development of both brothers, forcing them to re-examine the very basis of their Christian faith, and leading them to a liberating and profound experience of the love of God and of their own acceptance by him through faith. Many of the basic features in later Methodism emerged and were practised in Georgia, such as the use of hymns, enabling the laity to take on limited responsibility, and the value of placing people into small groups for growth and fellowship. Also John Wesley added to his knowledge of several languages, including French, Spanish, Italian and German; he continued to read extensively; he saw slavery at first hand (when visiting South Carolina, since it was initially banned in Georgia), learning to detest it; and he first discovered there an abiding interest in work among negro peoples. The way was thus prepared for Wesley to give distin-guished and distinctive leadership within the evangelical movement, combining as he did to a rare degree the zeal of an evangelist with the insights and persistence of a social reformer.

It was John Wesley's rediscovery and practice of the great evangelical certainties, offensive to many at the time – that all can be saved, may know that they are saved, and may be saved to the full – which made Methodism a missionary movement, and helped to create a climate out of which the modern mis-sionary enterprise sprang and in which it flourished. Charles Wesley's hymns popularized Methodist emphases in the sharp, often bitter, confrontation with Calvinism, declaring such con-cepts as 'general grace', God's 'undistinguishing regard' and His 'universal love.' Notice, for example, the attack on debased Calvinism in every line of a hymn:

> Father, whose everlasting love
>   Thy only Son for sinners gave;
> Whose grace to all did freely move,
>   And sent Him down the world to save:

Help us Thy mercy to extol,
　Immense, unfathom'd, unconfined;
To praise the Lamb who died for all,
　The general Saviour of mankind.

It has been claimed that among the larger Protestant churches, Methodism is the only one which from the outset adopted a world view, and that the Wesleyan revival was essentially a reaction against narrowing concepts of the gospel and of the church, 'whether Calvinistic, sacerdotal, nationalist, or particularist of whatever kind'.[6] The fact that after his evangelical conversion John Wesley, despite claiming that the whole world was his parish, confined his own efforts to the British Isles, did not detract from the influence he had on wider mission. Through the supply of manpower for the New World, and his correspondence with Methodist leaders there, Wesley exercised a remarkable co-ordinating ministry across the Atlantic. His indirect influence was enormous, chiefly through the theological truths he affirmed, his commissioning of Thomas Coke as the superintendent of Methodist missions, and his acceptance of the need for American Methodism to plot its own course. The emphasis on fellowship, mobility, evangelical conviction without dogmatism, social commitment, lay involvement, and an awareness of being called and sent out by God, was bound to have repercussions for the wider world.

The Irish in World Methodism: a partial World Survey

It has long been believed, within Ireland and also much further afield, that Irish Methodism has from the beginning taken a keen and consistent interest in Methodism's world outreach, and indeed that Irish Methodists, despite being few in number, have played a significant part in such outreach. American voices especially have been raised to make strikingly eloquent claims on behalf of Irish achievements in this field, and, not surprisingly, these voices have been well received within Ireland and have frequently been re-echoed approvingly by the Irish. Thus in a speech delivered by Bishop Janes of the Methodist Episcopal

Church (MEC) in New York in 1866, it was stated that wherever English-speaking Methodism existed out of England, it had been planted by Irishmen, and that English-speaking Methodism was Irish Methodism the world over.[7] Significantly this speech was given in the presence of a visiting Irish delegation, and received greater coverage in Ireland than it did in the United States. A claim by the American historian Abel Stevens was not less sweeping. He wrote that Irishmen were to found, or to aid in founding, Methodism in the North American British provinces, in the United States, in the West Indies, in Australia, in Africa, and in India.[8]

Such generalized statements, however, need to be examined critically and seen in context before they can be properly evaluated. It is, for example, necessary to recognize that Janes' speech was delivered at a meeting specifically called to stimulate support for Wesleyan Methodism within Ireland. Given to an audience composed largely of Irish people and of Irish Americans, the speech is not the stuff of which objective history is made, however impressive it may have been on first hearing. It is indeed an injustice to Janes not to take into account the special nature of the occasion. It must be noted also that the speech contained several inaccuracies. It is necessary to indicate these since some of them have been handed down in historical folklore without being subject to normal scrutiny. Thus it is not true, despite Janes' claim, that an Irish minister introduced Methodism to Nova Scotia. The credit for this belongs to Yorkshire immigrants. Nor is it the case that an Irish minister took Methodism to Australia, though an Irish layman was prominently involved in Methodist beginnings there. Also John Summerfield, to whom Janes referred in recognition of his extraordinary impact in the early 1820s, was not in fact, Irish, although converted in Ireland. Other similar points could be made. The most serious criticism of Janes, however, is that he failed to acknowledge the contribution made by people of other nationalities, nor did he recognize the many ways in which Methodism within Ireland had itself been nurtured and supported by people from outside. Alongside the claim by Janes that the Irish Wesleyan Church was 'the mother' of the American Methodist Church, and that Ireland not only supplied the first Methodist ministers to the American Church but continued to do so, we need to set the measured terms of an editorial published in Toronto in 1872 and entitled 'Claiming Rather Too Much'.[9]

Richard Carwardine's recent research into the obituaries of almost three thousand ministers in the MEC between 1771 and 1865 also helps us to recognize that Janes' claims were exaggerated. In those cases in which information is available regarding the country of origin of preachers, the British and Irish-born element came to only nine per cent. Commenting that the overall figures hide the shifting pattern within the period, Carwardine makes an interesting observation:

> In no decade before 1830 did the English-born entering the ministry outnumber the Irish; before then 61 per cent were Irish and 36 per cent English. Thereafter the proportions shifted so far that 65 per cent English-born entered the MEC between 1830 and 1865; the Irish figure for the same period was 24 per cent . . . The change does not reflect any absolute decline in the Irish contribution to the American ministry, for the number of entering Irish-born shows a steady decennial growth. Rather it suggests some caution on the part of the English . . . in the generation or so after the Revolution.[10]

While all these qualifications warn us against getting things out of proportion, they do not mean that the Irish did not play a significant part in Methodism's outreach. Carwardine has established that within the MEC those preachers who were Irish-born were as much as 31 per cent of the total number who came from Ireland and Britain, and it is not difficult to illustrate that among them were several Irish preachers who made outstanding contributions. The same is true of Irish lay people, not only in America but further afield as well. They too contributed much.

Among important Irish 'firsts' in various parts of the world, to which more detailed reference will be made, are Laurence

Coughlan in Newfoundland; Barbara Heck, Philip Embury and Robert Strawbridge in the United States; James Lynch and George Erskine, as part of the pioneer missionary team which went to Ceylon, led by Thomas Coke, the founder of Wesleyan Methodist overseas missions; James Lynch, who also went to Madras; John McKenny in Cape Colony, South Africa; and William Butler in Mexico. Others included the following – William Hammett, the first Wesleyan missionary to St Kitts in 1787 and to Jamaica in 1789; John Stephenson, the first Wesleyan preacher in Bermuda in 1799, who preached without local authorization and for his pains had to serve a six months' gaol sentence; James McMullen, the first Methodist missionary to be appointed to Gibraltar, who died with his wife in 1804 within weeks of their arrival, both victims of an outbreak of cholera; and John Ross, a colour sergeant with the 59th Regiment in Hong Kong, who gathered a Methodist class around him in 1849, and whose letter to the Missionary Society in London encouraged the sending of the first Methodist preacher in 1851.

The links between Methodism in Ireland and in North America as a whole have been particularly close, and note is taken at this point of some Irish people who contributed significantly in the United States.

Edward Dromgoole (1751–1836) came from near Sligo, was brought up a Roman Catholic, and became an itinerant preacher in the MEC from 1774. When lack of provision for married preachers forced him out of the itinerant system whereby Methodist ministers are regularly moved, he continued to be involved as a local preacher and a successful businessman. The Dromgoole Papers, being letters written to him chiefly by influential circuit-riders (travelling preachers) between 1778 and 1798, and also between 1802 and 1812, provide a fascinating insight into Methodism as it spread along the eastern seaboard. Of particular interest are those letters commenting on slavery.

William Ryland (1770–1846) became the minister of the notable Foundry church in Washington from 1820 to 1822, and from 1825 to 1827. Andrew Jackson, one of several Irish-born

Presidents of the United States, often heard him preach, and appointed him Chaplain at the Navy Yard. He was also elected Chaplain to both Houses of the Congress of the United States.

Charles Elliott was born in Co. Donegal in 1792, and emigrated to the United States in 1816 with his mother and her eight other children. A factor in their decision to emigrate was that since Elliott was not an Anglican it would have been difficult for him to continue his education at Trinity College, Dublin. An early description of certain of his physical features and characteristics did not flatter him, and gave but little indication of the distinction he was later to achieve:

> His speech was generally somewhat broken, giving unmistakable evidence of the country of his birth; his attitude and gestures were awkward and void of dignity; his appearance in and out of the pulpit indicated the most profound disregard for dress, being too much occupied with more important subjects than the wardrobe, the toilet, or looking-glass; and besides all this, his close application to study so affected the nerves of his face as to produce a most singular twitching, drawing his face and mouth into the most grotesque appearances imaginable.[11]

Despite such handicaps Elliott held professorships, was the editor of important journals, wrote several books (particularly on Roman Catholicism and on slavery), and became President of Iowa Wesleyan University. The following excerpt from one of his pamphlets gives an indication of the vigour of his opposition to slavery:

> It makes very little difference, in estimating the evil of slavery, that there may be many slave-holders who are mild and merciful masters, who have the interests of the slaves at heart, and are anxious to ameliorate their condition. All this cannot rectify the incurable evils of the system; these are beyond the reach of individual benevolence.[12]

James Caughey was born in Northern Ireland in 1810.

From a Presbyterian background, he renounced Calvinism after emigrating to the United States, and became an MEC preacher. After an unexceptional start, he became widely known on both sides of the Atlantic as a travelling evangelist and revivalist. He met with a varied response particularly from within Wesleyan Methodism in Britain, many ministers and lay people becoming sharply divided over him, partly because he was not covered by normal connexional discipline. He had arrived from America without an invitation, had worked extensively within Methodism without official recognition by the Conference, and was not answerable to the authority of the Conference. Conflict reached a peak in 1846 when he was denied the use of Wesleyan pulpits and premises. Caughey exerted an important influence within Britain. Much of his appeal lay in the sharp contrast between the extravagance of his oratory and the formal style of other preachers of the period such as Jabez Bunting. His career provided one of those comparatively rare moments when American Methodism directly influenced the movement in Britain.

Another important strand of Irish influence on the American scene, to which too little attention has hitherto been paid, was that of dissidents from Ireland including Robert Strawbridge, James O'Kelly, William Hammett, the pioneer missionary to St Kitts and Jamaica, and Alexander McCaine. These were leading opponents of developments in the beliefs and practices of early mainstream Methodism in America, who took their opposition to the lengths of forming protest splinter movements. The spotlight over the years has fallen on more traditionalist figures such as Barbara Heck and Philip Embury, and it is only in recent times that the contribution of these dissidents has been acknowledged. That the four named were all Irish (O'Kelly was probably born outside Ireland, but of Irish parents), and that there were points of contact between them, merits fuller examination than has yet been undertaken.

More than any other person, **Robert Strawbridge** was responsible for precipitating a dispute over the administration of the sacraments which threatened to disrupt the early Methodist movement in America. He has the dubious distinction of having been officially criticized by the first Conference of Methodist preachers to be held in America, in 1773.

Ordained an elder in 1784, **James O'Kelly** was an early champion of those who opposed the authority of Methodist bishops. In the General Conference of 1792 he proposed a resolution upholding a right of appeal over stationing. The resolution was lost, but this issue long remained a matter of sharp debate within the MEC. O'Kelly, together with a few other preachers, withdrew from the Church and formed the Republican Methodist Church. In 1801 this became known simply as the Christian Church, and finally united with the Congregational Church. A later generation of reformers revived O'Kelly's 'republican' principles, and established the Methodist Protestant Church with which McCaine was also associated.

To **William Hammett,** whose health was broken by persecution in Jamaica, belongs the distinction of forming the first schismatic Methodist denomination within America, pre-dating that of O'Kelly who, however, had been in opposition earlier. Hammett had been taken by Thomas Coke from Jamaica to Charleston, South Carolina, in 1791, in the hope that he would recover his strength and be able to return to the West Indies. Things, however, did not work out as anticipated. Instead Hammett engaged in a bitter dispute with Coke and with Francis Asbury, the joint Superintendents of the work in America, over developments within Methodism, rejecting the episcopal system, siding with O'Kelly on the right to appeal with regard to stationing, arguing for the need to make provision for married and retired preachers, and supporting the idea of a larger General Conference composed of at least two-thirds of the preachers. Six other preachers are known to have associated themselves with Hammett's Primitive Methodist Church. This brand of Methodism was introduced into the Bahamas, where it continued at least into the 1820s.

Alexander McCaine, a Dublin Roman Catholic, owed much to Hammett, having been converted under him. He became a MEC preacher in 1797, and although for a time he was a close associate of Asbury, he later opposed him and threw his weight behind the idea of a larger Conference. He made highly unfavourable comparisons between the early Christian church and developments within the MEC, rejecting the episcopal system and becoming a founder of the Methodist Protestant Church. This became a significant branch of Methodism within the United States, and was a partner in the union of American Methodists in 1939.

The importance of these dissidents lay in the protests they raised, and the questions they posed, about a series of sensitive and interlocking issues concerning church government and practice. The dissidents were firmly convinced that the MEC was moving in authoritarian and unbiblical directions. The fact that at least two of the group had taken the radical step of first breaking with Roman Catholicism, in order to embrace Methodism, helps to account for their fierce opposition to what they interpreted as the loss of fundamental freedoms and the introduction of unscriptural practices. It is significant too that the issues and questions they highlighted persisted long after the dissidents themselves had been silenced. Some have remained as Methodist preoccupations into the present century. It should, however, be acknowledged that some of the dissidents were themselves notably authoritarian in approach, and did not welcome criticism. As is often the case, they prized the freedom to protest but did not go out of their way to afford it to others.

Ireland's involvement in the Wesleyan Methodist Missionary Society (WMMS), Methodism's chief official channel for world outreach, will now be examined under two headings, finance and personnel. The Irish were not significantly inolved in other Methodist missionary organizations. Some preachers, notably William McClure, went to Canada with the Methodist New Connexion.

The Level of Financial Support for the Wesleyan Methodist Missionary Society

Occasional remarks and sets of figures in the nineteenth century suggested that the Irish compared favourably with Methodists elsewhere in their giving to overseas missions. A statement by William Arthur in Leeds in 1865, followed by an analysis of giving, made it clear that the average per member for the Missionary Society at that time was greater in parts of Ireland than elsewhere. A comment in the Canadian *Christian Guardian* in the same year concluded that Irish Methodists, though far from being the most wealthy in the world, contributed the largest amounts for overseas missions in proportion to their numbers.[13] It would be quite wrong, however, to assume that this was a uniform pattern throughout the century. Indeed the Irish themselves frequently expressed disappointment at the level of their achievements in comparison both with their own expectations and with what was done by others, particularly within Ireland. Statements by the Rev. Hugh McKeag, the Secretary of the Hibernian Auxiliary (which promoted the interests of the WMMS within Ireland), are particularly telling. He wrote in 1902:

> We are just where we were thirty-five years ago. Our expenditure on missions twenty-five years ago was several thousand pounds more than it is today. At the earlier of these dates the Church Missionary Society raised about the same as we did; its income now is about three times as great.[14]

Just over a year later he commented further on the same theme:

> When all is said in mitigation, the great fact remains that the income has not kept pace with the increase of the Church's numbers and wealth, nor even of its generosity in other directions. We have had to stand by and witness other and much younger societies far outstrip us in aggressiveness.[15]

In assessing the level of support for overseas missions within Irish Methodism we must also take account of the money Ireland received from the WMMS for the Irish Mission which worked in Irish-speaking parts of Ireland. The statistics published by the Missionary Society in the second half of the nineteenth century, which differ slightly from those appearing in Ireland over the same period, because of variations in the method of analysis, make clear that up to the end of the nineteenth century, contrary to what has normally been assumed, Ireland received considerably more from the Missionary Society than she officially remitted to London through circuit contributions. It should however be recognized that these figures did not include amounts received in London direct from individuals in Ireland and also from Juvenile Offerings raised officially by children on behalf of home and overseas missions (from 1895 these latter amounts were divided equally between home and overseas). When these sources of income are also taken into account, it has been argued that a different picture emerges. Thus the Mission Committee in Ireland claimed in 1888 that when this necessary adjustment is made, contributions from Ireland exceeded the incoming grants by not less than £17,000 in the preceding twenty years.[16] In 1895 Dr McMillen, a member of an Irish deputation to London, estimated that from 1818 Irish giving had exceeded grants received by £30,743.[17] Even if these claims are allowed in full, however, it is clear that the level of giving within Ireland for overseas missions fell far short of what has often been assumed.

Decade	Income from Irish circuits to the Wesleyan Methodist Missionary Society through the Hibernian Auxiliary	Expenditure on the Irish Mission by the Wesleyan Methodist Missionary Society
1850–1859	£42,255.0.7	£52,818.18.0
1860–1869	£33,927.11.1	£56,475.0.10
1870–1879	£43,641.10.10	£60,184.7.7
1880–1889	£50,597.11.7	£60,300.6.0
1890–1899	£44,974.0.2	£55,150.0.0

Irish Personnel serving Overseas through the WMMS

Turning from the subject of financial support for the WMMS to consider Irish people who served overseas under the WMMS, one is immediately struck by the unevenness of the supply of Irish missionaries. From 1786 until the death of Coke in 1814, Ireland merited the description of being Coke's chief recruiting ground. Thereafter, until the widespread resurgence of missionary interest and activity in the closing decades of the

nineteenth century, Ireland supplied surprisingly few missionaries. Thus as many as sixteen ministers from Ireland were
appointed to the Caribbean between 1786 and 1812, and only
four were appointed in the remainder of the nineteenth century,
the last reaching Jamaica in 1828. Also, although two Irishmen
accompanied Coke on his voyage at the start of the Ceylon
mission in 1813, and another joined them in 1816 from Cape
Town, no more Irish ministers were appointed to Ceylon within
the nineteenth century.

A careful study of the only available missionary candidates'
papers reveals that at least a small number of enquiries from
ministers and lay people continued to be received by the Missionary Society throughout the century. In 1820 and 1821 consideration was given to the possibility of a printer from Louth
serving in The Gambia. In 1825 and 1826 Matthew Lanktree,
whose father served in the Irish Mission, corresponded about an
overseas appointment until ill-health made such service impossible. In 1831 John Barry, on furlough from Jamaica, wrote from
Co. Cork on behalf of a local teacher who was interested in
working overseas. In the same year Robert Lindsay, a probationary minister in Co. Mayo, placed himself at the disposal of
the Missionary Society. There was also an enquiry in 1831 about
an educational position in Nova Scotia, and another concerning
a young woman willing to serve overseas as a governess. In 1833
a teacher who was also a local preacher asked about the possibility of an appointment in Canada. In May 1838 William
Darby, a probationary minister in Portadown, indicated that he
had a strong call to work overseas:

> I have offered myself for a Foreign Mission through our
> District Meetings to the Conference for the last three years,
> and with no effect. I now at the instance of some of my
> brethren apply to you. . . . I have no objection to labor in my
> own country. I will yield to no man in warmth of attachment
> to Ireland, and to Irish Methodism.[18]

In fact Darby remained in Ireland, and eventually entered the
ministry of the Church of Ireland. In the late 1850s Thomas

Johnston wrote about a teaching position in Newfoundland, indicating that his brother in Toronto might be interested.

It seems that none of these people actually served overseas with the WMMS. This in itself is not unusual. Some of the enquiries were essentially of a tentative nature, and in at least one case serious ill-health intervened. What is strange, however, is that over such a long period there were so few successful applications from people in Ireland to serve with the WMMS. One suspects that there was an agreement, however unofficial, between leaders in Ireland and Britain that Irish involvement in overseas service be discouraged at least for a period. Thus an article appeared in *the Irish Evangelist* in 1868 claiming that:

> Many have at various times desired to go 'where Christ is not named,' but for many years there has been no open door. Those in authority said – 'We have only a sufficient number of candidates for the Ministry for the wants of Ireland; we can spare none for the heathen.'[19]

Apart from this personal expression of opinion, however, I have not come across any official statement that it was not possible for the Irish to continue to serve overseas with the WMMS. There would appear to have been an understanding of an informal nature that people from Ireland should not be recruited. The quotation from Darby, already given, suggests that he came up against such a 'policy' when he first expressed interest in working overseas. Two sentences in a letter written as early as 1821 by John Wiggins, who formerly worked in Jamaica, convey a similar impression:

> The idea has gone abroad here that the Committee do not intend to employ any Irish Preachers in future. I suppose there is no truth in this report.[20]

The experience of Ebenezer Webster towards the end of the century is also relevant. When he first offered for missionary service, he claimed that he was informed that there was no arrangement whereby Irish ministers could go overseas.[21]

In the absence of explicit statements of policy we can only

speculate as to the reasons behind the significant reduction in the number of Irish missionaries serving overseas. The more formal style and structures of the Missionary Society, in contrast to the enormous personal appeal of the charismatic Coke, was probably a factor at least in the early years of the WMMS. Also some of the Irish missionaries serving under Coke had to be disciplined or gave up early. This is not to suggest, however, that the failure rate among the Irish was significantly higher than for other people, or that it led to an anti-Irish policy in recruitment. An increasing desire to consolidate the work within Ireland itself, particularly in Roman Catholic areas, against the background of the steady, occasionally dramatic, losses incurred through emigration, was presumably the major factor and would have received the approval of the official leadership in Ireland as well as in Britain. It should, however, also be recognized that the form of relationship which Ireland had with the WMMS, permitting it at best to have only a subordinate role, stifled rather than encouraged involvement.

Towards the end of the nineteenth century factors began to operate which added considerably to the impetus for missionary activity. Included among these were an upsurge in interest among university students and increased demands from the white colonies for support. As opportunities increased, the Missionary Society recognized what Coke had always known, namely that Ireland had resources to share with the wider world and that enabling her to do so would increase, not lessen, the effectiveness of witness within Ireland itself.

World Outreach, More a Peripheral Interest than an Urgent Concern?

Methodism's main convictions about mission – that the church is a missionary movement rather than a self-propagating and self-preserving institution; that mission is world-wide, is initiated by God himself, and demands the response of the whole church – were shared by Irish Methodism. These and other basic truths were ably expounded by Adam Clarke and William Arthur,

Portrush

themselves Irish. Affirming such truths, and even devising appropriate structures to express them, is, however, one matter. Implementing them on a significant scale is quite another. In chapter 2 official structures and procedures are examined to see whether they helped or hindered Irish Methodists in their response to the challenge of world mission. Here it must first openly be acknowledged, however, that many did not respond at all, not because of inadequate or unsatisfactory structures but because they lacked vision. Then, as now, the church as a whole failed to be renewed for mission, and progress depended too much on committed individuals, families and other outstanding groups. A Dublin layman, Alfred Deale, taking part in correspondence in the *Irish Christian Advocate* in 1895, which called attention to the need to re-awaken missionary interest and involvement, summarized the situation well when he stressed that a great deal still had to be done before mission became a central theme for rank and file members in the church.[22] An earlier correspondent who signed himself simply 'W.A.J.', and whose letters helped to spark off the correspondence, had written unflatteringly of the Hibernian Auxiliary, describing it as 'a very slumbering organization, with a high-sounding title', and adding:

> Certainly we hear the name, at least once a year, when it makes a spurt with the missionary deputation; but after that it seems as if it fell once more into a semi-comatose condition.[23]

It is to this organization, and the body to which it was an auxiliary, that we must now turn.

The Missionary Society –
Helping or Hindering Mission?

=

Three Phases in Methodism's Missionary Response

Allen Birtwhistle has pointed out that there were three distinct
phases in Methodism's missionary response, culminating in the
creation of the Missionary Society.[1] The earliest phase lasted
until 1786, and was characterized by the efforts of committed
individuals who took initiatives without the official backing or
support of the home church. In the second phase the Methodist
Conference undertook responsibility for overseas missions, and
in the third the WMMS came into being.

John Wesley himself made a major, though indirect, contribu-
tion in **the first phase** when in 1758 he preached in a house in
Wandsworth High Street at a meeting attended by Nathaniel
Gilbert, a distinguished lawyer and Speaker of the House of
Assembly in Antigua, in the West Indies. Gilbert had read
Wesley's *Earnest Appeal to Men of Reason and Religion* (1744) with
great profit, when he was ill in Antigua, and indeed it was with
the main aim of hearing Wesley preach that he made his way to
England. Two of his negro servants accompanied him to the
meeting, were converted, and were subsequently baptized by
Wesley. On his return to Antigua in 1760, Gilbert summoned
all his slaves into his home, and proceeded to tell them what
Christ had done for them and for all men. A Methodist Church
was thus begun in Antigua long before the first missionaries
were appointed.

Even Coke's *Plan of the Society for the Establishment of Missions among the Heathens*, published late in 1783, has to be seen in the context of such unofficial initiatives. It called for a mission to non-Christians in the British dominions in Asia, and the Society's membership was to be made up of individuals who contributed at least two guineas a year, and who at a general meeting would set up a committee, appoint a secretary, and prepare and send out missionaries. In the first list of subscriptions published in connection with the Society, amounting to just over £66, it is interesting that more than £14 had been received from Dublin. There is no firm evidence, however, that the first general meeting (called for 27 January 1784) actually took place. It is possible that Wesley himself vetoed it. He would certainly not have approved of the measure of independence envisaged for the Society; and events in America were soon to demand his close attention and that of Coke, as Methodism there moved towards autonomy in the wake of the War of Independence.

The **second phase** lasted from 1786 to 1813, and the Methodist Conference itself, rather than a voluntary society as in the 1784 Plan, undertook responsibility for overseas missions. Coke directed the mission (the term 'agent' was used officially of him in 1799), and received increasing help which, however, was sometimes seen by him as interference and resented.

Prior to the annual Conference in 1786 Coke prepared *An Address to the Pious and Benevolent, Proposing an Annual Subscription for the Support of Missionaries in The Highlands and adjacent Islands of Scotland, The Isles of Jersey, Guernsey, and Newfoundland, the West Indies, and the provinces of Nova Scotia and Quebec*. Wesley wrote a preface to it, and the whole was approved by the Conference in July. Also with the blessing of the Conference, Coke sailed soon afterwards with three missionaries, two of whom were designated for Newfoundland (including the Irishman, William Hammett) and one for Antigua. This was the beginning of the fulfilment of Coke's desire that the Methodist connexion should be 'a seminary to fill the vineyard of Christ with devoted labourers'.[2] The Constitution of the Overseas Division of the Methodist Church (Methodist Missionary Society) recognizes the significance of the 1786 Conference, seeing it as 'the beginning of

Methodist overseas missions', with the Conference itself under-
taking responsibility for 'the initiation, direction and support of
overseas missions' from that date.

Irish involvement was a prominent feature in this phase. The
first subscriptions for overseas missions (over £20) were reported
to the Irish Conference in 1786, even before the new approach
to missions had been approved by the British Conference. An
Irish preacher serving in Dublin, the distinguished Adam
Clarke, was one of nine members appointed to the first Missionary Committee in 1790, with the task of sharing responsibility with Coke for the management of the work in the West
Indies. After several preachers had been sent to the West Indies,
it was resolved at the Irish Conference in 1800 that every missionary should indicate his willingness to return to Ireland upon
completion of his period overseas. Chairmen of Districts in
Ireland were asked in that year to look out for suitable candidates
for overseas service. In 1808 arrangements were made at the
Irish Conference for a collection to be taken in all congregations
for overseas funds. Rudimentary though these and similar
developments in Britain and Ireland were, it is clear that the
structure of what became the Missionary Society was gradually
emerging.

The **third phase** commenced in 1813, hastened by Coke's
imminent departure for Ceylon and the need for alternative
arrangements through which the church could continue to be
involved officially in overseas missions. The first Auxiliary
Missionary Society was established in Leeds in October 1813,
and other Districts quickly followed, soon to be organized at a
national level under the Wesleyan Methodist Missionary
Society. Almost immediately features began to emerge which,
in modified forms, still survive. In 1814 a 'Penny a Week
Society' was formed in Edinburgh. Two years later Juvenile
Missionary Associations (JMA) were started in several cities and
in Kingswood school. A missionary magazine, *Missionary Notices*,
was published for the first time also in 1816; the first mention of
collecting boxes is made in 1817.

It should be noted that from the beginning the WMMS was

unlike most other missionary societies, whether denominational or undenominational. It was not a voluntary missionary society in the normally accepted sense of individuals choosing to belong to it, but 'the Methodist Church itself organized for Overseas Missions'. *Every member of the Methodist Church was automatically a member of it.* It should, however, also be recognized that the creation of the Society, and the fact that it had a separate budget, were an acknowledgement that direct Conference management of overseas missions had been a failure.

Developments in Ireland kept pace with those in Britain. On 5 May 1814 a Missionary Society was formed for the Dublin District which became a national body three years later, known as the Hibernian Auxiliary to the WMMS. The Juvenile Missionary Association, encouraging support for the parent WMMS, was active in the Dublin area from 1816, with annual reports being published from 1818. By 1827 there were branch Societies in Whitefriar Street, Abbey Street, Donnybrook, Ringsend and Kingstown.

The WMMS in Britain called as early as 1818 for the formation of Ladies' Branch Associations in connection with District Auxiliary Missionary Societies, but there is no evidence of this challenge having been taken up in Ireland. There are, however, references to a Ladies' Juvenile Association (in connection with JMA) in Dublin in 1825. Work specifically by women on behalf of women overseas gained fresh impetus, however, with the formation in London in 1858 of 'The Ladies' Committee for the Amelioration of the Condition of Women in Heathen Countries', and there was an early response to this within Ireland.

Occasional Papers were published by the Ladies' Committee in London from 1859, and in August 1860 a printed appeal was sent out. This called for local committees to be formed, for money and materials to be sent, and for female missionary candidates to offer as a means of supplementing the work of the parent Missionary Society and of advancing Christian outreach among women overseas. Included were these stirring words:

Now is the time for the Ladies' Committee to be encouraged and established. They have taken a step in advance, and must not be allowed to retreat. Who will come to their help? Is there not in every city and town, and at least in every Circuit in Great Britain, a company of women zealous for God, and full of compassion for Heathen women? . . . Let Christian women throughout Great Britain be of the same mind with the Ladies' Committee, and labour with them in the Gospel; and women throughout the Heathen world shall bless them and thank God for them.[3]

Although addressed specifically to British Methodist women, the appeal appeared in the *Missionary Notices* and was therefore circulated within Ireland. It was not the sort of challenge which Irish Methodist women would ignore, and indeed they did not. There is evidence of a women's missionary meeting being held in the Centenary Methodist Church, St Stephen's Green, Dublin in 1864; of gifts from women in Belfast around the same time; and of a missionary 'Association' for women in Belfast in 1865. By 1870 such Women's Associations were in existence in Belfast, Dublin (at Kingstown, Abbey Street and the Centenary church) and Portadown.[4] Even more significantly, one of the two Beauchamp sisters who served overseas (A. M. Beauchamp in India and Ceylon, and Charlotte E. Beauchamp in South Africa, both from 1869) first had her offer of service considered at a committee meeting in London in October 1864. Here therefore are much earlier roots of what is now known in Ireland as the Methodist Women's Association, the centenary of which was, however, observed in 1984.

In tracing the beginnings of Methodist overseas missions Birtwhistle looked for two distinguishing marks – an official and collective effort in the name of the Church, and initiatives towards those who would then have been regarded as 'the heathen overseas'. It is certainly the case that a beginning on this basis was made in 1786. It would be wrong, however, to assume that Methodist missions were ever simply 'to the heathen overseas'. The truth has always been more complex, as indeed William

Arthur indicated when he addressed the Anniversary Meeting of the WMMS in 1848. Speaking of the threefold nature of the Missionary Society, he said:

It is not merely a Missionary Society to the Heathen; but it is, first, a Colonial Missionary Society; it is, again, a Continental and European Society; and it is, finally, and most largely of all, a Missionary Society to the Heathen.[5]

It was for this reason, Arthur contended, that as a colonial Missionary Society the WMMS was heir to the first official initiatives in sending preachers to North America. There is a case therefore for suggesting that Methodist missions began with the appointment of Richard Boardman and Joseph Pilmoor as the first preachers to America in 1769. In the same way, Arthur stated in his speech, the WMMS was currently involved in South Africa, Australia and New Zealand. He pointed out also that as a continental Missionary Society the WMMS was engaged in work in nearby nominally Christian countries such as France; and that as a Society to the heathen, it had its major involvement in several non-Christian countries. Arthur's influential voice and pen were repeatedly used against any tendency to restrict the range of mission or to limit the involvement of the Missionary Society. As he wrote compellingly towards the end of the nineteenth century:

Some would limit mission work. No missions in Christian countries: it is an affront to a baptized people to be treated as if they were heathen. No missions where a Bishop, whether Anglican, Greek, or Roman, is in possession: it is an offence against episcopal order. No missions to Jews: they are incorrigible. No missions to Mohammedans: they are harder than the nether millstone. No missions to Buddhists: Buddhism is better than the Gospel; and so forth. And I once heard, even in the Methodist Conference, no missions in Roman Catholic countries. All these limitations of mission work are vanity. To all men everywhere must we go.[6]

This is not to suggest, however, that the work of the WMMS

was diffuse or ill-defined. Clarification as to specific functions was given from time to time. Thus the Missionary Secretaries in London wrote officially to the Irish Conference in 1819, as a reminder that the task of mission stations in Ireland was not simply to supplement the work done in ordinary Methodist circuits. They were rather to initiate new outreach into Irish-speaking areas. It was similarly made clear in New South Wales in 1835 that WMMS resources should not be devoted solely to work among British settlers. Contacts with aborigines had also to be developed.

A study of the Irish Mission throws into sharp relief the complexity of relationships between Methodism in Britain and Ireland, making us aware of both strengths and weaknesses.

The Irish Mission

The Irish Mission was launched at the Irish Conference in 1799, with Dr Thomas Coke presiding. From the outset it was administered separately from the normal circuit-system in Ireland which was the responsibility of the Irish Conference. The Mission was directed from London first by Coke himself and later by agents appointed by the WMMS. Coke undertook to raise the funds as part of Britain's total missionary contribution. Three general missionaries were appointed under the Irish Mission in 1799, with authority to move freely throughout the country, unhampered by circuit boundaries. In addition local mission stations were established, some with schools attached. By 1823 there were twenty-one of these, in each case with missionaries appointed, twelve of whom were considered competent to preach in the Irish language.

Nothing accounts more for the wide dispersal of Methodism in Ireland than the work of the Irish Mission, but, on the debit side, anxiety arose in Britain over the WMMS being responsible for financing it, on the grounds that funds raised for the Society were intended for overseas missions and not for mission in these islands. In July 1819 the Missionary Secretaries in London wrote to the Irish Conference to remind it of the strict limits governing the use of WMMS money in Ireland:

> That the Missionary Fund is raised for *Foreign objects*, & cannot consistently be applied to the enlargement of support of our Work at Home: that the Irish Mission has indeed been considered as an exception to this General Rule, because the Committee have felt an earnest desire to afford every possible assistance in the great work of promoting the moral & religious improvement of Ireland ... but in order to continue this mode of asistance it is absolutely necessary that the money sent from England should be bona fide & exclusively applied towards the support of those of your Missionaries only who can & do preach or teach in the Irish language, & whose labours are generally devoted to those parts of your country in which your Regular Preachers do not exercise their Ministry.[7]

By 1871 a limited transfer of control of the Mission stations to the Irish Conference took place, but the WMMS continued to provide grant-aid for the Irish Mission. Ireland for its part still raised money for the work of the Missionary Society as a whole. In 1871 the grant from England was £6,664. By 1905 it had fallen to £4,100, the number of mission stations having declined significantly, with some becoming part of the circuit system. The Irish Methodist historian, Lee Cole, has described the procedure which he suggests had evolved for handling the finances.

> The Irish Methodist Church collected a sum of about £4,000 each year for Foreign Missions, and on the other side of the account received a grant of about £4,000. By a simple and natural arrangement of contra-account there was no interchange of cheques and the amount of money collected in Ireland for Foreign Missions was not sent to England, but was set off against the grant that was due to Ireland.[8]

This is an over-simplification, however, and does not do justice to the variety of practice that emerged. In 1895, for example, it was recommended that the money raised in Ireland for the Missionary Society should all be remitted direct to the Mission House. Yet at other times correspondence between Ireland and London sometimes alluded to the 'missionary balance' along the lines indicated by Cole, with the balance being understood as the difference in the amounts given by the Missionary Society to Ireland and received from Ireland. Thus in 1882 a letter was sent to Dublin:

> Permit me to urge upon you, and your dear Colleagues . . . to use all possible measures to restore your old custom, of remitting to us, for the evangelization of the world, some acceptable balance.[9]

Reference has already been made to the unease felt in Britain about money for mission being spent in Ireland. A related problem arose in Ireland over money raised for the WMMS. Should this money be used to help pay for the Irish Mission or for mission overseas? Confusion over this surfaced from time to time, and can only have blunted Irish financial support for the WMMS. Such confusions were aired in the Minutes of the Missionary Society for October 1816 when it was stated:

> That Mr. Kean of Dublin be informed that the Committee have no authority to determine how the monies raised for the support of Missions by the Irish Brethren shall be applied as they conceive that that is a matter to be determined by the Irish Conference, yet they give it as their opinion, that as in the pulpit & in public meetings the people were urged to contribute to the Mission Funds under the express assurance that their object was to support foreign as well as home Missions some part of the monies raised in Ireland ought in fairness to be applied to the support of the gospel abroad, and to be transmitted to the general Treasurers of the Methodist Missions for that purpose.[10]

In 1822 William Reilly, a preacher who had served in the Irish Mission, felt compelled to publish a pamphlet entitled *An Answer to several Charges brought by some Anonymous Persons against the Methodist Missionary Society of Ireland*. Reilly stated that:

The leading accusation against us, is, that we misapply the monies, which he says, are raised under the impression that they are for foreign objects, but that they are applied to home purposes, and that we studiously conceal our Irish affairs from view.[11]

In rebutting the charges, Reilly argued that Ireland had given more money to the WMMS than it had received; that the Irish Mission had been established by people in Britain, and was paid for by them; and that:

Since the commencement of our Society, any liberal friends, who wished to contribute to our foreign mission, or Pagan Schools exclusively, their contributions have been acknowledged and applied accordingly.[12]

Even this reply, however, reveals ambiguity.

A letter written by one of the Missionary Secretaries in September 1824 followed a different line from that taken in the Committee Minute of October 1816:

I am desired to state most explicitly, that from the beginning it was always assumed that the *whole sum* raised by the Hibernian Wesleyan Missionary Society (deducting expenses only) should come to the account of our General Treasurer.[13]

In 1859 a letter written in 1842 by one of the missionaries involved in the Irish Mission, and sent originally to Dublin, was forwarded to London. Part of it ran:

As to 'the Missionary balance,' it has gone among the clergy of Ireland thro' the Agent of the Church Society, that all the monies raised for Missions *remain in Ireland*. Does not that same Miss. balance countenance this conclusion? One of the clergy of this city refused peremtorily to give a subscription the other day until he was assured it should go *exclusively* into the *foreign* channel.[14]

A covering letter commented that similar views were still being expressed. Apparently some potential subscribers still required assurance that their contributions would be used only for work overseas.

Even by the end of the century the issue had not been resolved. In April 1898 the *Irish Christian Advocate* quoted a certain 'Layman' who had written elsewhere about the implications of Anglican support for Methodist missions:

I have been informed on good authority that out of every £5 subscribed in Ireland with the object of sending the Gospel to the heathen by Wesleyan Missionaries £3 goes to the Irish Mission i.e. to support Irish Wesleyan Ministers. As a considerable proportion of the £5 is given by Church people, it is well they should know . . . they are also subscribing for the support of work which is directed mainly to the break-up of the congregation to which they belong.[15]

A few months later it was alleged that the claim that money collected for overseas missions was in fact diverted for use at home, came from those who themselves contributed nothing and were hostile. It was acknowledged nonetheless that damage had been done by such allegations, and the suggestion was made that a return to an earlier practice would lead to an improvement:

Let the sum we collect in Ireland for the Foreign Mission Society go to the support of missionaries who shall be sent out by the Foreign Missionary Society in London, as missionaries supported by the Irish contribution, and then let the sum given to our missions in Ireland be given, as it originally was, as a gift from the English people to help us to carry on our missionary work in this country. I think this plan would be far more satisfactory to all parties, and it would give an impetus to our Irish Methodists in feeling that they were supporting their own men, and induce them to give more liberally to the foreign work.[16]

As has been seen already, however, such an approach created problems for Methodists in Britain. It seems extraordinary that the anomalies in the arrangements should have been allowed to remain for so long, and that by the start of the twentieth century the problem was still unsettled.

Britain and Ireland, Unequal Partners in Mission

The constitution of what is now the Overseas Division of the Methodist Church (Methodist Missionary Society) contains an article devoted entirely to the Methodist Conference in Ireland, making it plain that Irish Methodism undertakes and conducts its work overseas through the Methodist Missionary Society, and that it takes its place within the committee structure of the Missionary Society. Up to the end of the nineteenth century, however, Ireland had no direct involvement in the formation of missionary policy or in making decisions. The Hibernian Auxiliary was strictly on a par with Auxiliary Societies in overseas Districts, having no executive authority. Its role was simply one of promoting the concerns and work of the parent body. There was no direct Irish representation on committees outside Ireland, the only Irish people involved being those who had left Ireland and settled in Britain, becoming part of Wesleyan Methodist life and structures there. Adam Clarke, William Arthur and William McArthur were outstanding examples.

As early as 1808 difficulties arose over the partial equipping in Dublin of two overseas missionaries, it being made clear that Ireland was not to incur any expenditure on the supply of such articles as books and cloth. By 1892 the Hibernian Auxiliary did not even have responsibility for working out the itineraries of visiting British deputation speakers. At the end of the century sharp differences arose between the two Conferences over the cost of training ministers in Ireland for work overseas, and the Irish Conference requested a grant from the Missionary Society to help defray its expenses in the case of two missionaries. The reply sent from Britain again underlined Ireland's subordinate role:

In the opinion of the Committee no payment should be made, on the ground that places on Mission Stations are granted to Irish Probationers at the request of the Irish Conference, though the Missionary Committee has at the time trained men in waiting who would occupy the said places if Irishmen were not applicants. The arrangements under which Candidates from Ireland for Missionary work are received were adopted by the Conference of 1886, and do not make reference to any payment for training. If the Irish Conference objects to these arrangements, it is open to it to send its approved Candidates to England to pass the usual courts of examination in this Country and to become Ministers of the English Conference in the ordinary way.[17]

This reaffirmation of the 1886 arrangements raises questions about a claim in Alexander McCrea's *Irish Methodism in the Twentieth Century* which Frederick Jeffery has more recently repeated:

In 1890 a new arrangement was made between the Irish Conference and the Missionary Society whereby ministers going out from Ireland should retain their connection with the Irish Conference and should be free to return to the work in Ireland from the Foreign Field. . . . The fact that our missionaries still remain members of our Conference and Church leads our people to a personal interest which could not possibly be theirs if in giving our young people to the work it was necessary to transfer them to the English Conference.[18]

Neither the Irish and British Minutes of Conference, nor the Minutes of the Hibernian Auxiliary, provide evidence of a new arrangement being made in 1890 or at any time in the last decade of the nineteenth century. The 1886 arrangements set out regulations applicable to Irish-born missionaries whether they retained their links with the Irish Conference or transferred to the British. Jeffery's claim that for many years ministers who became missionaries had to transfer to the British Methodist Church does not appear to be correct. Undoubtedly factors arose which encouraged some missionaries to choose to transfer to the British Conference prior to going overseas, or to work in Britain upon their return from overseas, but there was no compulsion for them to do so. Indeed the Missionary Society took the line that Irish-born missionaries, unless they had transferred to the British Conference, should return to Ireland after completion of their overseas service.

A Better Way?

Dissatisfaction with the form of the relationship between Methodists in Britain and Ireland, and also with the manner in which Methodism had been administered within Ireland, led to different approaches being suggested. They were voiced, however, only by individuals in an uncoordinated manner.

Patrick Ffrench, who served in the Caribbean from 1818 to 1827, wrote in 1828 from near Cloughjordan to London, favouring the integration of Methodism in Ireland and Britain, and claiming that otherwise the work in Ireland would steadily decline.[19] This, however, was but a passing reference in his letter, and there is no reason to suppose that it was a view which commanded widespread support. Indeed the opposite was more probably the case. Ffrench's missionary colleagues in the West Indies had accused him of serious mental instability in 1825. Their actual words, contained in a formal resolution, were that he displayed 'extreme imbecility and want of apprehension'.[20] Since he was still recovering from a serious illness when he wrote to London, and bearing in mind that he had returned to Ireland only a year earlier, it can be assumed that what he was advancing was a personal view. Interestingly, however, the same idea surfaced again forty years later, when two articles appeared in the *Irish Evangelist* arguing the case for the creation of a single Methodist Conference in the United Kingdom. One of the advantages their anonymous author saw in what he called the 'junction' of the two Methodist Conferences was that he believed there would be a greater missionary response. It would then be as easy, it was affirmed, for people to go overseas from Ireland as it was from Yorkshire![21]

Less radical were the more frequent pleas for a different form of partnership with Britain which would enable Methodists in

Ireland to identify more readily with overseas missions. A returned missionary writing to the *Irish Christian Advocate* in 1895 asked whether the time had not come when Ireland should send a few missionaries 'direct to the foreign field', with Irish Methodism perhaps assuming responsibility for a new area being considered at the time.[22] The same paper reported an extension of this kind of thinking when it referred to the meeting of the Sligo District Synod in September 1906. A speaker there suggested more direct responsibility for Ireland in association with the Missionary Society:

> The Missionary Society might give the Hibernian Auxiliary a district in India, another in China, and another in Africa to take care of in conjunction with the committee in London. Irish missionaries might be sent to these by preference, and Irish contributions ear-marked for the support of the work in those mission areas.[23]

Such suggestions for a new form of partnership are entirely understandable, given the lack of Irish involvement in policy-forming and decision-making to which we have already referred. It is in this context too that we can appreciate the warm response within Ireland to the different style of approach adopted by the Christian Endeavour movement at the end of the nineteenth century. In co-operating with the Missionary Society in sending Robin Booth as a medical missionary from Cork to China in 1899, and in calling for prayer and practical support specifically for his work, Christian Endeavour was responding to the need which many felt for some form of personal identification with overseas work. Irish Methodism, it was claimed in the *Irish Christian Advocate* in 1898, at last had a missionary whom they could 'look on as their own'.[24] The level of financial support for Booth was, however, disappointing.

The WMMS contributed much to missionary outreach in and through Ireland. Through the Irish Mission the influence of Methodism was spread widely, if rather thinly, throughout the country. The WMMS was also the body through which Irish

Methodists officially fulfilled their missionary obligation. It was their window on the world, and the door through which many passed to be involved directly in overseas service. Upon their return to Ireland overseas missionaries helped to make their fellow-countrymen more aware of world issues, and sharpened the mission of the church at home. There is no doubt, therefore, that if there had not been the opportunity of being involved in overseas missions through the WMMS, Irish Methodism would have lost much through lack of a wider challenge and stimulus. Too small and too weak a church to take many official initiatives on its own, particularly in the crippling mid-century years of famine and emigration, the temptation to which it has always been exposed – that of losing its own soul in attempts to preserve its life – would have been stronger and more influential than ever.

The benefits would have been even greater, however, had there been a clearer financial policy and, even more significantly, had real progress been made in enabling Ireland to play a more responsible part in the affairs of the Missionary Society. Mature partnership, in which each party realizes his potential and derives full benefit from his involvement, is only possible when responsibility is shared. Such partnership is possible, given a right spirit and attitude, irrespective of the comparative strengths and weaknesses of the partners. Britain, however, was always dominant, more a patron than a partner, a benefactor rather than a brother; and in consequence the relationship for each was less fruitful than it might have been. It could also be argued that this unequal relationship inhibited growth towards maturity within Ireland itself. In the New Testament all Christians are seen to possess gifts (charismata), which they are to use in accordance with the grace God has given (Romans 12.6). Only thus can there be continued growth in Christ and fulfilment in mission.

There was nevertheless another very important factor in the Irish contribution to Methodism's witness overseas. When in the several decades immediately following the formation of the WMMS, the relationship between Britain and Ireland was least productive from the point of view of co-operation in overseas missions, large scale *emigration* – in itself so destructive an influence – became the major means whereby Irish Methodism remained creatively involved in the wider world.

– 3 –

Emigration – Losses and Gains

=

Emigration has undermined Methodism in Ireland from its earliest days, frustrating its hopes and rendering it permanently weak. There is, however, another side to the story. What was stated in the *Irish Evangelist* in 1867 with regard to America has in fact a much wider application, that 'during the past century the weakness of Methodism in Ireland has been the strength of Methodism in America'.[1]

The Extent of the Problem

Methodist emigration cannot of course be viewed in isolation. It is only a tiny aspect of a major historical process upon which recent writers have thrown much light. G. O'Tuathaigh has drawn attention to an estimate that in the years preceding the Famine, between 1780 and 1845, about 1.1 million people from Ireland emigrated to the United States and Canada, of whom about 400,000 left during the decade commencing in 1831.[2] David Fitzpatrick points out that emigration peaked during the decade 1846–1855, when about two and a half millions left the country in response to the Famine and to the social revolution which followed.[3] According to J. Lee, a further three and a half million Irish people emigrated between 1856 and the start of the First World War.[4] Ireland under the Union (1801–1921) was 'a land which most people wanted to leave', losing a larger proportion of its people through emigration than any other country.[5]

Virtually every English-speaking country experienced extensive Irish settlement. Around 1890 only three-fifths of those born in Ireland were still at home, with three million living overseas. The United States contained nearly two-thirds of the Irish overseas, and at different periods Canada and Australasia each accounted for about one-tenth.

The religious professions of emigrants were not systematically recorded. Protestants, however, made up about two-thirds of the Irish population of Ontario through most of the nineteenth century. They also contributed heavily to Irish settlement in New Zealand, many of them 'Ulster Scots', since New Zealand had a strong Scottish tradition. By contrast, Protestants accounted for about only one-fifth of state-assisted Irish emigrants to New South Wales.

Continuous statistics on **the emigration of Irish Methodists** are not available for the period prior to 1830, but earlier occasional references sometimes contained illuminating local detail. For example, Wesley himself wrote of the effect of emigration on the Palatine community in Ballingrane, Co. Limerick. The Palatines were German Protestant refugees who left the Palatinate in the Rhine valley because of religious persecution. In 1709 many went to England, and between five hundred and a thousand settled near Rathkeale in County Limerick. Their industrious and distinctive way of life frequently drew favourable comment from social and agricultural observers in Ireland. Some, however, lapsed from the practice of religion, to be recalled to it again from 1749 onwards under the influence of Methodist open-air preaching around Limerick. Then, about fifty years after they had first settled in the area, their original leases ran out and much higher rents were demanded. This in turn led many to uproot themselves again, some emigrating to America. Wesley was appalled at the deterioration he witnessed in the Palatine settlement when he visited it in 1765:

> About noon I preached . . . to the small remains of the poor Palatines. As they could not get food and raiment here, with all their diligence and frugality, part are scattered up and

down the kingdom, and part gone to America. I stand amazed! Have landlords no common sense (whether they have common humanity or no), that they will suffer such tenants as these to be starved away from them?[6]

In 1818 a decrease in general Methodist membership was partly accounted for 'by emigrations to the Canadas and other places . . . In one Circuit alone, 120 emigrated'.[7] In 1823 a total of nearly five hundred members was reported as having emigrated, and it was noted that whole families had gone to America and whole societies had been dispersed.

From 1830 figures for emigration have been printed in the Minutes of Conference. The following Table summarizes the membership loss in Irish Methodism through emigration:[8]

1830–1839	5,593
1840–1849	8,665
1850–1859	6,811
1860–1869	5,340
1870–1879	3,682
1880–1889	4,717
1890–1899	3,725

More than a thousand members were reported as having emigrated each year in 1831, 1847, 1848, 1849 and 1850, the last four coinciding with the worst effects of the Famine. Not surprisingly, the Irish Methodist membership which stood at 44,000 in 1844 had, by 1900, declined to only 27,461. Even allowing for other factors in this numerical decline, it is clear that emigration had greatly weakened the church.

Of course the loss through emigration should not be seen merely, perhaps not even primarily, in terms of numbers. Within the church it would appear that the key people in local communities often emigrated. They at least possessed sufficient drive to seek to improve their prospects in the New World. In 1835 it was reported that many holding important public offices had emigrated, and in several cases whole congregations had been scattered. In 1841 the annual Reply from the British Conference to the Irish Conference stated that it was painfully discouraging to witness the departure of the best people from year to year. In 1847 Thomas Waugh, an Irish Wesleyan preacher, claimed at the Annual Meeting of the WMMS in London that 'hundreds and thousands of our very best and most industrious people have fled to America'.[9] In 1848 it was stated that in many localities classes had been broken up, centres where ministers had been provided with accommodation were closed, and congregations had been scattered. In 1851 it was affirmed in the annual Address to the British Conference that 'multitudes in the middle class', people among whom potentially the most productive work could have been carried on, had gone away. The same trend continued throughout the century. Thus in 1886 it was stated that large numbers still emigrated – by then the annual average was in the region of five hundred – and the comment was added that emigrants consisted 'chiefly of the young and energetic'.[10]

Emigration on such a scale was bound to have a debilitating effect upon Methodism in Ireland. Class leaders, local preachers, and other lay people capable of providing leadership, left the country; and, in the wider community, large numbers with whom an initial contact had already been made and through whom more fruitful contact might have become possible, also fled the country. A report published in 1870 summarized the position well:

> True religion as soon as experienced awakens in the minds of youth the spirit of enterprise, and between discouragements at home, and the attraction of America and the British colonies in the southern world, flourishing societies and congregations are often decimated.[11]

Causes of Emigration

Here again Methodist comment must be placed within a wider setting. O'Tuathaigh has pointed out that there was a serious failure in the potato crop in 1817, leading to severe distress. Again in 1821 there was further widespread failure of the potato crop, particularly west of a line from Londonderry to Cork. On both occasions private charity was augmented by public works schemes in an effort to alleviate suffering. Throughout the 1830s scarcely a year passed when partial crop failure was not reported in the west.

William Forbes Adams has made similar points, concluding that the four years ending in 1823 constitute one of the blackest periods in the social history of Ireland. According to him, agrarian outrages, which had been less frequent in the few years immediately after the famine conditions of 1817–18, reappeared with increased bitterness late in 1820, particularly in Galway and Roscommon. Such disturbances took on a more religious dimension in the 1820s due to the prolonged campaign for Catholic emancipation.[12]

O'Tuathaigh claims that a state of near anarchy existed in many parts of rural Ireland in the early 1830s, with a vigorous campaign against the payment of tithes sweeping the country in the winter of 1830–31. The crime list for 1832 (over 9,000) showed 242 murders, over 300 attempted murders, and 568 cases of arson. Bitterly resentful that the Emancipation Act, from which Roman Catholics had expected so much, had in fact left their basic condition unaltered, many peasants turned again to secret societies in the hope of finding an instant remedy, and assaults on persons and livestock increased sharply.[13] Pre-famine emigration was, then, dominated by such 'push' factors as economic deprivation, lack of employment opportunities, crop failure, rural unrest, and religious tension. Adams summarized the compelling motive for emigration in this period in a single word, 'distress'.[14]

In the post-famine period 'pull' factors came into play increasingly. Prominent among these was a powerful foreign demand for immigrant labour, as expressed for example by the United States, and the growing influence of 'chain migration'. The urban sector in the population in the United States rose from 11 to 46 per cent between 1840 and 1910. Natural increase and rural-urban migration could scarcely have generated this transformation, although it is admittedly difficult to assess the

particular contribution of the Irish in this process. It must, however, have been considerable given that the rapid urban expansion in America in the middle of the century coincided with the
heaviest influx from Ireland. Through chain migration the
selection of future emigrants lay largely with those who had gone
before. At first efforts were made to reassemble household units
in the New World, and then the process gradually broadened to
include communal replanting. State aid was significant in
encouraging Irish movement only in the cases of Australasia and
Canada.

Irish emigrants were well suited for the role of servicing other
people's industrial revolutions. Their background had been one
of enforced idleness and ignorance. They were now eager for
work, to better themselves and their families.[15]

Methodist comment on emigration prior to the Famine re-
affirms the 'push' factors already indicated. The Annual Address
in 1823 from Ireland to the British Methodist Conference commented on 'outrages, robberies, burnings, and murders'.
Societies had been scattered, property destroyed, and preachers
attacked:

> In such circumstances of desolation and poverty as have suc-
> ceeded the insurrectionary state of this country, when tens of
> thousands of the poor are begging and starving in several
> counties, when trade is depressed, when there is no market for
> agricultural produce, and when anxiety and fear have come
> upon the land like an armed host; it is not to be wondered at
> that our beloved Societies should have had a large portion of
> the common affliction . . . Whole families have emigrated to
> America as their only place of refuge, and, in consequence,
> whole Societies have been dispersed.

In 1827 the annual Irish Address to the British Conference spoke
of 'commercial depression' in both Britain and Ireland, and
claimed that many people in Ireland had been 'obliged to yield
to the pressure of the times, and remove to distant parts of the
earth'. In 1837 the story was the same. 'The still prevailing political and religious contentions, which have so long disturbed and

afflicted our population, have kept up the spirit of emigration.'
Five years later the Address to the British Conference noted that
'the continuously agitated, distracted, and impoverished state
of our country . . . is a great impediment in our way and draw-
back upon our prosperity', and had consequently led to a dis-
tressing level of emigration. Thomas Waugh claimed in a speech
to the Anniversary meeting of the WMMS in London in
1847:

> Society seems to be uprooted. As for our religious societies I
> know not what to tell you about them. Starvation has driven
> those who had realized a little, and were in independent cir-
> cumstances, from the country . . . We look for hundreds and
> thousands of them in vain.[16]

In the post-famine period the situation was still as bad according
to the annual Report of the WMMS. Political events in the
United States were a complicating factor:

> Emigration to an unusual extent, occasioned by a series of bad
> harvests, and loss of trade, chiefly caused by the lamentable
> civil war in America, has thinned our ranks, and in many
> places narrowed the field of our operations.[17]

A notable comment on emigration from Lord Dufferin and
Clandeboy, the Chancellor of the Duchy of Lancaster, appeared
in the *Irish Evangelist* in 1872. Its background was a defence of
landlords against the charge of 'extermination'. Dufferin's view
was that the chief cause of emigration was the systematic discouragement, indeed the ruthless suppression, of Irish industry
by Britain over a period of centuries:

> In the suppression of Irish manufacturing industry . . .
> we have evidently the original and principal cause of the
> excessive emigration from this country. Since that time
> successive agitations, to which all Governments of what-
> ever shade of politics have pandered, have discouraged
> the investment of capital, and thereby prevented the
> general resuscitation of that industry.[18]

That Dufferin's view was not questioned or modified, either in
the issue in which it appeared or in a subsequent issue, is surprising even allowing for the fact that Dufferin was a Cabinet
Minister. Irish Methodism prided itself in loyalty to Britain, and
was seldom openly critical of the role of Britain in Irish affairs.

The influence of Roman Catholicism was believed to be
another factor in the economic distress of Ireland. Wesley himself held this opinion. David Hempton has suggested that he
shared the anti-Catholic sentiments of his times, albeit for sup-
posedly liberal reasons, and that he saw in the Roman Catholic
Church an institution that merely contributed to the poverty of
the Irish people. The close ties between the people and their
priests did not promote such necessary virtues as individual self-
improvement and freedom of choice. This conviction hardened
further among Methodists at a later period when political pressures become more urgent in the Bunting generation.[19] Hempton
states that

> when the economic condition of Ireland became a major con-
> cern in the years preceding the famine, the Methodists in
> England and Ireland were convinced that the propagation of
> the Gospel was the best solution.[20]

A similar attitude prevailed in the post-famine period. William
Crook, an Irish Wesleyan preacher, argued in 1866 that whereas
Protestantism raised people's living standards Roman Catholic-
ism kept them poor:

> It is POPERY that has impoverished them and kept them
> down, shedding its baneful influence . . . over all . . . as seen
> in Spain, beneath the sunny skies of Italy, and in poor priest-
> ridden Ireland. On the contrary, it is PROTESTANTISM
> that has elevated . . . the sturdy inhabitants of Ulster.[21]

In the wake of the Famine the British Wesleyan Conference
offered comment in the same vein on the relationship between
economic distress, emigration and religious truth. Consider,
for example, the official Reply to the Irish Conference in
1847:

It is unnatural for man to leave the home of his fathers. . . .
It must cost these wanderers the most painful pangs to tear
themselves away from all which they hold dear. Their
humanity, their religious attachments, their relative affections, must all be outraged. It does not become us to review
the causes of this evil, further than to remark, that in a country
which is constantly expatriating her children, expelling them
from their homes, and sending them as exiles in distant lands,
there must be something radically and almost universally
wrong . . . We may venture to express our belief, that the true
remedy is the preaching of the Cross, and the influence of
religion.

This commitment to the gospel as the solution for Irish post-
famine misery is paralleled by the British Government's equally
inadequate reliance on laissez-faire economic principles. Both
positions are of course more distasteful in retrospect than they
were at the time.

The Positive Side to Emigration

It says much for the faith and insight of Irish Methodists that
they recognized that emigration was not wholly evil. Supreme
among the benefits flowing from it was the strengthening of the
world church. Thus in 1827 it was stated that 'Ireland has been
for years a nursery' from which many people had gone to be
added to the membership of the church in other parts of the
world.[22] This advantage was recognized outside Ireland too, and
in 1833 the Reply from the British to the Irish Conference
claimed that 'although it was painful for Ireland to part with its
people, it was comforting to know that their loss sometimes led
elsewhere to the furtherance of the gospel, and to the extension
of the . . . kingdom'. In 1841 it was said of Irish emigrants that
some went to swell the numbers, and increase the efficiency, of
'other branches of the great Methodist family', and some carried
their religion 'into the heart of the wilderness', laying there the
foundations of new churches. In the Irish Address to the British
Conference in 1844, it was affirmed with reference to emigration:

Our loss ... is alleviated by the persuasion that, like the Christians dispersed 'through the persecution that arose about Stephen,' they will go 'everywhere preaching the word,' that 'the hand of the Lord will be with them,' and that by their instrumentality a great number will 'believe' ... This hope is warranted by the reviving fact ... that Methodism was introduced into the United States of America by emigrants from this country.

In 1849 the Address of the British Conference to the Irish Conference spoke of 'emigrant witnesses for Christ' rendering 'a blessing beyond all calculation'. In 1857 a message from the General Conference of the MEC commented 'that the very foundations of our American Methodist Church' were laid by Irishmen, and that a large portion of her ministry and member-ship were natives of Ireland. In 1870 the Annual Address to the Methodist Societies in Ireland claimed:

Emigration is not to be viewed *only* in its depressing aspects. The removal of many from our country – if a local and tem-porary loss – has been a wide and permanent gain' Churches large and fair', founded or strengthened by them, are now a great and constantly increasing power for good in the earth.

Three years later it was again stated in the Address to Method-ists in Ireland:

You cannot place your foot on any colony of the British Empire that does not include a convert of that little Irish Methodist Church. Though kept weak by a continual drain of emigra-tion, she has contributed to the strength of every stem in the Methodist plantations. ... She has yielded more ministers than any Church of similar size in the world.

In 1884 in an Address from the Irish Conference to the General Conference of the MEC, it was claimed:

You have more Methodists in New York or Philadelphia than we have in Dublin or Belfast; and in all the leading cities of the Union Irish Methodists are among your most prominent members and most efficient office-bearers.

The MEC Conference again expressed indebtedness to Ireland in 1886:

Both in our ministry and in our laity, Ireland is largely represented; and the quick intelligence, the ready wit, the lively sympathies, the fervent piety, and the steady principles of Irish Protestantism are with us everywhere esteemed as most valuable elements in our religious life. You have greatly enriched us.

It is little wonder, then, that in 1867 an article in the *Irish Evangelist* made the claim which we have already quoted, that the weakness of Methodism in Ireland had been the strength of Methodism in America.

It must be acknowledged that those who emigrated did not always retain their faith. As was admitted in 1841, many lost 'all sense of religion in the trials and anxieties of a settler' due to the lack of church services and of close pastoral care.[23] In a booklet written after extensive preaching and money-raising tours in North America, an Irish preacher, John Ker, noted that some people's piety could not withstand the voyage across the Atlantic.[24] This trend was used to encourage support for the efforts of the WMMS to build up the colonial church. Attempts were also made to alert prospective emigrants to potential dangers overseas, and to offer them practical advice. Thus a letter from the United States in the *Irish Christian Advocate* in 1885 encouraged people to carry letters of commendation from their ministers in Ireland, and to seek out an MEC minister immediately upon arrival in America.[25] Some months later another letter appeared in the same paper, this time from Australia, giving advice to young Methodists who emigrated there. They were urged not to stay too long in large cities after their arrival and were encouraged to take the first job offered to them, being warned against alcohol and exhorted to avoid bad company and to be regular in church attendance.[26]

It should be admitted too that even those who held on to their faith were not always wholly an influence for good in the lands and churches of their adoption. In this aspect of church life, as in others, over-simplified 'success stories' tend to be handed on from generation to generation. Reality was frequently more complicated than religious nostalgia would allow.

Regrettably little original material has come to light to show what kinds of attitudes Irish Methodist emigrants took with them. Did they, for example, carry strong anti-Roman Catholic or pro-British sentiments? Here indeed would be a fruitful field for further research. It is interesting to note that the Palatines embraced the Empire Loyalist cause, travelling across the border to Canada in the aftermath of the American War of Independence. As already indicated (in chapter 1) it does seem that the line on some issues taken by influential dissidents in early American Methodism was strongly influenced by earlier Irish experience.

To return to the positive aspects of emigration, it is significant that the official *Manual of the Laws and Discipline* of Irish Methodism claims that the Methodist Church is itself one of the least results of the Methodist revival in Ireland, since throughout its history hundreds of its members have annually found a home in other lands where they played a leading part in establishing churches. This is perhaps best illustrated not by drawing upon official church statements but by citing examples from individuals in different parts of the world.

John McKenny, writing from New South Wales in 1839, referred to the great number of immigrants who took an interest in religion, and proceeded to draw attention to the role of two Irish lay people who had been centrally involved in outreach in new places:

At West Maitland, the new Chapel is ready for the roof. At Patnuck's Plains, thirty miles beyond Maitland, Mr. Kingsbury has given us ground for a new Chapel, and will supply, as a donation, the bricks necessary to build it. This place is visited every third Sunday by Mr. Lidsam, a Local Preacher from Ireland, who has had the honour of commencing the work at Maitland . . . At Wollongong . . . we have a Society which has been raised by the exertions of Mr. Robinson, a Local Preacher and leader from Ireland, who built a chapel in Fintanagh at his own expense and made it out to our connexion just before he left home, he is a sound Methodist and of course anxious that a Preacher should be appointed.[27]

This was the James Robinson, of Fintona, to whom reference was made in C. H. Crookshank's *History of Methodism in Ireland*. In 1842 McKenny added a covering letter to a request being forwarded to the WMMS in London, asking that a preacher be appointed to Wollongong and a church built. The first signature, as one of two local preachers, was that of Robinson. There were by then, claimed McKenny, fifty-two full members and five on trial. The Lidsam to whom McKenny referred was Jeremiah Ledsam, who is said to have arrived in Sydney with credentials from the Irish evangelist Gideon Ouseley and other Irish preachers. A coachbuilder and auctioneer, Ledsam settled in Maitland where he preached at first in his own home and then for some years rented a billiard room at an annual rate of £20. He is thus credited with having introduced Methodism into the Hunter River district, where in time it became both strong and lively.

Printed sources have tended to reproduce the same letters and references when illustrating the strength of Irish lay influence in Methodism in the United States of America and in Canada, but have scarcely mentioned the important personal material contained in such journals as the *Christian Guardian*, a Canadian weekly published in Toronto from 1829. Thus in the obituary of Mrs Barbara Shillington in 1871 (she had been born in Ireland in 1779 and proceeded to Canada in 1819), it was stated that her descendants numbered over two hundred and that most of them were members of the Wesleyan Methodist Church in Canada. Two of her grandsons, Robert and John J. Hare, became ministers in Canada.

The strength of Irish Protestant influence in New Zealand

has already been noted. In 1883 David Brown, formerly of Belfast, wrote from Ashburton (New Zealand) that Irish Methodism was strong in the area, as indeed it was all over the country.[28] The Rev. S. H. MacDade commented form New South Wales in 1886:

> We rejoice in a large membership, five congregations, an efficient staff of local preachers, and good financial resources. In the vicinity of my residence there are many families who some twenty years ago emigrated from various parts of the North of Ireland.[29]

Visitors to North America frequently confirmed what official church statements occasionally acknowledged, that Irish immigrants were often to the fore in Methodist life in the land of their adoption. In 1887 an Irish preacher visiting Philadelphia wrote to the *Irish Christian Advocate*:

> To name all the Irish Methodists who came up to greet me at the altar would require too much of my time, and to print them too much of your room, and so I must only say that they represented many countries, many circuits, and many families, from Limerick to Ardara.[30]

An aside in the official history of the WMMS is significant in what it implies of the Irish contribution to world Methodism through emigration. After paying tribute to the influence of Cornish lay people among gold diggers in Victoria, the authors claim that next to Irish immigrants they had been the most important lay propagators of Methodism in the colonies.[31]

In assessing the role of Irish Methodists overseas it is wise to keep in mind that the emigration of lay people was probably more important than the missionary strategy of the WMMS.

– 4 –

The Laity, Primary Agents of Mission

=

The vital influence of lay people in the life and outreach of the church has often been neglected. This oversight, however deplorable, is to some extent inevitable given that those who have been ordained occupy the main positions of leadership within the church. It is, for example, normally only the names and appointments of ministers which are listed in records, and when official church histories are compiled it is easier and more convenient to trace and assess the contributions of such full-time servants of the church. The fact should not be lost sight of, however, that countless lay people – only a few ever remembered by name, men and women, lettered and unlettered, rich and poor, people of all ages and races have consistently been true to the faith over the centuries, and have thus fulfilled a crucial role in the life and work of the church. By crossing frontiers and travelling to the ends of the earth, or by being faithful at home, many of them have been primary agents of mission.

The laity selected for special consideration in this chapter have in most cases already been recognized as having played a significant part in the life of the church overseas. Their contribution is here reassessed in the light of recent information and comment, and is presented 'warts and all'. However, because of the way the church is organized and church history is recorded, trace will have been lost of the contributions of other outstanding lay people. In these unsatisfactory circumstances, an incomplete account of the role of the laity must be accepted as being better than none.

Forerunners of the First Missionaries

Earnest lay Christians or enquirers – both nationals and ex-patriates – frequently awaited with eagerness the arrival of the first missionaries appointed to new areas. Indeed in most cases the missionaries would not have been sent at all had it not been for the repeated requests and promises of support which such lay people forwarded to missionary executives and other church leaders.

A letter from 'Kurrachee, Scinde' (presumably Karachi in Pakistan) on 10 November 1855 provides an example of the prominent part the military often played in this connection.[1] It tells how soldiers from several different denominations met to-gether in a Wesleyan church for prayer and fellowship, although no Methodist preacher had ever been appointed to the region. The work had started ten years earlier when a Sergeant-Major McBride, who originally came from Banbridge and who had himself been converted in the West Indies, was given permission from the military authorities to build the first church there. Although McBride himself had died in 1846, in a cholera epidemic in which three hundred of his comrades also perished, the work was carried on by successive regiments. As the letter commented:

> If ever the Wesleyan Missionary Society sends a Missionary to Scinde, he will find a place of worship ready built for him.

Even Methodist hymn books were in regular use!

In a detailed study of the role of lay pioneers in the first phases of **American Methodism**, the distinguished historian Frank Baker has concluded that with one exception the major lay figures had all Irish connections.[2] Ireland had itself presented a formidable challenge to the first preachers coming from Britain – due, Baker suggests, to such characteristics of the Irish as sturdy independence, emotional fervour, robust physique and dogged endurance. Once the Irish were won, however, they became, according to Baker, strong champions of the Methodist cause whether they remained in Ireland or travelled overseas.

Foremost among the Irish pioneers in America whom Baker listed was a familiar trio, Robert Strawbridge ('a powerful dynamo of evangelism'), Barbara Heck and Philip Embury (the latter, 'a slow-burning fuse' compared with Strawbridge). The fact that, although not ordained, Strawbridge became a recognized itinerant preacher and was listed in the Minutes of Conference, largely rules him out for our purposes in this chapter. We shall, however, consider whether it was he who formed the first Methodist society on American soil.

The date and location of the first Methodist society in America has been a matter of keen debate among historians. The issue at stake is whether the first society was formed in New York in 1766, following the initiatives of Philip Embury and Barbara Heck, or whether it was in Maryland at an earlier date in association with the work inspired by Robert Strawbridge.

The main facts have long been established so far as New York is concerned. Embury and Heck grew up in the immigrant Palatine community in Co. Limerick. They were cousins who were attracted to Methodism following preaching tours in the area by John Wesley and others. Indeed in 1758 Embury, a carpenter by trade, was placed on the list of reserve for the itinerant ministry in Ireland. In June 1760 he and Heck, with their respective spouses, were prominent members of a group of emigrants who, against the background of soaring rents, sailed from Limerick for New York.

Embury and some of the other Palatines worshipped with the Lutherans in New York, thus renewing the denominational link their forefathers had earlier enjoyed in Germany. For six years he took communion in the Lutheran church, having his children baptized there, and teaching in a church school. Then in 1766 he was challenged by Barbara Heck to start a Methodist society because of the drift into religious indifference of some of their fellow Palatine immigrants. Meetings were started in his house which were later moved to an upper room and to a rigging loft.

John Street chapel was built in 1768, with Embury doing some of the carpentry work himself and preaching at the opening service.

The case for Maryland is much less certain since no one knows precisely when Strawbridge emigrated to America. He was born at Drumsna, Co. Leitrim. Like Embury, he may himself have heard Wesley preach; he probably came under the influence of Laurence Coughlan in the early stages of his religious experience; and he spent some time in Sligo and Tandragee before emigrating. Nineteenth-century historians were divided on the question whether he had arrived in America in the early 1760s or came in 1765 or even later. It is now commonly believed he arrived between 1760 and 1766, and that he started preaching more or less immediately.

In 1916 a joint Commission representing three major branches of Methodism within the United States, presented a report on the origins of American Methodism to the General Conference of the MEC. In this it was claimed that Strawbridge settled in Sam's Creek in Frederick County, Maryland, in 1761; that he baptized a child in 1762 or 1763; and that he began forming Methodist societies as early as 1763 or 1764. A minority report was also produced, however, which opposed these conclusions. Subsequent attempts have failed to resolve the issue, and in 1933 the historian William Sweet concluded that it was a type of controversy which could not now be resolved since conclusive documents on both sides were missing.[3] From an Irish point of view it is perhaps important only that it be acknowledged that Embury, Heck and Strawbridge were all Irish-born.

When the first Methodist society was formed in New York, Embury took office as the 'first trustee, first treasurer, first class-leader, and first preacher'.[4] After the appointment of official Wesleyan preachers to the city by the British Conference in 1769, however, he led several families to establish a new settlement on a tract of land in the Camden Valley which was northeast of Albany though still in New York state. There he again established a society, this time at a place called Ashgrove, being the first society north of New York. He was assisted by Thomas

Ashton, another Irish-born layman who had earlier settled in the vicinity. Embury was appointed a Justice of the Peace for Albany County, but died suddenly in 1773 as a result of over-exertion. A not uncommon account described him as quiet, diffident and melancholy,[5] and the impression is often given that Heck was the real driving force behind much of what he did. Attempts are now being made, particularly by historians who favour New York's claim to have been the location of the first Methodist society, to present Embury in a more forceful light. Attention has recently been drawn to the fact that in the autumn of 1772 he conducted the first Methodist preaching mission in New Hampshire, riding on horseback through dangerous terrain for about a week. His preaching on that occasion is said to have made a deep and lasting impression, leading to a religious revival.[6]

Whatever view one takes of Embury, the overwhelming impression of his cousin Barbara Heck is that she was a most forceful personality who exerted a strong influence on everyone around her. She has been credited with persuading Embury to resume preaching in New York after a lapse of six years. The building of the Methodist chapel in John Street, New York, owed much to her initiative, and she was also instrumental in forming Methodist classes wherever her family settled.

Perhaps the most remarkable contribution of Heck and Embury should be seen not so much in whatever personal initiatives they took, but rather in the strength and resilience of the Palatine community as a whole. Such close-knit community life, with personal religion a dominant element, is vitally important for the creation and development of new communities. This was convincingly demonstrated wherever the Palatines settled, in New York from 1760, in the Camden Valley from 1770, and in different parts of Canada from 1778 onwards as part of the exodus of Empire Loyalists in the wake of the American War of Independence.

Turning from Methodist beginnings in America, we find that one of the earliest Methodist classes in **Australia**, indeed possibly the first, was formed by an Irish layman called Edward Eagar, at Windsor, New South Wales, in 1812. Eagar was referred to in Crookshank's *History of Methodism in Ireland* simply as 'Mr E—', but the other details which are given are substantially correct. Until recently the main known features of Eagar's life were as follows – he had been educated for the Bar, but on committing forgery and being convicted he was sentenced to death. In prison he was visited by Methodists from Cork, under whose influence he had a spiritual awakening and became a reformed person. The death sentence imposed on him was commuted to life transportation, and he was sent to New South Wales where he was employed as a teacher and started taking religious services around Windsor, forming a Methodist class. Another Methodist class had also been started around the same time by others in Sydney, which led to a request being forwarded to London for the first Methodist missionary to be appointed. Samuel Leigh was the person sent, and upon arrival he stayed with Eagar and was introduced by him to the Governor. Thus began what was destined to become a large and influential Methodist Church.

Even a generation later than Crookshank, J. E. Neill was still unable or unwilling to provide Eagar's surname, claiming that perhaps the most remarkable instance of Ireland's contribution to Methodism in Australia was through 'an unnamed Irishman who had been educated for the Bar'.[7]

Additional information has more recently come to light about Eagar, much of it directly relevant to our particular field of interest, as a result of which Eagar emerges as a complex character who, if anything, appears to have been even more significant than had previously been recognized. Some of the material, however, raises questions about Eagar's integrity and also the depth of his religious conversion.

From an article in 1963 by Noel McLachlan,[8] we learn that Eager was a son of Richard Eagar who owned an estate in County Kerry in the parish of Killarney, his ancestry ensuring him a place in Burke's *Landed Gentry of Ireland*. He was tried in 1809 'on a charge of having uttered a forged bill of exchange' and was sentenced to death, the death sentence being commuted by the personal intervention of the judge. There is, however, an account in the *Sydney Gazette* which states that it was the influence of the Irish bishops, prompted by Eagar's conversion, which saved him from execution while his accomplices were hanged. On his arrival in New South Wales in July 1811, he carried a letter of commendation from the prison chaplain in Cork, and was assigned to the household of the Rev. Richard Cartwright, an Anglican chaplain, to act as tutor to his children. Soon he was also engaged in organizing Bible classes in the area around Windsor.

A letter from Eagar himself, sent to Cork and dated 20 June 1812, is the first item (by more than two years) in the WMMS archival materials on Australia.[9] It contains a great deal of interesting information. In it Eagar referred to the 'little plan' he had adopted 'of holding prayer meetings, visiting houses and families and sick persons'. He was, he wrote, attending to these activities without drawing too much attention to them, and then he added:

> To my great surprize Rev. Mr. Cartwright proposed that I should on sabbath days assist him in going to some places in the country round about, where people seemed willing to attend public worship.

Eagar declined to do this at first, not being sure that he had received a call to engage in such work. He agreed in the end to do so, however, urged on by the three Anglican chaplains who also assured him of the Governor's backing:

> At length seeing that the thing came on me unexpected & unsought for by me . . . I thought it was my duty to comply. Accordingly I have begun to go to some districts around. My plan at present is after service to expound & enforce a portion of Scripture in a free way. . . . I do not yet see that I am called to *preach* the Gospel.

In view of all that he had been through he felt it had been

right to exercise caution and await 'indubitable evidence' that
God had called him. He then continued in the letter:

> I have formed our little company into a class. This we hold
> on Sunday mornings. We also meet on Sunday, Tuesday &
> Friday evenings. I hold a meeting in the country on Thursday
> evenings, on Sunday forenoon & afternoon. I go to the outer
> districts sometimes a dozen miles – the people of this country
> are dreadfully profane and hardened in sin, and were it not
> that I myself was as profane and hardened a wretch as lived,
> I would be ready to say it was impossible to make any impres-
> sion on them.

He pointed out that two other people, sent from Britain specifically as teachers, were 'old Methodists', and that they too had
started Methodist classes and had written to the British Conference for a preacher.

McLachlan's article has added greatly to the positive things
which can be said about Eagar. He received a conditional pardon
for his past offences from the Governor in 1813, and became
involved in a sizeable practice as a law agent and attorney in
Sydney. In 1815, however, a judge refused him authority to act
in the courts because of his criminal background, and also called
his legal qualifications into question. Eagar was therefore compelled to switch from law to trade, and for some time engaged in
a successful business partnership. Indeed he became one of those
behind the founding of the Bank of New South Wales. He was,
however, barred from officially becoming a founder director on
account of his 'convict past'. He was also effectively a founding
member of other institutions such as the Benevolent Society and
the Society for the Protection and Civilization of the Distressed
Islanders of the South Seas. He is regarded also as having been
one of the first settlers to show a practical concern for the welfare
of aborigines.

Eagar's high standing in New South Wales was recognized in
a striking manner when he was appointed secretary of a committee which drew up a petition to the Prince Regent in 1819.
This sought such reforms as trial by jury in the criminal and

civil courts, and the removal of certain restrictions on external trade. The petition received the support of the Governor who emphasized that it had been signed by virtually everyone of rank and wealth within the colony. A seventy-three page document written by Eagar himself accompanied the petition, providing a comprehensive critique of the existing state of affairs in the colony.

McLachlan notes Eagar's marriage in 1815; his absolute pardon by Governor Macquarie in 1818; and the fact that in the Annual Report of the WMMS in 1823, Eagar and his wife are listed as the highest contributors in New South Wales (giving more even than the Governor).

His research has, however, also uncovered much less complimentary information about Eagar's life. He was, for example, greatly involved in litigation. This, though, was not unusual at that time. Church leaders in Australia, after being initially impressed, had reservations about him. Some of his business ventures went disastrously wrong, causing considerable suffering to members of his family and to others. Errors have also been found in his church accounts. It is however, his behaviour in London, after he went there in 1821 to represent the views of the colonialists on the need for reform, that raises most questions. Not only did he totally neglect his family back in New South Wales from then onwards, never returning to them, but as early as 1823 he had an affair with a girl of sixteen, and in the end lived permanently with her. In all she bore him ten children. None of this, however, detracts from the importance of Eagar's work in London on behalf of colonial reform, through his pamphleteering, lobbying, and published correspondence. His letters and articles often appeared in the Australian press. McLachlan has discussed Eagar's contribution in this field in considerable detail, and as a result he has found it necessary to modify at least at one point the findings of Professor A. C. V. Melbourne in his outstanding study of the constitutional development of New South Wales. Melbourne's position, normally accepted, is that prior to the end of 1822 no one in New South Wales had seriously considered the possibility of imposing limitations upon the executive and legislative authority of the governor. McLachlan's contention is that on the contrary:

the class of emancipists which matured during Macquarie's regime did produce a positive political manifesto and that the role of one man, Edward Eagar, in the agitation for self-government, has been substantially underrated.

From the church's point of view, it is not easy to assess the value of Eagar's contribution in the light of the less savoury material which has emerged concerning his morals. His early initiatives on behalf of Methodism were, however, undoubtedly significant. McLachlan, although drawing attention to Eagar's faults, has no hesitation in claiming that 'he can still be regarded as a pioneer of Methodism in Australia'. James S. Udy, a contemporary Australian churchman and historian who is familiar with the material contained in McLachlan's article, has likewise concluded on the available evidence that Eagar cannot be denied an important place among those pioneering lay Methodists who, despite their faults, tried to live out their Christian faith in the crude and cruel settlements of New South Wales.[10]

A Friend in High Places

Sir William McArthur is an outstanding example of the significant part played by influential and committed lay Christians in securing support for the church and in contributing to its outreach. The son of a Wesleyan preacher, he was born in Co. Donegal in 1809. His interest in overseas missions became apparent at an early date, and continued throughout his life. Prior to their settling in London in 1857, he and his wife often provided hospitality for visiting missionary deputation speakers in their Londonderry home, and the local newspapers covered missionary anniversary meetings at which he presented the annual report. He took part in the anniversary meetings of the WMMS in 1855, and thereafter did so on many occasions.

Even though he was resident in London he maintained close links with Methodism in Ireland, and was thus included in a three-man delegation from Ireland to America in 1866, when the centenary of Methodism in the United States (referring back to the initiatives of Embury, Heck and Strawbridge) was celebrated. The delegation was given the task of raising money for an endowment fund for Methodist College then being established in Belfast, in which McArthur took a special interest. For part of their time in America McArthur stayed with William Butler, the Irish pioneer missionary in India and Mexico. McArthur claimed on this visit to the United States that:

> There were more Irish Methodists in New York than in Dublin, and in the American Union than in Ireland. There were at least three hundred Irishmen in the ministry of the Methodist Episcopal Church.[11]

A circular issued by him and the other surviving member of the delegation (the third had died suddenly at the start of the tour) stressed the importance, from the point of view of the United States and of Canada, of maintaining an evangelical witness in Ireland in view of the high rate of immigration. Of Irish Protestants, whom they regarded as being socially and morally superior to Irish Roman Catholics, they observed that in America:

> Many of them have become leading merchants, bankers, doctors, lawyers, statesmen. They are generally an educated and prosperous class, and are so thoroughly in sympathy with Americans and American institutions that they are but seldom recognised as Irish.[12]

In commenting on an aspect of the political struggle going on in America between the Democrats and the Republicans, McArthur made it clear that he favoured the Republican policy on extending the suffrage to emancipated negroes. Half a million negroes were members of the MEC and more than a million others were influenced by it. In advocating reform, however, McArthur showed that his motivation was not altogether altruistic. Extending the vote to Blacks would lessen the influence of Irish Roman Catholic immigrants, he argued:

Their admission would prove a counterbalancing power to the Irish element, which has become very strong, and is likely to do mischief. Converted blacks are surely as well qualified to exercise the franchise as the low Irish who infest the large towns and form the very scum of society in them.[13]

McArthur became Liberal MP for Lambeth in 1868, and used his position in Parliament to press the claims of far-reaching national and international concerns. He opposed the opium trade with China in 1869, claiming that it had been 'a great hindrance to the spread of the Gospel in China'.[14] In 1871 he detailed maladministration in Sierra Leone and in the Gold Coast. In 1876 McArthur moved a resolution in Parliament on The Gambia, and addressed a meeting of the Aborigines Protection Society.

In 1872 he helped to mount a campaign on behalf of the annexation of Fiji to the British Empire, which eventually proved successful in 1874. His brother Alexander and William Arthur were also both committed to this cause. Alexander had emigrated to Australia because of ill health, started mercantile houses there, became a magistrate, and was elected to the House of Assembly in New South Wales. He managed to get a resolution on Fiji through that House, and Arthur wrote a pamphlet in an effort to alert the British public to the issues. William McArthur argued forcibly for the creation of a British protectorate, maintaining that this was in accordance with the wishes of the chiefs and native peoples concerned. He also pressed the point that it would be an effective way of putting a stop to the kidnapping of Polynesians, part of an illegal labour traffic at the time. An opponent in Parliament sneered that the House was being asked to annex Fiji 'lest 20,000 ferocious mountaineers should eat up 150,000 Methodists'.[15] Two years after the annexation was achieved, a suggestion was made that Fiji might be renamed 'McArthur's Land', in view of the significant part which William McArthur had played in having it placed under British protection.[16]

The high offices McArthur held (Sheriff of London and

Middlesex, Alderman, Member of Parliament, and Lord Mayor of London), were vantage points from which he sought to exert a strong moral influence, enabling him to commend to a wide public the many good causes which were close to his heart. The use of his personal wealth, acquired in his pursuits as a successful businessman, also reflected his humanitarian and Christian concerns. As well as being active in local church life, for example in Sunday School teaching, he also came to the fore in wider national matters. He was involved in Methodist publishing, and in attempts to enable the Methodist Church to respond more adequately to the challenge of the London metropolitan area, and in educational initiatives. Overseas missions were a deep and abiding interest, and in 1883 his close association with the WMMS was recognized in his appointment as its honorary treasurer.

In 1885, following the defeat of Gladstone's second administration, when McArthur himself was coming under pressure from a local radical group within his own party, McArthur was strongly defended by the famous preacher, C. H. Spurgeon. In a letter to the press, Spurgeon reminded people of McArthur's 'liberal support of every movement for the benefit of our fellow-men, and his zeal for the interests of the oppressed in all lands'.[17] This internal dissension opened the way for a Conservative victory at the November election, McArthur losing his seat after seventeen years. He died just under two years later, in 1887.

McArthur was a notable example of those people referred to in the Preface who regarded themselves more as 'British' than as 'Irish'. His class consciousness emerged at various points. It was particularly evident in his association with the comments quoted earlier which expressed strong negative sentiments about 'the Irish element' in North America, and also when in 1886 he referred to Irish Methodists as 'a body composed chiefly of the upper middle class and a substantial yeomanry'.[18] Such an attitude has frequently been a factor in severely limiting the effectiveness of mission, making it difficult for some groups to respond. Without detracting from the many positive initiatives which McArthur took through the WMMS and in his public service, it must also be acknowledged that apparently his zeal on behalf of the world's oppressed, of which Spurgeon wrote, did not noticeably encompass some in need who were much closer at hand, that is Irish Roman Catholics. In this he was not of course unique. People are frequently not prepared to face the domestic application of their wider sympathies.

The First Lay Missionaries

The first Methodist lay missionaries from Ireland were women who were appointed especially for work among women and children overseas. Most prominent among them were Annie Wood and the sisters, Charlotte E. and A. M. Beauchamp. Others included Charlotte Lowe, who worked as a teacher in Madras from 1891 to 1895 (until her marriage to the Rev. E. W. Redfern); Isobel Hoey, the daughter of a Methodist minister, who taught in Colombo from 1891 to 1895; and Liz Teasey, another teacher who was stationed mainly at Badulla, Ceylon, from 1895 to 1907.

The Beauchamps' service in Africa and Asia was unspectacular and distinguished mainly for its length and devotion. A. M. Beauchamp – her Christian names were not used – taught in Bangalore, India, from 1869 to 1876, and in Batticaloa, Ceylon, from 1876 to 1880. Upon resigning her position, she attempted to run a private school in Calcutta from early 1880 (her brother-in-law, the Rev. G. Baugh, was stationed there), but when this venture failed she re-entered missionary service and was appointed to Point Pedro, Ceylon, in 1881. She served in India again from 1884 to 1895. Then, following a brief period of retirement in Youghal, Ireland, she was again appointed to Point Pedro in 1898, retiring finally in 1905. Charlotte Beauchamp's service was slightly shorter. She taught among the Pondo in South Africa from 1869 to 1896, being based for a long time in Emfundesweni. Her work was often made difficult by serious political and community unrest, and in 1881 her nearest white colleague lived thirty miles away. A tribute to her work at that time stated:

The girls' school in charge of Miss Beauchamp has been well attended. The number of scholars has increased, and some of the young . . . wives of our Native Agents and local preachers have received instruction in reading, writing and sewing. Some of the elder boys also have received lessons from Miss Beauchamp, the day school teacher being unable to teach in English . . . By carrying out her noble resolve to remain on the Station during the absence of a resident Missionary she has been the means of keeping the Mission property from partial destruction and the people from discouragement.[19]

In contrast to the Beauchamp sisters, Annie Wood, a teacher from Cork, was adventurous and high spirited, showing herself capable of taking unusual initiatives. She was based at Canton, China, from 1885, training Bible women. After a period of furlough, she returned to China in 1892 accompanied by her fifteen-year-old sister, Connie. Another sister, Fanny, qualified as a doctor in Edinburgh in 1900, and was appointed to India. During a plague in Canton in 1894, when feelings were running high against medical missionaries, Annie Wood and a woman colleague were both at risk. They kept a boat moored on the river at their back door, ready for a quick escape if necessary. A few months later Annie wrote that while her work among the women still gave grounds for encouragement, the plague, riots, and war were making things very difficult.[20] In the light of such obstacles it is remarkable that she remained in China until 1904.

Possessing considerable literary skills, Annie Wood published articles and pamphlets which reveal outstanding qualities. Her descriptive powers are a strong feature of her writing. For example, in describing a journey by canal and river, she wrote:

At the turning of a corner another page in this new book of nature was turned, and we saw a sudden mountain sloping down in steady grandeur to the harvest plain, dotted with its grey clan villages in nests of trees, and edged by the grand curve of the wide water plain over which we were steaming, which also had its water-villages of boats anchored in neighbourly clusters. A great page of parables was spread out before us, beginning and ending with a silent sermon from the mount. But the sad part of it was to see the women everywhere at such hard work; deeply touching to see the *Je ne sais quoi* of rounded limb and tender movement clad in coarse blue cotton jacket and short trousers, bare-footed, muddy to the knees, yet standing to watch us as we passed, with something so delicately human in the pose that one knows certainly that it is a woman.[21]

Touches of humour often shine through her writing:

A wife-beater in Canton gave up beating his wife because he had become a Christian, and then she began beating *him* for the same reason, until she was converted too, and then they agreed to influence each other in a less violent fashion.[22]

Her thumb-nail sketches of people are often illuminating, saying as much about her own beliefs and values as about the people described. She commented on a teacher in a rural area:

The school-master is a typical country pedant whose learning has come from books, so that he is a disciple of books rather than of the men who make them, and has grown something like a book himself. Silent, absolute, full of respectable information, though his binding is greasy and worn.[23]

Though a firm believer in 'one brotherhood'[24] composed of people of different races, she frankly acknowledged the reality of racial difference. Describing a scene during a missionary tour far from the city, she confided:

The women and children came around me, and we all tried to feel that we were members of one family and thoroughly happy together; but it wouldn't quite do, the racial 'something' is felt all the more in closer contact, and sitting there in the unlit chilly twilight or moonlight I felt glad that I had only come after all for a few days.[25]

On another occasion cultural differences came to the fore, when she attempted to share her faith with a non-Christian woman:

My emotions were worked up to the point at which you grasp a person by both hands and look lovingly into their eyes; but emotions do not shake hands in China, being too highly civilised for that, they simply illumine the face and shine from the eyes, so I only let mine do that – hers responded, and so we left her.[26]

Above all Annie Wood longed that those among whom she worked, mainly women and children, would learn of their heavenly Father's love. Trusting in Jesus, they could then be publicly received into the church through baptism. Those whom she thought of as shackled by fear, false religion and sin would thus discover personal freedom and peace.

In offering insights arising from her experience in China, she sometimes posed a challenge to attitudes at home. For example, in describing 'the foreign field' as 'an admirable back-garden' for social experimentation, she pointed out that those at home who are shy about having women doctors for themselves are enthusiastic about sending them to Eastern women. How strange, she wrote

that the call to our women to advance in medical science and in the study of theology, and then to travel thousands of miles alone, and to live alone in a foreign land, should come from the intensely feminine women of the East.[27]

It has not often been acknowledged that women missionaries played a part, however indirectly, in advancing the role of women in the allegedly progressive West. It happened, Annie Wood implied, because whereas there were difficulties in having new things attempted at home, women missionaries were able to prove their worth and abilities overseas.

When Fanny Wood was interviewed for overseas service in 1895, she was found to be 'a fine-spirited girl'. Her sister Annie was certainly that, and was also a person of remarkable courage, insight, and sensitivity. The role of such gifted lay people, alas so often ignored, cannot be exaggerated when one seeks to assess the effectiveness of mission.

– 5 –

Canadian Case Study

=

If we focus on Canada, the influence which the Irish exerted on Methodism in one country, through those officially appointed by the church and those who emigrated, can be studied in depth. Methodism made an important, if neglected, contribution to Canadian religion prior to the formation of the United Church of Canada in 1925. The preacher and author, William Crook, had this in mind when he claimed that it would take a considerable volume to trace the influence even of Irish Methodism on Canada.[1] Within the brief compass of this chapter, however, at least the main features and personalities of this contribution can be indicated.

Putting the Record Straight

An article by J. I. Cooper which appeared in 1955 in *The Journal* of the Canadian Church Historical Society, entitled 'Irish Immigration and the Canadian Church before the middle of the 19th Century' referred to Anglican, Presbyterian and Roman Catholic influences but made no mention of Canadian Methodism's indebtedness to Ireland.[2] Cooper did refer to Laurence Coughlan's work in Newfoundland as a missionary of the Society for the Propagation of the Gospel (SPG), but his Irish Wesleyan background was overlooked. Two points should therefore be affirmed at the outset. Methodism generally was a major influence in the early development of British Canada, and the Irish element within Canadian Methodism has been significant.

Methodism was the largest Protestant denomination in Canada at the start of this century. There were then 916,886 Methodists, 842,442 Presbyterians, and 681,494 Anglicans. There were at the same time two and a quarter million Roman Catholics. In a total population of 5,371,315 in Canada in 1901, those of Irish origin numbered 988,721 (18.41 per cent).[3] On statistical grounds alone it would not therefore be unreasonable to expect a discernible Irish influence in Canadian Methodism.

The Irish contribution has at times been acknowledged. Thus the Minutes of the Canadian Wesleyan Methodist Conference stated in 1864:

> We hold ourselves under obligation to the labours of our Irish brethren for many of the most valuable men in our church and ministry in this country, from its early history to the present time.

In putting the record straight, however, we must take care not to go to the extreme of exaggerating the role of the Irish. Such a warning was issued in the *Christian Guardian* (published in Toronto) in 1872 when it was under the editorship of the Irish-born E. H. Dewart. Of North American Methodism as a whole he wrote:

> The obligations of American and Canadian Methodism to Ireland have been in late years an oft repeated ground for appeals on behalf of Irish Methodism. . . . There is no disposition in either Canada or the United States, to deny any obligation we owe to Irish Methodism. . . . (But) it is only in a limited sense that Irish Methodism can be regarded as the parent of American Methodism. The honor of planting the first seed is justly due to Irish Methodists. But the whole of American Methodism has not grown from that root. There have been many more important plantings from England.[4]

Since the Irish were the largest ethnic group in southern Ontario, the major area of Methodism in Canada, Dewart's comment was probably more applicable to the United States than to Canada.

Ireland and Methodist Beginnings in Canada

One source has summarized Methodist origins in Canada as follows:

> To fix the exact date when Methodism had its beginnings in any locality is almost as difficult as to fix the moment when a seed begins to germinate. . . . But there is a close approximation to historical accuracy in saying that Methodism began in Newfoundland with the advent of Lawrence Coughlan in 1765; in Nova Scotia with the coming of a party of Yorkshire emigrants in 1772; in Lower Canada with the preaching of Tuffey, a commissary of the 44th regiment, in 1780; and in Upper Canada with the coming of the Hecks, Emburys and others to the banks of the St Lawrence in 1778.[5]

Significantly all the people to whom reference is here made, with the obvious exception of the Yorkshire immigrants in Nova Scotia, were Irish-born or had strong Irish connections. Coughlan, the Newfoundland missionary, was an Irish Roman Catholic who became a Wesleyan preacher in Ireland and Britain, and although serving in Newfoundland under the auspices of the SPG continued to regard himself as a Methodist and corresponded with John Wesley. Tuffey, about whom little is known, is traditionally referred to as Irish. The Hecks and Emburys were, as we have seen, Irish Palatine families who emigrated from Ballingrane, Co. Limerick, in 1760. They settled first in New York, proceeded one hundred miles north to the Camden Valley in 1770, and then moved on to British America.

Other early pioneers not mentioned in the quotation but to whom reference is made in published histories included Major George Neal, James McCarty, and Thomas Dawson. While the first two had strong Irish connections, it is probable that neither was actually born in Ireland. Thomas Dawson is the least known of this trio. He was a native of Co. Monaghan who joined the army at the age of sixteen, and served in America until Lord Cornwallis's surrender to Washington. He returned to Ireland where he again served in the army, as paymaster under the Earl of Bellamont, finally withdrawing from military service in 1799 and taking a civilian position in Dublin with the same nobleman. After the Earl's death he purchased six hundred acres in Prince Edward Island as a family investment. Leaving Ireland in March 1801, he and his family reached their destination in June 1801. Dawson was immediately struck by the profound spiritual deprivation of the colony. In his earlier days he himself had drifted from the church, but he had later been converted and was by then a convinced Christian and a local preacher. Long-term plans for his family were set aside as he travelled to as many settlements as possible to take services, often at great risk because of the absence of proper roads and bridges. Dawson, although physically strong, wore himself out and died in March 1804. Accounts of his life were published in Methodist circles and so impressed one man, Joseph Avard, that he organized a party of emigrants from Guernsey to form a Methodist colony in Prince Edward Island. In a follow-up to this initiative, letters were exchanged between Avard, Adam Clarke, and Thomas Coke, resulting in the first Wesleyan missionary being appointed to Prince Edward Island.[6]

The attitude of immigrants – the Irish often prominent among them – was crucial for the early progress of Methodism. Some even requested that Methodist preachers be sent to them before they sailed from Ireland. Thus on 20 June 1819 a group of emigrants on board the ship *Camperdown*, anchored off Limerick, forwarded this message to Methodist leaders in London:

The vicissitudes of life has (*sic*) caused us to leave our native land and take our flight to Canada and as we were brought to the knowledge of the truth as it is in Christ by your Ministry nourished and brought up under your fostering care as members of the Methodist society in connexion with you, we think we have still a claim on your paternal care altho at a distance from our native country, we therefore request that you dear brethren and the Miss. Committee in England will take our cause into consideration and send us preachers from England and Ireland.[7]

At least two priminent Palatine names, those of Switzer and Ruckle, are among the more than fifty signatures on the document. In view of earlier comments about the attitudes of Irish emigrants, it is interesting that one of the factors used to boost their claim for Wesleyan preachers was their loyalty to Britain and dislike of American republicanism.

John Carroll's *Case and his Cotemporaries* (*sic*), chronicling Methodism from its beginnings in Canada to 1855, is an invaluable source of information on many topics including the role of Irish immigrants and Irish-born Methodist ministers in both the American-based MEC and the Wesleyan Church originating in Britain. Thus we are told that in 1820–1821 in the Smith's Creek circuit:

> the preachers began to follow the immigrants who were threading their way into South Monaghan and Cavan, among whom there were several English and Irish Methodist families ... The Morrows and others were among the latter. In the District conference ... an Irish brother, who lived far back in Cavan, was authorised as a local preacher ... This was Moses Blackstock.[8]

Blackstock, who had been born in Co. Cavan, Ireland, subsequently became an ordained minister and rose to the positions of Chairman of District and President of Conference.

Immigrants did not always retain the denominational allegiance they held in Ireland. In the early 1820s, within the site of what is now Toronto airport, we find a good example of this:

> Mr. Aikens ... was a grave and godly Presbyterian from the north of Ireland, who, finding no fellowship but among the Methodists, with his excellent wife, cast in his lot with that people; and their house became a home for the pioneer preachers.[9]

Two sons of the Aikens' family became prominent citizens of Canada, and a grandson was Lieutenant-Governor of Manitoba from 1916 to 1926.

In 1824–1825 the Rev. John Black, who was Irish-born, assisted another minister on the Rideau circuit (in the region of present day Ottawa). Black commented on his work:

> I took the back ground. Most of the inhabitants were immigrants from Ireland. In the fall of 1824, the roads being bad, I had to leave my mare at a friend's and walk from place to place – hard labor. I have heard that the love of Christ draws men through fire and water. I know that his love and the worth of souls drew me through swamps.[10]

John Huston, another Irish-born minister, was said to have 'had a toilsome, muddy ride from the Thames to the Richmond circuit' when taking up a new appointment in 1829–1830. However

> he 'took' at once most wonderfully with his fellow countrymen, the Irish, of those settlements. A revival commenced which was upheld by prayer meetings, and went on with great power, at every appointment all over the Circuit.[11]

Disbanded soldiers of the 99th and 100th Regiments, recruited from the Dublin area during the Napoleonic Wars, together with civilians, settled the district between 1817 and 1826.

A reference to Wesleyville, west of Port Hope, in 1831–1832 spoke of 'a very interesting mission, populated to a considerable extent by Methodists from Ireland'.[12] To the north was the Irish Methodist township of Cavan. Many other illustrations could be given from Carroll's volumes.

T. W. Smith provides a notable example of similar beginnings in part of New Brunswick.[13] When a Wesleyan preacher ventured for the first time as far as the north-west branch of the Miramichi river in 1828, he was warmly received into the home of 'the leader of the Irish settlement' in the area. This was Robert Tweedy, an Irish Methodist who with his wife had settled there some five years previously. Class-meetings had helped to nurture their faith in the absence of preachers. Three sons from this family later entered the Methodist ministry, and a grandson became a professor at Mount Allison University, Sackville.

This began as a Methodist educational institution on the initative of a benefactor whose family had emigrated from Ireland.

Irish Methodist Ministers in Canada – Towards a Comprehensive List

There is no complete list of Irish-born ministers and probationers working in Canada before the end of the nineteenth century. Extant materials on preachers in all the branches of Methodism are incomplete and do not always contain details of country of origin. This is particularly true of those relating to the late eighteenth and early nineteenth centuries. The list compiled in connection with this work is the most complete available.[14]

The total number of ministers exceeds 220, of whom at least 16 became Secretaries of Conferences, 51 Chairmen of Districts, and 32 Presidents of Conferences. It is important to see statistics such as these in an Irish context. In 1866, when there were only 167 Methodist ministers in Ireland, Sir William McArthur, while a member of an Irish Methodist delegation to Canada, wrote that 'not less than 170' ministers in Canadian Methodism were 'directly or indirectly the fruit' of Irish Methodism.[15] This was probably an underestimate since as many as 134 people on the list were ministers in Canada at that time. These, by McArthur's defintion, would have been predominantly the 'direct fruit' of Irish Methodism, and doubtless there would have been many others who were 'indirect fruit' in the sense of being descendants of those who had earlier emigrated.

In the case of 164 people their county of origin in Ireland is known. As many as 29 came from Fermanagh, 12 from Tyrone, and 10 from each of Armagh, Cavan and Sligo. Of the thirty-two counties in Ireland, only seven, i.e. Clare, Galway, Kerry, Louth, Meath, Roscommon and Waterford, failed to supply at least one.

In view of the preponderance of ministers coming originally from Co. Fermanagh, a letter from Benjamin Sherlock published in Ireland in 1885 is particularly interesting. Sherlock himself was originally from Co. Mayo, and he was writing from Ontario:

> In Canada we have townships almost filled with natives of Fermanagh and surrounding districts . . . and the majority of the Methodists on some circuits, and a large proportion of them in many, are in this or the last generation from the same section. And they are, generally speaking, earnest, sound, prayerful, and consequently worthy representatives of Irish Methodism.[16]

The proportion of Irish-born ministers in some of the various branches of Methodism in Canada was as follows. The Methodist Episcopal Church in Canada had 11.6 per cent (23 ministers out of 198) in 1833. In that year the majority of the members of the MEC in Canada agreed to become a Wesleyan Methodist Conference in connection with the British Wesleyan Conference. In 1874 a total of 12.54 per cent of the ministers (132 out of 1,045) of the Wesleyan Methodist Church in Canada were Irish-born. In the same year, the ministry of the Canadian Methodist New Connexion Conference was 11.61 per cent Irish-born (36 ministers out of 310).[17]

The smaller branches of Methodism are on the whole poorly documented. They are therefore omitted from the list except when information about individuals happened to be available. With regard to Primitive Methodists J. D. Hoover states that:

> Surprisingly, many Canadian Primitives had Irish origins, mostly in the Northern Counties . . . The Primitive Methodists, however, had an extremely weak cause in Ireland. Consequently, many of the Canadian Primitives with Irish origins were either former Wesleyans or former Presbyterians.[18]

This illustrates a point already made, that emigrants did not necessarily retain the denominational allegiance they had in Ireland.

A few of those ministers who served in Canada had already been ministers in Ireland or elsewhere. Others had been active as lay people in Ireland, some as local preachers. Some few individuals had drifted from church life in Ireland, and then were spiritually awakened in Canada or in the United States. Some emigrated as children, and even as infants. Despite such a variety of background a common thread is discernible in the great majority of cases, with religious faith being often a dominant force in their family life. Reference is frequently made in their obituary notices to Christian nurture as an important factor in their early upbringing either in Ireland or Canada. In this sense a genuine connection can be observed, even when they emigrated in infancy, through the strength of Christian conviction and devotion being passed on in family life.

Some ministers were of course recruited directly as a result of initiatives taken from Canada, particularly towards the close of the nineteenth century. A letter illustrating this point appeared in Ireland in 1884, written from England:

> I have this week received instructions to secure several additional young unmarried local preachers who feel called to the work of the Methodist ministry, for circuit appointments and missions in New Brunswick, Newfoundland, Nova Scotia etc. . . . Preference is given to men from twenty-four to thirty years old . . . English, Scotch and Irish Methodist preachers are alike acceptable, and . . . regret has been expressed that more Irishmen have not hitherto offered.[19]

In response to this F. E. Whitham wrote from New Brunswick in February 1885, counselling caution. He had himself gone to Canada from Dublin about two years earlier, following a similar invitation. He described the country, the people, and the work, mentioning several difficulties such as loneliness, isolation, and the preponderance of narrow sects. At the same time, he concluded, if God truly called a person it would be well worth embarking on such a venture.[20]

The General Board of Missions in Canada sent James Woodsworth on a recruiting drive in Britain and Ireland in 1895, particularly to secure ministers for the western prairies which were being opened up at that time. Dr Potts, himself a prominent Irish-born leader in the Canadian Church, wrote commending the visit. Woodsworth himself later confessed that he had not succeeded in finding many preachers in Ireland. He greatly regretted this since he believed the Irish had shown themselves capable of the adaptability required.[21]

Ireland and Methodism in Newfoundland

The Irish contribution to early Methodism in Newfoundland was remarkable by any standard and deserves special attention. Laurence Coughlan, who served as an Anglican priest in the Harbour Grace area from 1766, continued to regard himself as a Methodist while in Newfoundland, forming converts into classes. The strength of the Methodist element in his ministry can be seen from the fact that when Coughlan left in 1773, the Anglican priest who succeeded him encountered considerable difficulties. He was, for example, forbidden the use of the parsonage in Harbour Grace for some years until he agreed to pay rent, and when in 1775 he tried to enter the litle chapel in Carbonear the doors were shut against him. The local people made it clear that what they wanted was 'a Methodist preacher ... or a Presbyterian'.[22] This is the background to the unveiling of a plaque at Blackhead in 1983, in that part of Newfoundland, when the Moderator of the United Church of Canada marked the approximate site of the first Methodist church in Canada in 1769.

The first Wesleyan preacher specifically appointed to Newfoundland by the British Methodist Conference was John McGeary. The passing of an act of religious toleration in 1784 had eased the way for this. McGeary was also an Irishman, serving in Conception Bay from 1785 to 1788 and from 1790 to 1792. He had been a travelling preacher in America under Asbury, and was sent to Newfoundland after being interviewed by Wesley in England in late September 1784. Controversy surrounded his time in Newfoundland. His relationships with other people were poor, and when he married without obtaining the consent of his bride's father his withdrawal from the island became necessary. By the time William Black, the mission

Superintendent based in Halifax, Nova Scotia, visited Newfoundland in 1791, McGeary had already returned to the island. He left finally in 1792, and although he had been the only Methodist missionary on the island he was not replaced until 1794.

John Remmington was the next Irish Wesleyan preacher to minister in Newfoundland. He was born near Cloughjordan in 1772, and was appointed to Newfoundland in 1804. It was said that he was 'a lover of music, and a good singer'.[23] He encountered opposition, on religious grounds, from fellow Irishmen who had gone to Newfoundland as traders or fishermen, writing in July 1805 from Harbour Grace that he had 'been in perils among my own countrymen more than once in these parts'.[24] After being the sole Methodist missionary for two years he sailed in the spring of 1808 to England, returning to Newfoundland in late November accompanied by Ellis and McDowell, two additional Irish workers. Remmington finally left Newfoundland in 1810, writing of the dangers and difficulties of work on the island and arguing that for too long the mission had suffered from neglect. He himself had served it well, however, being credited with extending its influence as far as the Harbour of Trinity where for many years his name was remembered.

Samuel McDowell was a native of Dromore, Co. Down, who entered the ministry in 1808. He served in Newfoundland from 1808 to 1814 when ill health forced him to return to the British Isles. His letters spoke of improving relationships and also of steady progress despite set-backs:

While we have been wading through the deep waters of adversity, God has been graciously reviving his work . . . In the course of the last year there has been more, savingly converted to God, than any two former years since we came to the country.[25]

William Ellis was also from Co. Down, and served in Newfoundland until his death at Harbour Grace in 1837. He was the first Methodist missionary to be buried in the colony.

While serving in the Bonavista Mission in 1813/1814 he preached the first sermon heard at Bird Island Cove. Later this was renamed Elliston in his honour.

Ellis's letters are not easy to read. The Missionary Secretaries in London had great difficulty in understanding them and in the end had to request him to try to write more legibly. While his letters contain a great deal which is routine and even dull, they are occasionally enlivened by graphic personal references. Ellis's life was twice at risk at sea. He was injured in 1814 when his boat overturned, and he wrote of another incident from Adam's Cove in 1815:

> About two months since I was saved allmost by miracil from finding a wattery grave . . . Some of my fellow sailors were drownded; and the rest (four in all) were saved in the most wonderful manner – I received much hurt.[26]

In 1819 he described an unusual baptism involving a family of six Indians from Labrador. The congregation was moved to tears, he wrote from Port de Grave, as the Indians indicated to them by looks and gestures their common humanity.

Whereas his earlier letters had spoken of Anglican opposition, he was able to write from Burin in 1824:

> Prejudice is almost expireing . . . Almost every protestant in the place occasionally attend the House of God, from a conviction that Methodism is not at varience with the prayer Book of the Church of England.[27]

In 1826 he wrote from Blackhead of widespread poverty. 'I know maney families who have not a morcel of food for this long winter, except a scanty allowance of fish and potatoes.'[28] In the winter of 1826–1827, the weather was particularly severe:

> The snow was so deep that I had to travel part of the way on my hands and knees by which I got a bad pain in my back from which I have suffered much since nor is it likely to leave me.[29]

In 1834 there was another bad winter, and he wrote from Bonavista:

Hunger prevailed to such an extent that some of our people were not able to walk to the chapel, and some who left their houses hopeing to be able to go there, were not able, but had to be helped home again.[30]

Although arguing that the extreme poverty of the people made it difficult to concentrate on spiritual matters, he went on to describe in the same letter how a revival had in fact begun despite the severe physical distress of the people.

In his last years he expressed increasing concern for the welfare of his family in the event of his death or enforced retirement through ill health – he had six children when he died, the eldest being fifteen. In this connection he raised the possibility of an appointment to 'one of the British North American Colonies',[31] so that the period of his usefulness could be extended in a pleasanter climate. His last surviving letter, written from St John's in 1837, returned to the theme of family poverty. By then he had been forced into retirement, and was finding it impossible to make ends meet on an annual allowance of only £40: 'The children must remain destitute of clothing and education, and as far as I know we must beg our bread from door to door.'[32] Five months later, he was dead. One source commented that he had in the end been appointed to Bermuda for the good of his health, but weakness and death intervened before he was able to take up this fresh challenge.[33]

Prominent among Irish lay people who contributed to Newfoundland Methodism, were John Stretton and Arthur Thomey. They were engaged in the fishing industry, and took an active part in the work of the church. After Coughlan's departure from Newfoundland, they came to the fore in helping to maintain Methodist witness until McGeary's arrival more than a decade later.

In 1768 Thomey taught in a small school which Coughlan himself had started, but he had to give this up due to inadequate remuneration. Stretton, by contrast, had a wealthier background – Wesley received hospitality at his home in Waterford, Ireland. In 1788 he financed the building of a church at Harbour Grace, and frequently preached there himself.

Relationships between Stretton and others were often strained, however, and Wesley himself had to plead in correspondence for harmony to be restored. Stretton was strongly opposed to Roman Catholic influence. As he wrote at the opening of his church in 1788:

> This is the only thing at present that keeps up the Protestant name in the place . . . Few go to church; while popery, like a deluge, sweeps away all the rest.[34]

The formal establishment of a Methodist district in Newfoundland in 1815, with the creation of appropriate structures, proved to be of crucial importance in the development of Methodism on the island. It greatly facilitated the strengthening of existing work and ensured more effective planning for the future. Significantly there were by then six missionaries, with Ellis appointed as the first District Chairman. Of great importance also was the formal beginning of Methodist witness in the main city, St John's, in 1814. Remmington had called for such a move in 1810.

An Unusual and Unrecognized Contribution

It is not possible even to sketch the individual contributions of many more people. Only the barest mention can be made of a few, but even this is worthwhile to help provide a fuller account of the Irish contribution. Henry Ryan (1775–1833), probably born in Connecticut of Irish Roman Catholic parents, made a significant and colourful contribution to the growth of the Methodist Episcopal Church in Canada from 1805, particularly up to 1824. The splinter 'Ryanite' Church which he formed later, had primarily an Irish constituency. George Ferguson (1786–1851) is said to have epitomized the characteristic qualities of the early Canadian itinerancy. Matthew Richey (1803–1883) was a President of Conference, first principal of Upper Canada Academy, and biographer of William Black. James Elliott (1815–1892), a Secretary and Chairman of District and a President of Conference, was an outstanding preacher who played an important part in the conversion of Charles Freshman, for many years Rabbi of the Jewish synagogue in Quebec. Freshman subsequently entered the Methodist ministry. Wellington Jeffers was editor of the *Christian Guardian* (1860–1868), and an outstanding preacher. Edward Hartley Dewart was Jeffers' successor as editor of the *Christian Guardian*. Of him it was said that few had done more to determine the future character of Methodism. George Cochran was co-founder with another missionary of Canadian Methodism's first overseas mission, serving in Japan from 1873 to 1879 and from 1884 to 1893 and having a distinguished academic record. William Briggs was the Book Steward from 1878 to 1918. Under him the Methodist bookroom became the largest book and publishing house in Canada. John Potts (1838–1907) was the Church's Education Secretary for many years, and did much to strengthen its educational institutions.

Finally we turn to the unusual contribution of Edward Johnston. Little recognized hitherto, he is important not because his contribution was inherently distinguished, but because he threw into sharp relief the deep divisions which existed between Methodist Episcopals and Wesleyan Methodists. He also caused tension between Methodists in Britain and in Ireland.

Johnston was born in Co. Tyrone and entered the ministry in Ireland in 1809, being associated with the evangelist Gideon Ouseley. Responding to a Wesleyan Methodist appeal for ministers for Canada, he was appointed and travelled to Canada via New York in late 1817, enjoying friendly contacts with some MEC preachers in the United States. He and a fellow Wesleyan missionary colleague wrote to say that this experience had put them on their guard against too ready an acceptance of the criticisms made of MEC preachers. They added that when they reached Canada they would endeavour to collect and transmit to London the best information possible on Episcopal Methodism.[35]

In a long letter from Kingston in April 1818, Johnston wrote positively of the MEC and of the questions raised about relationships with the Wesleyans:

In every township in the Upper Province where there are Protestant settlers, the American preachers have followed them and preached to them the gospel and have formed circuits and classes and have now 20 traveling preachers and 31 local ps. and 1000 in society in this province; so you see how we are situated we must either confine our labours to the individual families who have heard but not embraced the gospel or otherwise go amongst their classes and try to take their ground. Several of the American preachers have waited upon me and proposed the following questions – did the British Conference receive a letter from our general Conference, can you tell the reason we have received no answer, do the Committee know the state of this country, do you think they wish you and your brethren to persecute us (as they call it) and divide our classes, do you think the Committee are determined to persist in trying to put us away from our people for whom we have laboured with tears these 26 years, do you think there will be no reconciliation, are we not all Brethren, do we not all preach the same doctrine, are we not all followers of Mr. Wesley?[36]

He went on to say that he had offered to go to Canada only because of a published appeal which had strengthened his own view that Canada 'was starving for the word of life'. In fact he now found not only fifty-one 'traveling and local' MEC preachers in Upper Canada, but also ten Anglican priests, twelve Presbyterian ministers, one German Lutheran minister, ten Baptist preachers and four Quaker preachers. They were all working among a scattered population whose 'morals . . . in general are better and their religious views less exceptionable than the generality of even the Protestants of our own Country'. On the political attitudes of the MEC preachers he added in the same letter that 'all the Methodist preachers both traveling and local in this country with the exceptions of seven are British subjects and have taken the oath of allegiance'. He concluded by seeking the advice of his superiors in London:

Your instructions . . . to me cannot come a day too soon that I may know how to act as I am sure they will be such as will enable me to go forward with my Bible in my hand and say this Book and the Committee authorises me to do so, for I dare not go in upon the labours of other Methodist preachers until I see the reasons made clear why I ought to do so, and I am the more causious in this as I have seen the evil of it so much in my own unhappy country.

Within months Johnston had taken things into his own hands, and decided to return home. He had found in Canada, he said in a letter to London,

that the business of a missionary . . . must be to keep up a religious war, and in many instances to be employed in making division in other Methodist societies (this I presume you are altogether unacquainted with).[37]

He had already negotiated a passage for Dublin and was ready to defend his actions.

Seeing that the destitute state in which the country was represented was only the exaggerated account of a few prejudiced individuals, and not being able to reconcile the work of division; and going on other men's labours and taking and keeping possession of Chapels built by them for the worship of *God*, and holding up a religious, and in some measure a political war, which in some instances have divided families, and speaking evil of each other as I could not reconcile these things with the word of God.

A letter written to Johnston, by now back in Ireland, in 1818 by one of the WMMS Secretaries expressed the strong disapproval of the Committee over his returning to Ireland without permission, especially since he had been informed that his complaints were being investigated.[38] Johnston was also informed that a request was being made of the Irish Conference

to take this case into their most serious consideration, as it is of the utmost importance to guard against any precedent which might encourage a similar dereliction of public duty in any Missionary in future.

The General Committee consulted with other missionaries in Canada before expressing its official attitude in a meeting in January 1819. Its conclusion was that Johnston's judgment had been impaired by his contacts with the American preachers, and that he had not been in possession of all the relevant facts. Some interference in the American work by the Wesleyans was, however, admitted, for which regret was expressed. No decision was taken to withdraw any Wesleyan preachers or to add to their number, and it was acknowledged that before any new preachers were appointed in the future a full statement should first be received in London detailing the specific need and commenting on the involvement of other religious bodies. Also it was agreed that those missionaries already in Canada should

> not . . . continue their labours in any station previously occu-
> pied by the American Brethren, except when the population
> is so large or so scattered, that it is evident, that a very con-
> siderable part of them must be neglected.[39]

A general instruction the Committee had given on 26 June 1818 was reaffirmed for the guidance of its Canadian missionaries:

> That it be communicated to the Missionaries there, that the
> Conference and the Committee never intended, that the
> Missionaries sent out by them should invade the Societies
> raised up by the Preachers appointed by the American Con-
> ference and to divide them; but that they should communicate
> the benefits of the Xian Ministry to those parts of the country
> where the inhabitants are destitute of them and to labour in
> those towns and villages, where the population is so large that
> the addition of their labours to those of other Ministers, are
> demanded by the moral necessities of the people.

The Irish Conference in 1819 treated Johnston much more leniently than the Committee wished or anticipated, appointing him as second minister on the Enniskillen and Brookeborough circuit. The Secretariat at the WMMS were unable to conceal their dissatisfaction with this, making a veiled reference to the affair in a circular letter sent to all missionaries in September 1819:

> Two Missionaries having, in the course of the year, returned home without leave from the Committee, they have been dealt with according to the nature of their case; and one of them, by the Irish Conference, much more mildly than he would otherwise have been, because information of some aggravating circumstances respecting his leaving his Station did not reach home in time. The Irish Conference, however, resolved in future to employ no man in the work at home, who should return from his Station without leave of the Committee.[40]

Johnston remained on the Irish stations for a decade, and then wrote to the British President from Monaghan in 1830, making another offer to go to Canada:

> When you read this you will recollect the conversation I had with you at the Conference in Cork when I told you of my feelings and convictions and sorrows respecting my return from the mission in *Canada* and the wish I had to return if possible and spend the remainder of my life in the good cause in that country. You stated to me the objection of a Family etc. . . . I take this liberty of addressing you as the President of the British Conference and making to you the following proposal as my boys will soon be fit to go to business – I offer to go as a married man without any children to pay all expenses of outfit passage etc. without any expense to the mission until I arrive on the spot.[41]

It is hardly surprising that his offer was not taken up, given the stir which his precipitate departure from Canada had caused earlier. He did, however, proceed to the United States upon his retirement, and died there in 1858.

When a church unites with others, there is a danger of its distinctive contribution being lost in the new body. Many believe that this happened to Methodism in the formation of the United Church of Canada, but there are now some encouraging signs that certain authentic Methodist emphases are being rediscovered. This poses no threat to the United Church's identity and unity, but rather adds to the quality of its life. Happily Methodism is now beginning to be associated in people's thinking with sound evangelism, relevant social witness and Wesleyan Catholicism, rather than with the emotionalism of a distinctively American revivalism.

– 6 –

Adam Clarke and William Arthur –
The Theology of Mission

=

Of all the people through whom Ireland contributed to world
Methodism, Adam Clarke and William Arthur were by far the
most outstanding. Their lives overlapped, and with Clarke
being a protegé of Wesley himself and Arthur living into the
twentieth century, they provide a striking study in the continuity of Methodism. They are also a reminder of the fact that
Methodism is a comparatively modern movement.

Adam Clarke was born in Co. Londonderry around 1760.
His career at school was undistinguished, but after he was converted and became a local preacher signs appeared of considerable latent abilities. He was invited to Bristol in 1782 to meet
Wesley, and so began a ministry which proved exceptional in
many ways. It has been claimed that his was the greatest name
in Methodism in the generation after Wesley,[1] and that he was
the most universal scholar of his time.[2] Three times President
of the British Methodist Conference, he did not lose touch with
Ireland, presiding over the Irish Conference on no less than four
occasions (in 1811, 1812, 1816 and 1822). He also worked in
Dublin in 1790, and founded six schools in counties Londonderry
and Antrim in 1831.

William Arthur was born in Co. Antrim in 1819, and entered
the Methodist ministry in 1837. After receiving training in
England, he sailed for Mysore, India, in 1839, remaining only
two years due to ill-health. Thereafter Arthur's ministry was
largely based at the WMMS Mission House in London. It has

been said that he possessed the eye of a statesman and the heart of an evangelist, and that probably no one had a more complete grasp of the missionary problems of his day.[3] Although earning a world-wide reputation as a preacher and lecturer and being based mainly in Britain, Arthur too kept in touch with Ireland. By a special arrangement he became the first Principal of the Methodist College in Belfast from 1868 to 1871, immediately following his presidential year in Britain. He also took a lively interest in Irish affairs, especially education, throughout his life and encouraged Methodists in North America to give financial support to the church in Ireland.

In their advocacy and involvement in mission, Clarke and Arthur had much in common. **First, both were missionaries themselves.**

Clarke took pride in claiming that he had first-hand experience of missions, as for example when he wrote in 1819:

> I speak not without knowledge. I was one of the first missionaries in the Connexion. I have variously suffered and bled in the cause. I bear about still in my body the marks of the Lord Jesus; I still feel the spirit of a missionary; and if I did not, I should not feel the spirit of a minister of Christ; and were there none other, even at this age of hoary decrepitude, I would volunteer my little services to the East, teach in the schools . . . at Ceylon; or enter on the Peninsula of India, to bear the seed-basket.[4]

Clarke's reference is to his period of service in Jersey, to which he had been appointed in 1786. He had this also in mind when in an address delivered in London in 1814 he declared that with the exception of those sent to America he was one of Methodism's first missionaries.[5] He claimed to know at first hand the 'heart of a missionary, and his labours' and to know what it meant to be outside the immediate protection of British law. At a much later stage in his life he again had direct missionary responsibility when he was given oversight of Methodist work in the Shetland Islands from 1825.

Arthur served in Mysore, and, although his term there was

short, it left a permanent mark on him. Thereafter his commitment to Jesus Christ was deeper. He emerged with a greater concern for the salvation of the world, and India always claimed a special place in his affections and interest. When he returned to England he vowed that the best of his strength would be devoted to advancing the interests of India.

Second, Clarke and Arthur each fulfilled a significant role in developing Methodism's official response to world mission. In 1790 Clarke was one of nine people appointed to a new Missionary Committee, to share responsibility with Coke for directing Methodism's work overseas. In 1813 and 1814 when, first at Leeds and later in other centres, District Missionary Societies were formed in a movement which prepared the way for the creation of the WMMS, Clarke was one of two Irishmen who were closely involved. His 'evangelical ardour, vast erudition, and unique personal influence'[6] gave prestige to these important early developments. Walter Griffith was the other Irishman. As President of the Conference from 1813 to 1814, he was in a unique position to support the Leeds initiative.

For almost the whole of his active ministry Arthur was directly involved in Methodism's official world outreach, serving in India and France under the WMMS, and having two lengthy periods as a Secretary of the WMMS, from 1851 until the mid 1860s; and again, after his term in the Methodist College in Belfast, from 1871 until his retirement in 1888. He was a particularly powerful advocate of work in India and Italy. He was also one of two WMMS Secretaries who met and prayed with a group of fourteen women in the Mission House in London in 1858. This led to the formation of the Ladies' Committee for the Amelioration of the Conditions of Women in Heathen Countries which in effect opened the door to much fuller participation by women in missions.

Third, Clarke and Arthur were keen language students. Clarke's facility with foreign languages added greatly to his contribution to the world church. It has been reckoned that he was familiar with as many as twenty languages and dialects, specializing in Oriental languages as well as in Latin, Greek and

Hebrew. This was the background to his appointment in 1808 as a member of the committee of the British and Foreign Bible Society (founded in 1804); and for ten years he was seldom absent from its meetings, advising especially on the translation of the Scriptures and constructing a scale of types for a Tartar New Testament to be used in the Far East. A claim that he played a unique part in translating an obscure inscription on the Rosetta Stone is, however, incorrect.[7]

Arthur too was gifted at languages. Disdaining the use of an interpreter in Mysore he applied himself rigorously and systematically to acquiring Kanarese.[8] His aim was to speak and preach as if he were a native. He listed four essentials in achieving this: a thorough knowledge of the grammatical and idiomatic structure of the language, an extensive vocabulary, an ability to write and speak fluently, and a correct pronunciation. He therefore noted new words, attempted to converse with people on all occasions, and insisted that his language teacher correct mispronunciations. He made rapid progress, reporting within months of his arrival in India that he could preach in Kanarese for half an hour, and that he could also offer extempore prayer. He was still not satisfied, however, and longed for 'unobstructed intercourse'.[9]

Fourth, Clarke and Arthur were both convinced of the uniqueness of Christ and of Christianity. In 1818 Clarke was given responsibility for the Christian training of two Buddhist priests from Ceylon. At the outset he affirmed two fundamental principles in working with them, that 'Christianity is indubitably true, comes immediately from God, and cannot be successfully controverted', and that 'other systems of religion are false or forged; and on them no man can rely, but at the utter risk of his salvation'.[10]

In his *Principles of the Christian Religion*, which was drawn up initially for the Buddhist priests and cited scriptural texts for each principle, Clarke affirmed that other religions did not, however, frustrate the work of God's spirit; for example in their followers becoming morally aware. One of the principles, the thirty-fifth, was that:

God sends his Holy Spirit into the hearts and consciences of all men, to convince them of *sin, righteousness,* and *judgement*; and that His *light* is to be found, even where His *Word* has not yet been revealed.[11]

The thirty-seventh principle ran:

By this light even the *heathens* are taught the general principles of *right* and *wrong*; of *justice* and *injustice*: not to injure each other; to be *honest* and *just* in their dealings; to abhor *murder*, cruelty, and oppression; and to be *charitable* and *merciful* according to their power.[12]

The thirty-sixth principle hints at an intermediate state between heaven and hell for those who died without the opportunity of responding to the gospel:

Those who have acted conscientiously, according to the dictates of this heavenly light in their minds, shall not perish eternally; but have that measure of glory and happiness which is suited to their state.[13]

In the thirty-ninth principle the basis of judgment for all peoples was summarized by Clarke in the following way:

God will judge the *heathen* by the *law* which He has *written* in *their minds*; and He will judge the *Jews* by the *Law* which He has given them by *Moses* and the *prophets*; and He will judge the *Christians* by the *Gospel* of Jesus Christ . . . and He will judge the Mohammedans according to the opportunities they have had of knowing the Gospel, and the obstinacy with which they have rejected it. And this will be an aggravation of the punishment of the *Jews*, Mohammedans and other unbelievers, that the Gospel which would have made them wise unto salvation, has been rejected by them; and they continue blasphemously to deny the Lord that bought them.[14]

The gospel, claimed Clarke, was '*a revelation from God*'.[15] It was 'the *means* of conveying *light* and *life* to the souls of men'. 'No power', he believed, 'whether *earthly* or *diabolic*, shall ever be able to overthrow it.'[16]

In January 1819 Clarke was able to write that the priests were making good progress. They were diligent in their studies, had an insatiable thirst for knowledge, were not prejudiced against Christianity, and showed a surprising ability to grasp abstruse subjects. In April he wrote that they showed an increased concern that others in Ceylon would learn of Jesus Christ.[17] Both priests received baptism in March 1820, and returned to Ceylon. As we shall learn from the chapter on James Lynch, criticisms were later expressed about their treatment in England, and their conduct in Ceylon.

So far as other faiths were concerned, Arthur's main contact was with Hinduism. His standpoint reflected the view frequently held at the time that 'that which is outside Christianity is wholly and hopelessly false'.[18] Appreciative of good qualities in many of the people whom he met – for example he often referred to their being courteous and hospitable – he nonetheless thought of them as people in moral and spiritual darkness. He thus wrote of his own part of India as a 'fine country . . . with its polished manners and dead souls'.[19]

Idolatry especially offended him. Madras, for example, he saw as 'a city given to idolatry'.[20] In the town of Gubbi, where he was based, 'there were temples; but no tower marked a sanctuary of the living God'.[21] Idols were impotent, utterly unable to save, he declared. 'Civilised, lettered, accomplished idolatry' struck him as 'the most startling thing on earth, man's worst curse, Satan's highest triumph'.[22] Nothing more dreadful could be conceived than to be

> transformed into one of these dark souls, bereft of the knowledge of the one holy and true God, of redemption, of the resurrection of the dead, or the life of the world to come.[23]

At times Arthur detected traces of earlier, less corrupt forms of Hinduism.[24] These had not been completely obliterated by developments such as the advance of Brahmanism and the spread of idolatry. It was, however, what he regarded as the inability of Hinduism to meet man's deepest moral and spiritual needs which encouraged him to press the unique claims of Christ. It was much more important to emphasize this than, for example, to expose the scientific inaccuracies contained in the sacred Shastras.[25]

Pardon was sought in Hinduism through such means as meditation, penance, ablutions, and the repetition of mantras; salvation was only to be found in a later life through re-birth. Not once, in all his earnest discussions with Hindus, had Arthur encountered a single person who had hope in this life of becoming a new and holy man.[26] Brahmans were unaware of experimental religion of this kind, Arthur claimed. 'Real, obvious demonstrable regeneration' in this life was to them a '*terra incognita*'.[27]

Christ, on the other hand, could certainly make people new here and now. It was his ability to renew man in God's image which made Christianity unique among religions. Protestant missionaries, as distinct from Roman Catholic ones, therefore looked for a change of heart rather than of ceremonial, not just a change of creed but a change of character in their converts. Their weapons were 'fair argument, wielded by vernacular addresses and publications'.[28] The making of compulsory disciples, through coercion or collusion with government, or through material incentives, was to be avoided as altogether unworthy. The aim was therefore to make Hindus aware of sin, and then to lead them to Christ. The fact that Hindus had some moral sense, however undeveloped, made such an appeal possible:

> Hindus have not the well-taught tender conscience of a Christian; but they have that light from God in Christ which enables them . . . to discern in good a beauty, and in evil a stain, which makes the choice of the latter defiling.[29]

As a missionary Arthur sought to tell idol-worshippers uncompromisingly that 'their god was an idol, that their services were folly, that their worship was sin', and that there was only one God and one mediator between God and man.[30] In describing the 'senseless, sinful ceremonies' of idol-worship, he wrote:

The din of the music, and the shouts of the throng, all mingling in one harsh clamour, seemed as the shout of Satan exulting in his wide-spread sway . . . O Spirit of the Lord, descend in thy mightiness, break the power that chains them now, and bring in all the blessings of the Gospel of Christ![31]

Fifth, Clarke and Arthur both emphasized the vital part to be played by the Bible in mission. Clarke was convinced of the inter-relatedness of Bible translation, preaching, and teaching, and it was therefore wholly appropriate that in his work with the former Buddhist priests he compiled *Clavis Biblica, or a Compendium of Scriptural Knowledge*, as an aid to their understanding of Christian fundamentals. This was later published for use in schools in Ceylon. Clarke, whose biblical scholarship was renowned, regarded the Scriptures as a revelation from God, being 'the only complete directory of the faith and practice of men'.[32] In *The Necessity and Existence of Missions* he gave his considered view on the place of the Bible in mission:

> Bible societies, and Missionary societies may, under God, convert the world, if they go hand in hand; I mean, if the Bible societies furnish the Scriptures for the heathen; and the missionary societies provide and support preachers to explain and apply those words of eternal life. But in multitudes of places the people cannot read the Bible; then they should be taught to read it: one part, therefore, of the missionary's work is to erect schools . . . Behold, then the grand system of agency for the conversion of the world. God commanding and influencing; the Bible declaring his will relative to both worlds; the missionary explaining and applying that word . . .; the school for the reception and instruction of the children of the heathen; and the Christian convert teaching the lessons of grace in the school.[33]

Arthur also wrote about the importance of Bible teaching in schools. One of many pamphlets written by him was entitled *Is the Bible to lie under a Ban in India?* Made available in 1859, it challenged Christian voters in Britain to press for a change in the law so that the Bible could be taught in Indian schools. Government by a Christian government should be openly Christian:

> The Koran of the Mussulman, the Zend Avesta of the Fire Worshipper, the Shastras of the idolater – some of them sanguinary, some foolish, others foul – are *taught* by the Queen's authority, and by liberal public grants. The only branded book is that on which the Queen takes her Coronation oath.

In the wake of the Indian mutiny Arthur was careful to make clear that he sought not the compulsory teaching of the Bible to all children in every circumstance, but simply the option of teaching it when the circumstances were considered favourable and the pupils themselves showed a willingness to be taught. Arthur was convinced that the absence of Bible knowledge had been a contributory factor in the mutiny, leading people to the mistaken view that Christianity approved of conversion by force and fraud. He also believed that the teaching of the Bible in India would do much to instil a deeper moral sense in native officials such as judges, magistrates, revenue officers, and police, and would thus contribute to justice in society.

Sixth, Clarke and Arthur were agreed that Mission is the vocation of all Christians and of the whole Church. Clarke saw Methodism essentially as a missionary movement. Preaching in London in 1814 he stressed especially the responsibility of all Christian ministers:

> It is my conscientious belief, that the same command is still *binding* on *every minister* of *Christ*; and will continue to be so, while there is one district of the globe, however small, unconverted to the Christian faith . . . Should not every minister of Christ lay this especially to heart, when there is more than half a world, after all that has been done, on which the light of the Gospel of Jesus has not yet shined?[34]

In a letter to the WMMS in 1819 he reflected first on how Methodism had initially committed itself to evangelism at home and then had proceeded to extend its influence to other parts of the world. 'We now feel that we are necessarily become a *Missionary People* and must spread ourselves', he wrote.[35] He also wrote on another occasion:

> Nothing can be more consistent with the genius and spirit of Methodism which so uniformly asserts and convincingly proves the love of God to the human race, than Missionary exertions.[36]

Arthur spoke of mission as 'the best of causes'[37] in which everyone had a part to play. Individual Christians became centres of Christ's mission force, and each church was an organized agency for conserving and diffusing that force. Speaking of the gift of the Holy Spirit at Pentecost, Arthur pointed out that each disciple had received the gift directly – it had not, for instance, been given first to the twelve to be communicated to the seventy, and then passed on to the others. Similarly, he argued, the task of mission was not one solely, or even in the first instance, for professionals:

> The multitude of believers were not mere adherents, but living, speaking, burning agents in the great movement for the universal diffusion of God's message.[38]

Seventh, Clarke and Arthur were convinced of the stimulus and creative interplay between mission at home and overseas. As with Thomas Coke, there was for them no negative tension involved in the dual concern for mission locally and further afield. Those who were keenest on overseas missions, Clarke claimed, had prospered most in their own souls, and 'through practical piety' became more deep and extensive in their local church life.[39]

As an old man, Arthur's enthusiastic commitment to universal mission remained unwavering:

> No Christian ought to look upon mission work as lying far off, and none should look upon any distance as putting the place beyond the pale of enterprise. First at home, next close by, and finally on to the ends of the earth, is our sphere.[40]

The lament over alleged waste of resources, even the loss of life overseas, did not dissuade him:

> The energy is not wasted, but returns into the bosoms of churches and of nations in the form of greatly augmented impetus to all holy deeds. The lives are not lost, but, whether 'broke by sickness' or cut off by persecution, they are the seed of the Church.

Eighth, Clarke and Arthur both recognized that God's mission was primary and definitive, and that the church's mission was therefore secondary and derivative. Clarke's *Principles of the Christian Religion* point to God's initiative in providing people with moral awareness and also in preparing the way for the offer of salvation through the gospel of Christ; and in what Clarke termed 'the grand system of agency for the conversion of the world' we have noted that the action of God in 'commanding and influencing' precedes the part to be played by the Bible, the missionary, and the Christian school.[41]

In his best known publication, *The Tongue of Fire*, Arthur took up and expanded this point even further, stressing particularly the vital role of the Holy Spirit in mission. God had spoken and acted decisively at Pentecost for the benefit of all peoples. A force had then been let loose which claimed all humanity. Without this power of Pentecost, Christianity degenerated into a human agency for social improvement, blessed with superhuman doctrines but destitute of superhuman power.[42] In his pamphlet *The Best of Causes* (1888), however, Arthur pointed to the Second Person of the Trinity in emphasizing the primacy of God in mission:

> When we speak of St Paul as the Prince of Missionaries, we mean of mortal Missionaries, for the true Prince was He who was sent of the Father, who, coming forth from out of the glory which He had with Him ere the world began, summed up His mission in the words: 'The Son of Man is come to seek and to save that which was lost.'

Ninth, both Clarke and Arthur believed that individuals and groups of people could experience personal renewal, and they recognized such personal change as a vital aspect of mission. Immediately before the public baptism of the two former Buddhist priests Clarke made clear to the congregation that he believed their hearts as well as their heads had been changed.[43] In one of his publications he affirmed that the success of a mission should not be estimated in accordance with the number of people attending the preaching or even seeking baptism. What was decisive in his view was the change effected in people's hearts and lives.[44]

Arthur argued forcefully on behalf of the power of the gospel to change people. Christianity's case depended on its continued ability from New Testament times onwards to make evil people good:

> To suppose that this power to regenerate man, and thereby to ameliorate human society, has been withdrawn from the Church by (God) . . . is to suppose, in fact, that *the one practical end of Christianity has been voluntarily abandoned* . . . If Christianity cannot renew man in the image of God, she ceases to have any special distinction above other religions.[45]

The convincing evidence for Christianity was found in men and women who had been regenerated.

Arthur consistently stressed that such personal renewal should not, however, be allowed to become individualistic. When the Spirit of God was active in people's lives, community was created. Christianity, he testified,

> seeks not the wilderness; she seeks not the few; she affects not little, dispersed, and hidden groups . . . She starts as the religion of the multitude; the religion of fathers and mothers, of traders, landowners, widows, persons of all classes, and of all occupations. She takes in her hand . . . an earnest of every nation, and kindred, and people, and tongue, of every grade and age, as if to expand for ever the expectations of her disciples, and impress us with the joyful faith that her practical redemption was for the multitudes of men.[46]

Finally, Clarke and Arthur both recognized that mission contained elements of what Arthur described as 'social revolution'.[47] In making this point it should none the less be acknowledged that they placed greater emphasis on personal renewal than on social change, and that they favoured a conservative and gradualist approach to social change.

Clarke was responsible for the Shetlands mission towards the end of his life. At first the mission's social emphasis was in terms of responding to the obvious personal needs of the islanders. 'Next to preaching Jesus', wrote Clarke to one of the missionaries, what was most required was taking practical initiatives to alleviate the condition of the poor, particularly the women.[48] He himself collected items, especially clothing, for the Shetlands. In 1826, however, he circularized the preachers, seeking a fuller account of the conditions under which the people lived, and asking what in practical terms would best 'ameliorate the condition of the peasantry'.[49] Another reference in 1826 suggests that he was at the time feeling his way towards a more radical programme of help:

> I wish to hit upon something that would give the poor some profitable winter employment. I believe I could get them a good portion of hemp, if they could spin their own lines, etc. Tell me in what we can help them.[50]

Clarke's published conclusions, following his second visit to the Shetlands in 1828, contained tentative suggestions to landowners to improve the conditions under which their tenants lived.[51] It should be openly admitted, Clarke argued, that 'the great mass of the population' live 'in a poor and wretched condition'. This did not mean that the islanders themselves were unaware of their suffering, or that there was an excuse for inactivity. A remedy had to be sought. His own approach was to suggest that fishing and farming be tackled as separate issues, and that tenant farmers be offered leases of nineteen or twenty-one years, with financial assistance on fair terms to help in the building of dykes and in the purchasing of stock and equipment. Clarke displayed uneasiness in thus involving himself directly in economics, but his interest in the spiritual health of the islanders had made him aware that civil and economic matters affected every aspect of life in the Shetlands. He also believed that 'such a systematic and universal change and improvement' would benefit not only the tenants but also the landlords.

Arthur showed a greater awareness than Clarke of the social implications of mission, and was convinced of the need for social justice. It was his view that nothing short of the general renewal of society ought to satisfy the Christian. 'The Gospel is come to renew the face of the earth', he wrote.[52] Such things as slavery, class alienation, child neglect, commercial fraud, and bad housing were thus legitimate objects of concern.[53]

Politicians in their efforts to improve society made the mistake of focusing solely on the reform of institutions, forgetting the need for fundamental change in people's moral condition. Good institutions did not themselves lead to the regeneration of society, although they had incalculable value in embodying and conserving personal values and goodness. Among people who were deprived and unprincipled, however, they would not themselves survive.

In such a situation Arthur was convinced that 'the only way to the effectual regeneration of society is the regeneration of individuals'.[54] Christians, however, had much to do if social regeneration was to become a reality. Although Christianity raised the level of conscience in a community, and thus laid a foundation for social improvement, it could not be assumed that proper moral principles would inevitably and spontaneously be given legitimate social expression. South Africa and Ireland give a strikingly contemporary ring to Arthur's acknowledgement that

> fearful social evils may co-exist with a state of society wherein many are holy, and all have a large amount of Christian light.

Arthur stressed that Christians have to avoid complacency, and that serious and sustained study was required in the urgent task of applying Christian principles to social evils:

To destroy all national holds of evil, to root sin out of institutions, to hold up to view the Gospel ideal of a righteous nation, to confront all unwholesome public usages with mild, genial, and ardent advocacy of what is purer, is one of the first duties of those whose position or mode of thought gives them an influence on general questions. In so doing they are at once glorifying the Redeemer, – by displaying the benignity of His influence over human society, and removing hindrances to individual conversion, some of which act by direct incentive to vice, others by upholding a state of things, the acknowledged basis of which is, – 'Forget God.'[55]

It is in this context that we note what was Arthur's most radical concern, that for racial justice. Following what he considered to be biased coverage in the British press of an uprising of black people in Jamaica, Arthur delivered a speech which was published in London in 1865. He examined three questions – whether, as had been alleged, the revolt proved that Blacks were sub-human; whether the method of suppressing the riot upheld the view that white West Indians were morally superior to black West Indians; and whether the rights of Blacks were safe in the hands of former slave owners? Among Arthur's points were the following – that Christians must stand by the oppressed ('when the powerful revile the mean, the place of the Christian is beside him with whom he will share reproach, not praise').[56] The Blacks appeared to have rebelled not because they were inferior or were too lazy to work, but because of the harsh conditions under which they suffered. In resisting oppression they were not reacting differently from other people under similar circumstances, and it was perhaps surprising that violence had not erupted sooner. Contrary to what the press had said, missionaries were among those who exercised a restraining influence; and the actions taken to suppress the riot appeared to have gone far beyond what was justified. Arthur's view of the Black man was devoid of false sentiment:

When he does wrong, let us not extenuate it. When he is idle, licentious, or cruel, give his sins the right name, and call him to repent. But by every principle, Christian, manly, and true, let us face the people who say that such faults belong to his race and not to others. Man for man the West India blacks need not fear comparison with the whites, especially when comparative advantages are taken into view.[57]

Arthur possessed the ability of holding together what some have regarded as mutually exclusive elements in Christian mission, personal renewal and social renewal. It was the belief that renewal was needed on both fronts that made him ultimately optimistic about the results of mission. This is seen clearly in his attitude to the work in India. No one knew better than he that the church's resources were slender, and that the task confronting the church was enormous, yet he was convinced that an impact could be made on the nation as a whole. The social cohesiveness of the caste system which made individual conversions rare and difficult could ultimately enhance the prospects of fundamental change:

> Every individual who, overcoming the restraints of Hinduism, embraces Christianity, effects, however unconsciously, an achievement by which Asiatic superstition is one degree weakened, and the way to grace made, for the people of nations, one degree easier.[58]

The ties that bound people together in India were so strong that individuality as such did not exist.[59] Those ties increased 'the hope of universal regeneration' more than they diminished 'the facilities of partial change'. This sort of conviction was repeated with special reference to the subordinate position of women in *Women's Work in India* (1882):

> Every man who embraced Christianity became an instrument, however unobserved, of weakening the old customs which had for ages rendered the lot of women unchangeable. [60]

When the Society for Promoting Female Education in the East was founded, there were, he claimed, few people who looked upon it as the pioneer of a great historical movement. It was in this setting that Arthur wrote of Christian mission containing elements of a 'social revolution' and being 'disturbing to old-established ideas of social order'.[61]

We do less than justice to Methodism historically, and we run the risk of distortion or at least of imbalance in our understanding of mission, when we do not take account of the views of such significant leaders in the Methodist tradition as Adam Clarke and William Arthur. Much in their teaching is more or less predictable, including their uncompromising stand on the place of Christ, the uniqueness of Christianity, and the importance of the translation and distribution of the Scriptures; their emphasis on the initiative of God himself in mission and on the need for personal renewal; and their passionate commitment to mission and the clear recognition that it is properly a concern for the whole church and for every Christian. Less to be expected is Arthur's concern for racial justice and his recognition of the need for structural and institutional renewal as well as personal renewal. What perhaps is most impressive is not any one element in the teaching of Clarke and Arthur, but simply the range and inclusiveness of it all when taken together. We are certainly the poorer in our own understanding of mission if we do not draw and build upon such insights.

– 7 –

James Lynch, Reluctant Leader

=

Lynch's Life and Work – A Summary

A native of the parish of Muff in Co. Donegal where he was born in 1775 and was brought up a Roman Catholic, James Lynch became a Methodist by conviction while not yet a teenager. Little is known of the influences leading to this decision, or of the strains involved for his family. Evidence has now come to light that he kept in occasional contact with members of his family throughout his life, even while far from them. It is significant too that his nephew Samuel, son of his brother Hugh, became an MEC preacher in the United States.

James Lynch entered the Methodist ministry in Ireland in 1808. After serving for short periods in several northern circuits, he was accepted as a founder member of the pioneer missionary group which was sent out in 1813 under Thomas Coke to establish Methodist missions in Asia.

The East India mission had scarcely been launched before it became engulfed in a series of crises. As the seven missionaries embarked on two vessels in a convoy of thirty ships which set sail on 31 December 1813, they could not have guessed at the calamities which were soon to befall them. Seven ships were lost in a gale in the Bay of Biscay. Then the wife of one of the missionaries died on 10 February 1814. Finally, and of most significance to the mission, Coke himself was found dead in his cabin on 3 May. This loss was indeed a cruel blow for the missionaries, none of whom had been taken into Coke's confidence regarding detailed arrangements for the mission. Perhaps Coke had not laid the administrative and policy groundwork necessary for the smooth running of the mission. This would help to account for the horrendous financial difficulties soon to confront the mission. A recent comment by David Hempton is sharp and to the point, that Coke 'combined remarkable zeal with equally remarkable administrative incompetence'.[1]

In such highly unpromising circumstances, Lynch took over the leadership of the party since, by the common consent of his colleagues, he was the most senior missionary remaining after Coke's death. Lynch had of course no authority from London to become the leader, and when eventually word was received it was scarcely of a nature to boost confidence or to heighten morale. It simply stated that Lynch should continue as acting Superintendent until an appointment was made from England.

The party spent a month in Bombay, and then after sorting out some financial and other details they set sail again. They landed at Galle in Ceylon on 29 June 1814. A 'little conference' followed on 11 July, under Lynch's chairmanship, when the decision was taken to apportion the work on the basis of the two major languages of the area, Tamil and Singhalese. It has continued to be organized in this way ever since. Lynch, though to some extent responsible for the oversight of the entire mission, was appointed to the Tamil area and stationed at Jaffna which remained his base until he left for India in 1817. This move, like becoming leader, was not of his choosing.

Lynch's first intimation that he had received a request from Madras for a missionary to be sent, was contained in a letter to London in October 1816. What Lynch actually wrote to the Committee differed significantly from the version which was published in Britain and which has since appeared in print on several occasions. The published account presents the picture of a small, earnest group of lay Christians totally isolated in Madras, anxious to receive regular instruction but with no one at hand to help them. In fact the request came from five people who had previously belonged to a Calvinist congregation in Madras, and who now by preference sought Methodist teaching, having read some of the works of Wesley and Fletcher.[2]

The missionaries in Ceylon did not immediately respond to the initiative from Madras, feeling that they were already seriously over-committed. Their eventual decision was that one of their number, William Harvard, should be sent. This, however, was greeted with such a wave of protest within Ceylon, because of Harvard's involvement in the work of the Bible Society, that the decision was promptly rescinded. As a compromise Lynch himself was asked by his colleagues to proceed to Madras, to find out exactly what lay behind the request for help. Before he could leave on such an exploratory visit, however, word came through from the Committee in London that he had been appointed officially to Madras. As he himself openly confessed, this development struck him as a thunderbolt. He had neither sought nor anticipated the appointment, nor did he feel particularly suited to it especially in view of his acknowledged tardiness in acquiring Tamil. A reluctant leader yet again, he set sail from Jaffna on 23 January 1817, travelling in a small open boat just nine feet across, the journey to the southern tip of India taking thirty-eight hours. He thus earned the distinction of being the founder of Methodism's first permanent mission on the subcontinent of India.

On his way overland to Madras, Lynch was the guest of the Danish mission at Tranquebar where he was deeply moved when he visited the graves of Plütschau and Ziegenbalg, the first missionaries sent out under the King of Denmark's mission.[3] He preached for the first time in Madras on 2 March 1817, at a warehouse in Georgetown, and a chapel was opened there in 1822. An earlier chapel was built at Royapettah in 1819. Both sites have remained centres of vigorous church life.

Lynch's failure to acquire fluent Tamil undoubtedly restricted his effectiveness, largely limiting his influence to British civil and military personnel, but the importance of his contribution should not be underestimated. He judged that had he not gone to Madras when he did, the small society there could have been destroyed by dissension.[4] Had this happened, the possibility of advance from this strategic centre might have

been lost for another generation. He also had the task of super-
intending the mission as a whole, and revisited Ceylon occasionally in this connection.

Lynch was stationed at Madras until 1824, when he returned
to Ireland. He had hopes of going overseas again, mentioning
Upper Canada, South Africa, and Calcutta as possible destina-
tions in a letter to the WMMS from Newry in 1829.[5] His offer
was not taken up, however, and the rest of his active ministry
was spent in Ireland. He retired in 1842, and died in Leeds in
1858.

Lynch's missionary service highlighted a number of significant
issues.

Education, a Vital and Strategic Instrument

Lynch was convinced of the importance of education. In 1816
he wrote that without schools the opportunities for instructing
and training the native population would be much reduced, and
that there was indeed a case for launching 'a kind of *Missionary
School* Society' for the sole purpose of establishing schools.[6]
Extra money could be raised towards this without in any way
interfering with the general support of missions. Such an
approach would, in his view, prove to be the most effective way
of establishing the gospel in Ceylon.

In addition Lynch raised the possibility of a special kind of
school being created. The idea, which had arisen in conversation
with an Anglican chaplain, was that hand-picked boys should
be given training to enable them to become teachers and
ministers. He took up the theme again in December of the same
year with a suggestion that acknowledged his own inability to
master Tamil:

For a few months past my mind has been greatly exercised
about my call to India . . . My great dullness in learning the
native language renders me as nothing in a distant land, & I
have often almost determined to request liberty to fix myself
in some suitable place, & take a few pious native boys under

my care in hopes that God would convert them, & call them to the ministry, or that they might be useful interpreters. Indeed my mind has been deeply impressed with this for some time past, & I have little doubt but that this would be the way in which I could be most useful. We are all deeply sensible that unless God raises up native preachers our usefulness will be contracted indeed.[7]

This clear recognition of the strategic importance of a properly trained native ministry is impressive, and shows that without good Tamil Lynch had still a valuable contribution to make. Progress towards establishing such a ministry was nevertheless difficult as a result of negative racial attitudes. Lynch had referred to the need for such ministers almost a year previously when he expressed the opinion that 'until God raises up native preachers ... the labours of European Missionaries will be comparatively unfruitful'.[8]

One of the major educational questions considered by Lynch was whether mission schools should be openly and exclusively Christian. In a letter written in 1818 he showed an awareness of issues that still come to the fore in mission and educational circles, noting that there were two main points of view. The first he described in the following terms:

In several places schools have been established, wherein no religion whatever is taught; the books are selections of morality, both from Heathen and Christian authors – The conducters of these schools say, that by them the ability of reading the Holy Scriptures etc. is given to children – that when they arrive to maturity it is to be hoped they will read & judge for themselves, & ultimately embrace Christianity – & even tho they would not – that their strong prejudices would be removed – whereas if the Scriptures & Christianity were taught, parents would not suffer their Children to attend the schools & consequently they must live and die in ignorance – I believe untill lately very few called in question, or condemned this system.[9]

But there was another quite different approach:

Now there are Chaplains & Missionaries & others who are of a contrary opinion – they believe that schools under *them*, should be Christian schools – & that all Parents & Children should be informed – that Christianity & Heathenism, are completely opposite to each other – that the one is from & leads to Heaven; that the other is from the devil & man, & leaves men in darkness, & leads to Hell – They believe that from a conviction of these truths they should have nothing to do with softening down Christianity – & encouraging Heathenism – & that allowing Heathen books (however excellent their morality) to have the same place in school is, lowering the one & raising the other – It is granted that some of their morality is excellent – But it is only taught; how to practice they know not.

Lynch came down firmly on the side of the second approach, since the first resulted in few converts being made, and encouraged ungodliness even among Christians:

Does not the word of God command us as Christians to do all to his Glory, & in the name of Christ; & can he be glorified by any institution or labour, where the Lord Jesus is excluded – or where he is not directly taught to be the only Lord & Saviour of a fallen sinful world – Or how can any Christian with any degree of Faith pray for, & expect the blessing of God on such labours – & if the Grace of God does not affect the heart, of what saving advantage is learning – Or is it not rather a real hindrance to the Gospel when destitute of Grace.

People of other Faiths

Lynch's attitude towards the followers of other faiths was more open than might have been expected from some of his remarks on education. In commenting on idol-worship, Lynch drew a fascinating parallel with his own Roman Catholic background in Ireland:

In all places the Brahmins, & other sensible people confesst that their Idols are no Gods, & say they do not worship them – that there is but one God, who is the almighty Creator of all things, & who cannot be seen; but as he is in every place & fills all space, he is also in these images. Surely such a belief is not so absurd, as that of Transubstantiation, wherein it is believed that thousands of men at the same time, but in different parts of the world, make the real body & blood of Christ out of bread & wine – then worship it as God – & afterwards give this real Saviour to millions of people at the same time, & that each has eaten a whole & undivided Saviour, & yet we dare not say that none who believe this doctrine can be saved; & may we not have the same charitable hope of the poor heathen, as of pious, tho idolatrous, Catholics.[10]

In a subsequent letter he stated that he did not consider the people whom he had met to be idolaters in the sense condemned in the Bible. These views, arising from Lynch's experiences in Madras, contrast sharply with those expressed by Arthur after his period in Mysore over twenty years later. While Hindus had been taught to bow before idols, Lynch claimed that it was actually the invisible God whom they worshipped. He therefore confessed himself dissatisfied with the view that the mere accident of birth appeared to determine anyone's eternal destiny. Would it not be unjust for a person to be sent to eternal punishment simply because he had been born a heathen and had not had an opportunity of hearing the gospel? Just as the children of Christian parents cannot be held responsible for sin, or be regarded as sinners until they themselves have become conscious of God's law and have wilfully disobeyed it:

Children and heathens may be saved through the merits of the Lord Jesus though both may have been guilty of actions and of Idolatry which would be of a damning nature in one who had and was capable of understanding the law of God.[11]

Lynch's task in this situation was to introduce non-Christians 'to the knowledge and happiness of the children of God' through faith in Jesus Christ.

The Missionary Society Secretaries replied at length to Lynch in 1821:

> If you think that any of us have stated that the Heathen will perish because they have not the Gospel, you are mistaken. We do not think they will perish as heathens, that is, persons without revelation, but as sinners, violating the laws & the light they have. We believe in a law 'written in the heart' but if that be a law from God, it cannot prescribe idolatry, uncleanness etc.; it must on the contrary forbid them. Idolaters & immoral persons act contrary to the law written on their heart.[12]

Lynch had indicated that he could not accept that the salvation of the heathen was absolutely dependent upon his own preaching. The Committee recognized that Lynch was here raising fundamental questions about Christian mission and the role of missionaries:

> We do . . . believe that as wherever the Gospel is preached the means of salvation are multiplied, and the remedy applied in its strongest form, many will be saved by the gospel who would not be saved without it. If not why did Mr. Lynch go out to India? Why do we incur all this expense? How is it the work of a Minister to save souls if the same souls whom he instrumentally saves would be saved if he had taken no pains with them? . . . If the heathen are in that state of safety which Mr. Lynch supposes, they are not sinners; if they are not sinners, Mr. Lynch can neither preach to them the doctrine of repentance nor remission of sins. They are the ninety-nine who need no repentance. If he believes on the contrary that the mass of them are sinners i.e. that they violate some righteous rule which they either know or might know if they were disposed to enquire, though the knowledge of it may be dim & obscure, then he must believe them in danger, & there is no disagreement between us & him.

Unfortunately there is no surviving evidence to suggest that these vital questions were taken further in correspondence between Lynch and the Committee.

When Hindus reached the point of seriously considering becoming Christians, Lynch was fully aware that for them 'the breaking of cast' (*sic*) was a matter of the utmost gravity. This led him to question whether it was in fact a necessary step. He summarized the problem in 1818:

> Can a man be a real Christian & retain his cast? To retain his cast he must not eat certain kinds of flesh, nor eat with those who do eat such flesh; such as Europeans & Parriars; nor the food that Parriars handle or dress; neither must he marry outside of his own cast; & by breaking any of these rules of cast he is cut off from all connection (& all his posterity also) with his relations & his cast ... Is it necessary for a convert to Christianity to make such a sacrifice & cut himself off from all his friends; & become totally dependent on Christians for living & support; I cannot think that the Apostle Paul would have enjoined such a sacrifice.[13]

Was there not a way of avoiding this stumbling block, he wondered:

> Many have been prevented from embracing the Gospel in consequence of the Idea of the loss of cast being connected therewith – very few who wish to become Christians have the spirit of Martyrdom; or can forsake all & follow Christ – & to an Indian the loss of cast is worse than death – Why in general are they so much afraid to read our Books, or to hear the Gospel; they know that we wish them to become Christians; & with this they instantly connect the idea of the loss of cast.

Perhaps the matter of joining in Holy Communion with Europeans and pariahs could be made optional rather than obligatory. 'Might not a Brahman have Gospel love for me & to a Parriar tho he would not eat nor drink with us?', Lynch asked. He himself advanced the view that such things as reading the Bible, believing the gospel, abandoning idolatry, and being baptized, did not of themselves necessitate the breaking of caste.

Following receipt of Lynch's letter, the Committee replied in October 1818:

Resolved ... that on the subject of renouncing Caste he be informed that from the information hitherto obtained by the Committee, Caste appeared to be rather a civil, than a religious distinction, and if as Mr Lynch states, that the conforming to all Christian ordinances by Indian converts is not prevented by their retaining their Caste, it would be a very unnecessary opposition to the civil customs to interfere with the Caste of the Natives; and that the great object of Missionaries is to diffuse the great truths of religion with as little offence as possible to such prejudices and manners as do not imply any moral evil.[14]

It is surprising that in framing this reply the Committee did not appear to have any information on caste apart from that which Lynch himself had supplied; or, if it did, it made no use of it. No reference was made in the reply from the Committee to Lynch's point about the possibility of participation in Holy Communion with those of inferior caste being regarded as optional.

That such correspondence took place on vital and sensitive issues in the first phase of Methodist missions in India, is impressive. It must be conceded, however, that it is not clear at times whether the views being expressed by Lynch were strictly his own or those of other people. Whichever the case, it is still striking that he dared to state them, and that he received such a firm reply.

Questions of Race

On 29 July 1816, in the first Methodist Conference held in Ceylon, chaired by Lynch, a question was asked as to whether native assistant missionaries should be allowed to live under the same roof as European missionaries and eat at their table. The reply was that they ought not. This response was in sharp contrast to a letter which Lynch himself had written in 1814 within months of his arrival in Ceylon:

It is to be regretted that our European Christians, by their conduct, rather encourage ... cast. I cannot but detest a national custom which prevails, that no native, no not even a native Christian, is allowed to sit in the company of an Englishman. It is true that some of our countrymen who are in mind & station above the common ones, subject themselves to the censure of their imaginary superiors, by inviting a respectable native Christian to take a seat. But while we abhor the anti-Christian conduct, we feel very delicate at once to break through the custom.[15]

Evidently, in the course of only two years, Lynch had so shifted his position on racial matters as to endorse the kind of behaviour he had previously abhorred as 'anti-Christian'.

In two letters written in 1820 Lynch commented at length on what he regarded as the wholly misguided deference which had been shown to the two former Buddhist priests who had studied under Adam Clarke in England and who had since returned to Ceylon. They had failed to live up to the hopes held out for them, and in Lynch's view their usefulness had been marred for ever by their treatment in Europe. Too much had been made of them, and they had become unbearably proud:

Our friends in England do not know the Indian Character, or they would not have treated them with so much respect. Dr Clarke surely did not consult Sir Alex Johnson how they should have been treated. I am pretty certain the young men would not have presumed to look for a place at the Doctor's table, & they should have given the most satisfactory evidence of deep humility of soul before they were introduced in public at Missionary Meetings. I'm sure every Br. in India will be astonished that they had a cabin passage, an effectual way to render them worse than useless in India. It is well that they did not come to Madras. I had a homely room prepared for them, where they were to live & eat & sleep by themselves. ... Probably my Fathers and Br. may fear that I have a little too much of Indian pride. If so I fear every Br. in India has the same, and as a proof – at our last Ceylon Conference – we *unanimously* agreed not to go through the usual ceremony of ordination with our assistant Missionaries (at least for the present) even after they have travelled 4 years.[16]

Lynch's approach to such matters was shared by colleagues. Whilst showing a degree of benevolence at times, they also betrayed a total inability to regard native Christians as equals. In one case the ordination of a native assistant was delayed because it was believed that such a step would have made him intolerably proud. To its credit the Committee in London insisted that for native ministers the steps leading to ordination should be the same as for others. Once normal procedures had been completed, ordination could not be withheld. Lynch on one occasion objected to the Committee using a clerical form of address in writing to a native assistant, fearing that this too would encourage pride. When he learnt that one of the former Buddhists who had been taught by Clarke had introduced himself to the chaplain and another person at Trincomalee, and actually took 'hold of their hands, and shook hands with them', he commented that he was relieved that neither of them had come to Madras![17] One of the priests did go to Madras, however, and quarrelled with Lynch, who remonstrated with him that he should remain humble and always be grateful for what had been done for him.

As far as racial attitudes were concerned, it is clear that Lynch and his colleagues were greatly influenced by the Europeans around them. Their inability to treat native Christian leaders as equals detracts greatly from their willingness to develop a native ministry. It was their view that native ministers should be subordinated to expatriate workers.

Social and Community Dimensions of Mission

One of the most striking and important of Lynch's surviving letters deals with the social and religious conditions in Ceylon:

Before my arrival on Ceylon I had formed an idea that very little poverty and distress prevailed in it. I also expected to find a greater degree of the knowledge and practice of Christianity. But I have witnessed a great deal of the former and very little of the latter. Poverty, and indolence, and ignorance prevail to a great degree ... I have seen, and caused to be taken off the street, one dying ... I have seen native women with one, two, three, four or five children, the widdows and children ... whose husband and father were dead ... I have seen aged people in a starving state.[18]

In response to such poverty Lynch proposed that a poor-house or work-house be established in which people could be employed in picking, carding and spinning. Profits would then flow from the manufacture and sale of calico and muslin. Local Europeans would help to defray the initial costs of acquiring cotton, spinning wheels, looms and so on. 'About 600 pounds would commence the whole establishment', he wrote, and would support the children and poor till money was raised from sales. The parallel with what Clarke proposed for the Shetlands a decade later is intriguing.[19]

Lynch's colleagues were in agreement with the plan, and while he recognized the danger of having to spend too much time on such temporal affairs, he believed that the person employed in supervising the scheme would not be different from ministers at home who were also teachers, book stewards, and editors! He was also aware of the Committee's difficulty in meeting all its commitments, and felt that the extra money required could be raised by interested individuals at home. Another reason for establishing such an institution was to provide accommodation and employment for those who, upon becoming Christians, were socially isolated. Lynch wrote on another occasion pressing the need for settlements for 'heathen and Mahometan converts' who could not remain with their families and friends after they became Christians.[20] If they did not receive constant help and instruction they would become discouraged. In support of this he claimed that another missionary, John McKenny, had confirmed from his South African experience that such settlements were necessary because of the prejudice shown towards converts.

The Committee's response to Lynch was sharp and uncompromising. Under no circumstances, it was argued, should Lynch or his colleagues become involved in this type of scheme. Significantly the Committee's opposition was based not on grounds of cost or of Lynch's limited administrative ability, but rather on theological principles. He was informed that:

> The Committee have read with much concern your letter ... respecting your proposed plan of establishing a Manufactory etc. in Ceylon. They think it their duty to express their most decided disapprobation of the plan and solemnly enjoin both you and the Brethren to have nothing to do with manufactories or worldly traffic of any description whatever; but that you give yourselves entirely to prayer and the ministry of the word, not entangling yourselves with the affairs of this world that the word of the Lord be not hindered.[21]

Leaving nothing to chance, the Committee sent another letter two months later:

> The Committee totally disapprove of anything of trade, commerce, or manufactures carried on either by the schools or in connexion with them. There are strong temptations in the East for trade and commerce but all our brethren must keep themselves totally disentangled from the world. As men of God and Ambassadors for Christ your must have nothing to do with trade in any way whatever. Let the whole of your time and strength be given to the salvation of your own souls and of the souls of those among whom you labour.[22]

In a postscript the Committee underlined that while it would not object to lay people becoming involved in such projects, the preachers were certainly not to become entangled.

Implicit in the Committee's response to Lynch is the conviction that what was of paramount importance to Methodism were religious as distinct from social or political matters. Those promoting missionary interest at home had also to reckon with opponents who alleged that overseas missions were a mere cover for commercial exploitation. Some may have feared that practical projects such as that envisaged by Lynch would have drawn attention to the exploitation which already existed, posing a threat to British colonial interests and leading to increased hostility in Britain towards missions. As the work overseas developed, however, it became increasingly recognized that mission had to be expressed in ways relevant to people's total needs. Richard Watson's address to the Anniversary meeting of the WMMS in 1830, referring to slaves in the West Indies, had a much wider relevance, and reflected an approach which made the creation of practical programmes inevitable:

> All our Missionary enterprizes, all our attempts to spread Christianity abroad, do, in point of fact, tend to increase our sympathies with the external circumstances of the oppressed and miserable of all lands. It is impossible for men to care for the souls of others without caring for their bodies also.[23]

Lynch and the Missionary Committee – a Study in Relationships

Those who assume that the relationships between missionaries and the Committee which sent them overseas were normally trouble-free, cannot have examined the evidence. The surviving correspondence gives abundant proof of the serious misunderstandings and differences which arose between missionaries and committees. Whilst tributes to the quality of Lynch's work from those who observed it at close quarters were warm and fulsome, his relations with the Missionary Committee in London were strained almost to breaking point at times.

Sharp conflict arose, for example, over the question of the **length of missionary service.** Lynch protested to London in 1820 that some missionaries who had just arrived in Madras were saying that the Committee believed 'that all young men should come out for life'.[24] This had certainly not been his own thinking when he offered to accompany Dr Coke. Had it been 'intimated my remaining in India for life . . . I would at once have said I'll not go, & I believe several of my Br. would have said the same'. Lynch did not restrain himself on the matter:

I disapprove of such a question being put to any young man. Perhaps a few very timid young men or young men of more zeal than knowledge would give their consent, but I would not expect one in one hundred of them to continue of the same mind.

Arguing from personal conviction and also drawing on what he had learnt through observing others, he pleaded for flexibility and emphasized that those who agreed with him lacked neither love nor zeal. 'I know the real happiness of Home Work, & I may add the superior happiness of being a foreign Missionary . . . yet I cannot bring my mind to give up all hopes of returning to Europe.' In other denominations, he claimed, a rigid approach had led to undesirable results:

I have seen the baneful effects of life transportation on other Missionaries. The world has gotten too fast hold of them. They have sunk into comparative indolence & in a decline or decay of health the most unhappy feelings have preyed upon their minds.

Lynch's approach was upheld, and in the Minutes of the General Committee it was acknowledged that, despite the absence of written evidence, it appeared that the first missionaries did have an arrangement with Coke whereby they were to remain overseas only for seven years in the first instance. A scheme was therefore introduced to implement this in principle. It is interesting that it was unmarried missionaries who were allowed to return home first.

The most serious problems between Lynch and the Committee arose over **money**. From the beginning Lynch and his colleagues were well aware of the need for strict economies. When Ault, one of the original group of missionaries, died, Lynch admitted that he had long suspected that he had followed 'a too rigid system of economy to preserve health'.[25] Enquiries after his death confirmed that Ault 'had put himself upon a regimen of food on which no European could live in the country for twelve months'. A little later Lynch described various properties which missionary colleagues had acquired, and made the point that they were raising as much money locally as possible. In 1816 he confided that personal correspondence with friends in Ireland was proving too expensive since postage was so great.[26] After two weeks he wrote that the missionaries had entered into a solemn agreement to be as frugal 'as the safety of our health, & the prosperity of our work will admit'.[27] On an official visit to Ceylon as Superintendent eight days later, he wrote about a journey from Colombo to Jaffna which he had made by sea on the grounds of economy. He had suffered almost constant sea sickness through being exposed to the wind both day and night, and feared that his health had been damaged 'very materially'.[28]

Despite such care being exercised, the finances of the mission gave serious cause for concern from about 1817. Many factors were involved, including the inexperience of the missionaries over financial matters, difficulties in communication between the missionaries themselves (with Lynch far away in Madras) and between them and the Committee in London, differences in rates of exchange between Ceylon and Madras, and an over-simple assumption in London that the work overseas could come to maturity quickly and be self-supporting. Thus in February 1817 Lynch wrote from Madras to a colleague in Colombo:

> I think we should refrain from any new purchases or build-ings, till we have further accounts from our Committee. What will they feel & say on receiving all our bills since August last? As you have remitted to all the bren, I really wish to know how much you have drawn, & remitted to each station, since our meeting. I have requested this again and again, but you either cannot, or have not, done it.[29]

In May of the same year he wrote to London that the vast expenses being incurred by the mission had encouraged them to think seriously of not making any more purchases until they received clear advice from the Committee. In August 1817 he wrote from Colombo that he was surprised to learn that two of his colleagues, Harvard and Clough, had made two purchases in the course of the previous year without consulting either him-self or any of the other missionaries. Property had also been acquired at Galle, and in each case the missionaries argued that if they had not acted quickly they would have lost valuable sites and buildings.

Such was the background to an official letter written to Lynch from London in 1819:

> The Committee do not seem to understand the reasons of your erecting the building you mention. Such a measure should, whenever it is to any extent, be fully considered in its absolute necessity and its advantages. Every building must have repairs, which incur a certain expense, and what may appear to one Missionary desirable, to another who follows him, will appear the reverse.[30]

The financial situation continued to deteriorate. In 1821 a letter from London was addressed to Lynch and a colleague in Madras – 'we have grieved much over this subject . . . & should we have such another half year as the last has been I tremble for the consequences to our Eastern missions'.[31] A bill which Lynch had drawn in favour of Blanshards of Madras for £250 had been dishonoured by the Committee. Further action along similar lines might well become necessary. In the next month a meeting of the General Committee in London resolved as follows:

> *That* in consequence of Mr Lynch's irregularity and extravagance in his drafts on the Treasurers, and his drawing Bills to accommodate persons in India, by which the Committee have been put to great inconvenience, and the Society has been injured in its character, a letter be written to Mr Lynch, conveying the severe censure of this Committee . . .
> *That* Mr Lynch's conduct be brought before Conference as highly deserving the exercise of its discipline.
> *That* Mr Lynch be informed that the Committee prohibit his drawing any more Bills on the Treasurers, as such Bills will be dishonoured.[32]

Lynch was deeply shocked when he heard of these moves. In response to an earlier rebuke (details of which have not, however, survived) he wrote from Madras in May 1821:

How far I have erred through ignorance or want of thought, I dare not judge: but I acknowledge errors in both. I must conclude by stating that I fear my happiest days are over in India. A private letter of the strongest reproof, I trust would have been kindly received, and answered every intended purpose. But such a public and *recorded* mark of reproach is more than at present I can bear.[33]

Three weeks later he wrote a poignant letter of resignation:

I consider myself treated in the most disgraceful manner & unjustly sunk in disgrace both in the estimation of the Committee & in the public estimation in India ... My heart bleeds for the cause of God, a cause which for 20 years has been dearer to me than life. Every Brother on the mission is affected & distressed. Several of us with our present views & feelings cannot remain in India, but I now speak for myself. It may be 12 months from the date of this before the Committee can send one to supply my place. During 12 months *if spared so long* I shall consider myself bound before God to remain at Madras, but no longer. A disgraced Missionary I cannot be.[34]

In the meantime he wondered how the missionaries would survive on inadequate allowances. If more money was not forthcoming, some stations would have to be closed and some missionaries sent home.

Lynch continued to give expression to his distress in later letters, but by mid-1822 following further messages from London which he described as breathing 'a milder spirit than I have been accustomed to for many months'[35] he began to regain his equilibrium. He hoped it would be realized in London from a study of their accounts that they were 'not such careless men as approaches to wanton wastefulness'. The expenses of the mission had caused them 'hundreds of anxious hours & many sleepless nights'. In an appreciative reference to an affectionate letter he had received from the distinguished Richard Watson, he commented that 'a kind letter has been a strange thing to me for 13 months past'. By August 1822 relations had so far improved that he felt able to write:

> My painful exercises of mind about protested bills are now past – & were my publick censure by the Conference not against me I could feel perfectly resigned to remain in India, but as it is I must remain longer than I intended. The return of so many Bren. completely blocks up my way. I dare not leave . . . the work in the present state of things, & at present I bless God my soul is truly alive.[36]

In late 1822 further progress was made when the Committee resolved to recommend to the annual Methodist Conference in Britain that the previous resolution on Lynch's financial administration be withdrawn from the Conference Journal. His name was also restored to the list of those authorized to transmit official business on behalf of the mission.[37] This eased the way for Lynch to remain in Madras until 1824.

Poor communication between the missionaries and their London headquarters was undoubtedly a source of personal distress and was also a major factor in misunderstandings arising over policies and procedures. It will be remembered that Lynch and his missionary colleagues sailed from England on 31 December 1813, eventually arriving in Ceylon on 29 June 1814. In November 1814, six months after the death of Coke, Lynch wrote that he and his companions longed to hear from the Committee. He wrote again in June the following year that he was very uneasy 'on account of receiving no letters whatever from Ireland or England since I left there'.[38] Perhaps, he speculated, someone had been appointed to write and had failed in his duty. None of the missionaries had received letters, he claimed, though they themselves had written on several occasions from Bombay and also from Ceylon. They had seized every opportunity to write, and it was therefore particularly painful 'to find that almost every Englishman with whom we are acquainted has recd. letters'. In November 1815 he wrote again, trusting that the Committee would correspond with them and confiding that as yet they had not heard although 'several ships have put into Ceylon direct from England'.[39]

In a letter addressed to Lynch from London in March 1816 serious concern was expressed that he had not been receiving letters regularly from the Committee.

> It is impossible for me to express the pain of mind I have experienced in consequence of you not having heard from the Committee through my medium. I believe this is the twenty third letter I have written to Ceylon, and the fourth or fifth I have addressed to you. It is no less distressing than astonishing to me what can have become of them. [40]

Lynch replied in September 1816, saying that up to then he had received only three letters from the Committee, one from Adam Clarke, and one from another person.

Poor communication long remained a serious problem. In March 1819 a letter was sent to Lynch:

> I am sorry that you had not in October last received any letters from the Committee relative to your station at Madras, & I can assure you that since Conference, beside all other letters to you every one of yours has had a distinct answer. The letters I have sent are dated Sept., Oct. 28, Dec. 11, . . . & Jan. 22.[41]

A letter written by Lynch two years later provides a specific example of how such lack of communication led to misunderstanding. Following receipt of a letter from London Lynch protested that he had not, as indicated, received an earlier warning about the drawing of bills. There had been no previous hint of this, either directly or through anyone travelling to Madras.[42]

There was a further complication. In those early days the Missionary Committee, in the absence of regular information from its own missionaries, sometimes made decisions on the advice of people from overseas who happened to be passing through London (often on private business or on government service) or after hearing from only one missionary or other individual. However understandable in the circumstances, missionaries frequently had reason to object that the opinions expressed to the Committee in this way were wholly unrepresentative and did not facilitate taking proper or fair decisions. It was even less satisfactory when, as sometimes happened, the names of the Committee's informants were not disclosed to the missionaries concerned. This partly lay behind Lynch's objection in 1823:

> Were the *anonymous* charges gainst Br. McKenny rec'd. & passed at a full meeting of the Committee; or only at a meeting of the few? How would any Preacher in England like to be treated in the same manner? Such conduct was unlike *our* Committee, & foreign Brn. will never submit to it.[43]

Missionaries stood together in the face of such criticism from the Committee. Thus the Minutes of the Southern Ceylon meeting (Singhalese) in January 1822 declared with regard to allegations about financial mishandling:

> The Brethren are shocked to hear the charges which are preferred against them; which if true involves *moral guilt*; & as such utterly disqualify them for any longer sustaining the Office of Christian Ministers ... They are charged with '*committing outrages on the public confidence*' ... Wearisome days and sleepless nights have been the frequent attendants on our labours; some of the most painful anxieties that have ever distressed their minds have constantly been the expenses which have been incurred by a conscientious discharge of their duty to God ... & now what must their feelings be at the close of such exertions.[44]

They also affirmed their personal confidence in Lynch, paying tribute to his 'unimpeachable moral character and his rigid integrity'. His failure to send accounts from Madras until requested to do so, was due simply to his 'limited acquaintance with the usual forms of business'. Later in January, at the Tamil District meeting, Lynch resigned as Chairman but was immediately and unanimously reinstated. Great sympathy was shown towards him:

> We are exceedingly sorry that Brother Lynch's situation at Madras should have exposed him to the necessity of drawing bills for so large an amount, and which has subjected him to such severe censures from the Committee. We are not without hopes however, that the letters of explanation, read to this meeting by the Chairman, copies of which were sent home, will have had the tendency to soften those strong feelings . . . Had it not been for the very urgent requests of the Financial Secretary of the Cingalese district . . . the bill for £3,000 would not have been drawn.[45]

It is not surprising that against this background Lynch chose to return to Ireland in 1824.

Lynch also made an important though indirect contribution to mission in India and Mexico after his return from India, through his influence upon William Butler in Co. Down in the 1840s. Butler subsequently became the founder of the MEC mission in North India, and also played a leading part in helping to establish the MEC mission in Mexico. Even earlier, through correspondence with his brother Hugh and nephew Samuel (who had both emigrated to the United States), James Lynch gained an insight into the challenges faced by some of the early settlers in America and learnt of the beginnings of Methodism in the area to which his relatives had gone. Sickness and other family problems, occasional crop failures and hardship, and 'that disgraceful and *inhuman* traffic – Slavery' are part of the human drama which emerges in the correspondence,[46] and form the backdrop to efforts to make a home and also to help to establish the church in one small part of the New World. Samuel became an MEC minister in America. He served in the Ohio and Central Conferences, and was appointed Presiding Elder in the Delaware District. As a mark of respect for his uncle in Ireland he called his son James.

Mirrored in the family history of the Lynches from Co. Donegal there are many elements familiar to students of Irish

Methodism: the interaction between Protestantism and Roman Catholicism, the contribution to world mission of those sent overseas officially by the church, and the effects of poverty forcing many to leave Ireland in search of a better life elsewhere. Emigration had consequences for the world-wide influence of the church, and some of those who went overseas, such as Hugh and Samuel Lynch, played an important part in establishing the church in the lands of their adoption. Others, however, like James Lynch's own son (James married after his return to Ireland from India) sadly lost whatever faith they had amidst the demands and attractions of a bewildering new life in America.

Through the Lynch family, then, Ireland contributed in a remarkable manner to the spread of Methodism in countries as far apart and diverse as Ceylon, India, the United States and Mexico. James Lynch was the central figure in this. Circumstances forced him into positions of leadership which he did not seek and in which he plainly did not feel at home. He was a reluctant leader who became deeply scarred by the criticisms heaped upon him by distant superiors. Although he did not possess the intellectual and linguistic gifts of some of his missionary colleagues, he emerged in some respects as the most remarkable of those who sailed with Coke to Asia. He earned the unqualified respect and affection of his fellow missionaries, and so was chosen by them to preside over their affairs and to represent them in contacts with London. Of James Lynch, as of others who have made a significant contribution to mission, these words are particularly appropriate:

> Consider your call, brethren; not many of you were wise according to worldly standards, not many were powerful, not many were of noble birth; but God chose what is foolish in the world to shame the wise ... God chose what is low and despised in the world, even things that are not, to bring to nothing things that are.[47]

– 8 –

John McKenny,
Pioneer on Three Continents

=

Those whom later generations eulogize may well include some
who were yesterday's villains! The Chairman of the Tonga
District of the Methodist Church brought a charge against John
McKenny, arising from McKenny's alleged indiscretions on
board ship while travelling to New South Wales in 1836.
Although McKenny had by then more than twenty years overseas service behind him, the accusation was that he had acted
in a manner wholly 'unbefitting the character of the Christian
minister'. What grave sin or crime merited such comprehensive
condemnation? He had indulged in playing draughts on several
occasions 'to the great scandal of Methodism'![1]

Little is known of the early life of John McKenny. Born in
Coleraine around 1788, he had a Church of Ireland (Anglican)
upbringing. Then coming under Methodist influence, he entered
the Methodist ministry in 1813 and was appointed overseas,
sailing from Portsmouth in 1814. Thereafter there were three
phases in his life – in Cape Colony as the first Wesleyan missionary from 1814 to 1816; in Ceylon from 1816 to 1835; and in
New South Wales from 1836 to his death in 1847.

McKenny in Cape Colony (1814–1816)

The origins of Methodism in South Africa are still shrouded
in mystery, but the account of the conversion in Cape Town
of a young Irish soldier in the Royal Artillery, published in

1802, provides a glimpse into those beginnings:

> [I] found out four or five of the other regiments, who met
> together, and were called Methodists. We hired the use of a
> very small room in town for two hours in a week, to hold a
> prayer meeting: there we read, sang and prayed and at length
> I got faith.[2]

The room where they met became known as the Methodist
chapel, but it is uncertain how long this work continued.

McKenny arrived at Cape Town on 7 August 1814, but ran
into difficulties immediately:

> The Governor has refused to give me liberty to preach, but
> this is the more distressing as there is here a society of upwards
> of sixty members and many others who are very desirous of
> hearing the Gospel.[3]

The background to this difficulty was that among the Dutch
ordinances taken over by the British was one forbidding the
holding of religious services without the Governor's consent.
The Governor, Lord Charles Somerset, withheld permission
since the army already had their own Church of England
chaplains, and the Dutch Reformed Church, then established
in the colony, was not favourable to a ministry among Blacks.
The Governor had no objection to McKenny proceeding into
the interior and preaching to native people there. McKenny
believed, however, that he had been appointed by the authorities in Britain to minister in the first place to the soldiers and
other interested white inhabitants, and only then to local Blacks.
His protest that he 'had been educated as a member of the
Church of England' from his 'youth up', and that he would not
act contrary to the church's interests, did not, however, change
the Governor's thinking.[4] Indeed McKenny claimed that a
message was conveyed to him from the Governor to say that if
he attempted to convert any of the soldiers he would be considered 'a seditious person', and would be expelled from the
colony immediately. He wrote in December 1814 that whilst he
had met the leaders and local preachers in his own home, he

had not yet preached, adding that 'it is a sense of duty *alone* and not fear of *any punishment* . . . which influences me to act as I am doing in not preaching.'[5]

In May 1815 McKenny summarized 'the causes of the general prejudice against the Methodists'.

> First the very unfaithful conduct of some who have taken that name, secondly the mistaken zeal of those who possess very little information, and thirdly an entire misunderstanding of the nature of Methodism.[6]

This gives an important clue to McKenny's cautiousness. 'It is necessary,' he wrote, 'to be very careful that we do nothing, through mistaken zeal, that would injure the work.' Lack of communication from the Committee in London was an additional cause of anxiety and uncertainty. 'I have not yet received any letters', he wrote in August 1815. In March 1816 he stated:

> I feel much depressed and cast down upon account of my circumstances since I arrived here, and what has *greatly* increased my affliction of mind, is the silence of the Committee, but I must hope for better days.[7]

Since the restrictions on his activity were not lifted, McKenny felt obliged to transfer to Ceylon. Although assured that Cape Colony was not being abandoned by the Methodists – he had already been informed by the Missionary Committee that another missionary had been appointed – he doubted whether Methodism would ever meet with much success in Africa:

> Long before I left the Cape I was convinced that the interior of Africa is not likely to be a good soil for Methodism, as it is already almost overrun with Calvinism, all the Farmers are Calvinists and that of a very bigoted kind. . . . However I know that I may be mistaken, but experience will prove whether my views on this subject are correct or not.[8]

Fortunately McKenny's worst fears were not realized, and Methodism subsequently had a significant impact over a wide area. McKenny's comments at one point are still of course strikingly relevant. A rigid form of Calvinism today exerts an enormous influence in Southern Africa, providing a false theological basis for apartheid.

McKenny has been criticized as being 'all too acquiescent'[9] in his response to his treatment in Cape Colony, but full account must be taken of his special difficulties. He knew that Methodism was already seen in a bad light in the colony, and he was anxious not to make matters worse by acting contrary to the Governor's wishes. He had also requested the Committee to do certain things on his behalf in London, and was aware that some initiatives in this connection had in fact been taken which promised well. He therefore awaited further developments. In not taking up the Governor's suggestion that he might go into the interior, he genuinely believed that he was keeping faith with the terms of his appointment by Conference. These had been conveyed to him by Adam Clarke and Thomas Coke, and made it clear that he was to minister in the first instance to those who were inclined towards Methodism in Cape Town.[10]

McKenny in Ceylon (1816–1835)

John McKenny was one of three Irishmen (the others were George Erskine and James Lynch) in the group of seven ministers ordained by Thomas Coke in December 1813, prior to their proceeding overseas. All except McKenny set sail with Coke for the new East India mission. Thus when McKenny withdrew from the frustrating situation in which he found himself in Cape Colony, and joined the mission in Ceylon, he was renewing contact with those with whom he already had a great deal in common. As things turned out, he became by far the longest serving Irish preacher to share in the opening phase of the Ceylon mission.

McKenny's letters contain much of interest. For example, he expressed strong views on **financial matters**. On the prospect of the mission soon becoming self-supporting, he was firmly of the opinion that the Committee was far too optimistic. He wrote in 1817 that there was as yet 'not the most distant prospect' of this happening.[11] He argued strongly in defence of the missionaries in reply to the Committee's criticism of high expenditure.

In December 1821 he wrote to another missionary in Cape Town:

> I cannot say how *you* get on as to financial matters with the Committee, but this Mission has latterly got into sad disgrace. We were afraid that they were going to ruin us altogether as they talked of not paying down bills that had been drawn by Mr Lynch. . . . Poor Br. Lynch has nearly had his heart broken by the Committee's letters.[12]

Ten years later he was able to strike a much more confident note on finance:

> Our accounts were never more moderate or satisfactory; every Brother has steadily and conscientiously acted during the year on the principle of the strictest economy . . . and now our plans have attained such a degree of maturity . . . as to afford to the Committee a security that in future they will never have cause for complaint.[13]

In the **work among native Singhalese Christians**, McKenny was greatly distressed by the involvement of some of them in idol worship. He wrote in October 1819:

> How strange it is that so many of the *Pagans* of Ceylon should be called *Christians*! a few weeks ago I was called to witness a devil dance . . . in the garden of one of those *Christian pagans*! being informed of the circumstances, I went to the spot, and found the devil dancers hard at work in behalf of a young man, who was laid on the ground, and near death. . . . I called one of the capuas, or devil dancers, and asked him if he and his companions had engaged to cure the man, they said no. I then asked him why they attempt to deceive the people, and so greatly to disturb the dying man? to this they replied, that they were only doing as they had been desired by his relations![14]

More than ten years later he remained disappointed at the

lack of spiritual growth among the Sinhalese. After giving an encouraging report on English work (including that among soldiers) and on Portuguese work, he wrote rather despondently in September 1831:

> The poor Singhalese are a most discouraging people. Their character and circumstances is difficult to understand but still more so to explain; for not only their own system of heathenism, but everything connected with them is altogether against the Gospel. . . . In the West Indies the *bodies* of men are in slavery, but here their minds are bound with powerful chains.[15]

In January 1832 he referred again to the promising work among British soldiers, but then turned to the cultural differences which appeared to make progress more difficult in the work among other ethnic groups. In doing so he betrayed an attitude of cultural superiority which, though rare in him, was not uncommon in others at the time:

> I wish from my heart I could witness more frequently to conversions among the Dutch, Portuguese and Natives, as to these our minds are often painfully exercised, but we must not despise the day of small and feeble things; much good has been, and is being done among each of the classes referred to. But alas! they have not British minds, and they have a world of things against them which stand not in the way of a mind formed upon European principles. Yet the Lord can and will do the work.[16]

In July 1834 he was cautiously optimistic:

> There is much good doing in Ceylon, but the work is slow though progressive. How very different from its character in other parts of the world where a nation is born in a day.[17]

McKenny was of the opinion that in the past the wrong kind of incentive had been offered to people to become Christians and that this had led to deception:

If it should be asked why do those *pure Heathens* wish us to believe that they are Christians? The answer is at hand, because it serves their temporal interests. Thus by attempting to make them Christians, by holding out improper inducements, and without the use of the essential means of true conviction and conversion, the Singhalese people have been taught a system of the worst kind of hypocrisy and deceit. Surely there is not in the world a similar case of a nation sentimentally and practically Heathen, and at the same time professing Christianity![18]

McKenny had strong views too on **people of other faiths**, influenced by several contacts with Buddhist priests. In late May 1819 he and another missionary, Robert Newstead, visited a temple and spoke with the priests. Newstead described the senior priest as 'a very shrewd and clever man, but rooted of course, in his errors'.[19] McKenny had a further conversation of nearly two hours with one of the priests, and within a week Newstead reported that a priest had called with them to say that he was interested in forsaking Buddhism and embracing Christianity. While welcoming this promising development, they also regarded it with realistic caution.

In April 1827 McKenny described the conversion of a Buddhist priest in which he had played a part. The following is part of the priest's own story.

It is now fifteen years since I was constituted a priest of Budhu. For four years I held the office of Sameuers, or assistant, after which I was elevated to that of Upasampade, by which I was invested with all the honours and powers of the priesthood. During this long period I was diligently employed in reading the sacred books of religion in which I had been educated, in order to my being well informed on the subjects on which they treat, and to my obtaining the salvation of my soul. In addition to my own researches I had the counsel and instructions of several learned priests; but from all I have read and heard I can derive no comfort to my soul. . . . I was at last fully convinced in myself that there must be a Creator of the world, a

Saviour, and forgiveness of sin; and came to the conclusion, that there was no salvation for my soul in any other religion that is professed . . . but the Christian.[20]

In a letter written in September 1831 McKenny referred to a colleague's new tract which gave reasons for not being a Buddhist. He welcomed the interest and controversy it would occasion, and noted that it was being circulated in schools and other places. Someone had already set it to music in a traditional style, and there were reports that a Buddhist priest was preparing a reply. In McKenny's view this would enable a stronger case against Buddhism to emerge. 'It is reasonable to expect that their system will be shook to its very centre, then fall to pieces', he wrote, betraying an ill-founded optimism so common at the time.[21]

Along with other missionaries, McKenny was convinced of the importance of **education and of schools**. He wrote in October 1816:

I believe that all the Brethren are deeply impressed with the great importance of the subject of schools. If we can get schools established throughout the island *immediately and entirely under our own direction*, great good will arise from it. . . . It will become a powerful assistance to our Mission.[22]

A year later he wrote of his plans for school openings:

I am at present making arrangements for the establishment of seven, independent of my own school which I have at the Mission House, and I flatter myself that I can fairly calculate upon having in these seven schools upwards of six hundred children.[23]

In April 1818 he described the schools around Galle. Six schools had already been opened, more would follow, and he expected to have about fifteen hundred pupils in all. 'If the religion of Jesus Christ is to be established in this dark country', he wrote, 'it will be through the medium of Christian schools.'[24] The schools, he argued, although involving considerable expense, 'are to us the *key to the natives*; and promise to give our mission permanence and stability.'

McKenny occasionally commented on **disasters of various kinds** and reported serious outbreaks of disease. In June 1824 he described 'a dreadful epidemic' of what he called 'Kandian or jungle fever'.[25] It had been widespread for months, with thousands dying, public works on roads and bridges being suspended, and schools being closed. In July he reported further from Colombo:

> The hospital of this small garrison has exhibited, for some months past, one of the most dismal scenes I ever witnessed: for some time there was not less than one hundred individuals in it, principally laid up with fever, to which about fifty have fallen sacrifice.[26]

Apart from soldiers, only one European had died of the disease in Colombo, while hundreds of Muslims and Singhalese had perished. Special prayer meetings had been held in the Baptist church because of the emergency. Six years later, again in July, he wrote from Galle that fever and dysentery had prevailed throughout the villages, and that 'hundreds of old and young have been hurried into eternity'.[27]

One of the most significant **initiatives** McKenny took was to acquire a site of three acres at Colpetty, Colombo, in 1824, when the fish bazaar moved beside the original mission site. This action was not authorized by the Missionary Committee in London, and led to a serious strain in relationships, but it proved to be an inspired move. The church headquarters, the house of the President of Conference, and a college, all stand today at Colpetty. By 1830, however, McKenny's purchase of the site remained a contentious issue:

> If the Committee could have witnessed my exertions to save their funds and at the same time promote the interests of the Mission, they would have been much more inclined to have given me a vote of thanks than to have censured. . . . You have secured to the Mission a fine estate on very moderate terms,

which has been turned to the best advantage; of this you have been fully assured by the Brethren.[28]

McKenny argued strongly in October 1824 for a particular **method of working** – 'the experience of ten years *fully* confirms me in the unchangeable conviction, that the Brethren should go to their work as the Apostles did to theirs, by two and two'.[29] James Lynch's comments to the Committee about George Erskine's appointment to Australia make the same point:

> If Br. Erskine be sent alone to any Mission I fear he will sink into despondency. I am greatly grieved for his appointment & from a conviction of his usefulness in Ceylon & a firm belief that he will not be happy alone would not hesitate to say he should not be sent to Vandieman's land.[30]

McKenny, who had seen Methodism develop in Ceylon almost from its beginning, had high hopes for it as he prepared to leave the island:

> God is raising up in Ceylon Ministers of the sanctuary from lowest to the highest! We have two native assistants the sons of the caste of *toddy drawers* (one of the lowest among the Singhalese). We have one tailor, two doctors and one the son of a magistrate.[31]

In the long term he had no doubt that the future success of the church depended on the emergence of a strong native ministry. He had written earlier in 1834:

> The Lord has done much for us in giving us such able Assistants. It is, I am persuaded, by such men that the great work will in the end be carried on. . . . I am happy to say that we have the prospect of soon taking out a few others who are now labouring hard and successfully as Local Preachers.[32]

McKenny in New South Wales (1836–1847)

McKenny's appointment as Chairman of the New South Wales District was a turning point for Methodism in the colony.

Things had reached a distressingly low level before his arrival, with some missionaries divided among themselves, and also at cross purposes with local people and with the Missionary Committee in London. Among factors contributing to the strained relationships with London were delays in communication; uncertainty and disagreement over the District's role on such matters as the acceptance of candidates for the ministry, the stationing of ministers, and finance; and the feeling in New South Wales that one-sided and partial reports from anonymous sources were receiving too much credence in London. Relations deteriorated to such an extent that in 1831 a decision was taken to recall the Irish-born George Erskine who was then Chairman of the New South Wales District:

> The Committee being convinced of the inefficiency of Mr. Erskine for the Mission Work in general, and the duties of Chairman of the District in particular, as appears in the present languishing state of the New South Wales Mission, feel it their imperious duty to recall him home forthwith . . . Notice be given to the next Irish Conference that they must provide a Circuit for Mr. E. by the Conference of 1832.[33]

The Committee accused Erskine of laziness, weakness in observing the discipline, and engaging in property speculation. This was spelt out in a covering letter accompanying the formal resolutions:

> When the cause of God is at stake, we must be excused for dealing honesty & faithfully with those who are concerned, & whom, we fear, either retard the progress of the work of God by their conduct, or induce indifference & lukewarmness by their own want of energy, decision, or deadness to the world. This we are grieved to say, we fear has been your case. The cause of religion languishes, in our Societies, & a withering influence seems to rest upon them. This we fear has, partly at least, arisen from your want of activity & firmness, zeal not only as Chairman but as a Minister of the Gospel. We fear you have been far too wishful to gain property . . .[34]

Erskine of course denied these charges, and received support from a strongly worded message sent from New South Wales to London by stewards, leaders and other influential members. The message suggested that insufficient attention had been paid to the unique problems which arise in a penal colony. It also argued forceably that blame for the lack of spiritual progress lay with the people themselves and not with the missionaries and other church leaders. Erskine's ill health, in the form of an asthmatic condition, must also have been a contributing factor.

There is no denying the weakness of the mission. Membership returns in 1830 showed only one hundred and thirteen members in New South Wales, an increase of just thirty in ten years. J. D. Bollen's recent summary of problems facing the mission reads as follows:

> British irreligion, classes Methodism had not reached at home, now brutalized by the convict system, coarsened by the absence of restraints and refinements of civilized society, and by the material preoccupations of a land of tantalizing promise and sudden calamity.[35]

Seen in this light it is not surprising that progress was slow.

The decision to appoint McKenny as Erskine's successor indicated a clear vote of confidence by the Missionary Committee in his ability to rise to the challenge of such a dfficult situation. A letter from John Beecham, one of the WMMS Secretaries, written to McKenny before he took up his appointment, reiterated some of the mission's principles.

> The funds of the Socty. are especially designed for the support of Missions among the Heathen, & missionaries cannot be multiplied in an English Colony where the labours among the Settlers are unconnected with any efforts on behalf of the Aboriginal Inhabitants, excepting on the principle of their support being chiefly raised by those among whom they exercise their ministry. If a hopeful mission cd. only be commenced among those people, whose deep degradation excites a peculiar sympathy in their behalf, our Mission in New South

Wales wd. have a much stronger hold on the public mind in this country, than can possibly be the case, so long as it is confined to the Colonists themselves.[36]

It is questionable, however, whether such an approach was practical – or even right – at that stage in the colony's development. The need for a concentrated effort among the white settlers was self-evident, yet resources were severely limited. Any assumption therefore that the work could quickly become self-supporting was ill-founded, and the work among aborigines, already so frustrating, continued to encounter serious difficulties.

The underlying complexity of cultural differences was only slowly appreciated in **the aboriginal mission**, and little progress was made in McKenny's time despite much endeavour. In 1838 McKenny wrote of the Governor's special interest in this aspect of the mission's work. Three years later he reported that the aboriginal mission was not doing well, that the missionaries engaged in it were having problems in acquiring the language, and that questions were being raised about the continuance of government assistance.[37] By 1842 McKenny was forced to admit that the aboriginal mission at Bunting Dale had failed. Relationships between the missionaries involved in it were bad, and the senior missionary had accused some white settlers of being 'Murderers of the Blacks'.[38] The settlers, for their part, claimed that they had gone out to shoot kangaroos, although rumours persisted that they had instead shot 'black natives'. McKenny acknowledged that few aborigines attended the mission, and that many were dying of disease as a result of sexual intercourse with convicts. He wondered whether the mission was located too close to white settlements to prosper. This was a concern he had already discussed with the Governor:

> No success among the blacks can reasonably be expected unless the missionaries can make up their minds to go into the interior beyond the bounds of the dwellings of *white men*. The Governor quite agreed with me in this opinion, but observed 'wherever you go, the whites will soon follow you.'[39]

McKenny's achievements were largely in connection with **the colonial mission**. More than his predecessors, he recognized the importance of public affairs including relationships with other churches and with the government. Within months of arriving in the colony, he wrote:

> The Governor is now much more favourable towards us . . .
> I am on the best of terms with Ministers of other Denominations, and am so identified with religious Institutions and Public Charities that when it is required I can exert an influence which is valuable and weighty, though *not seen*. This indeed I consider my path of duty in a settlement like this, composed of such combustible materials. A man if he makes himself prominent as a leader in the reform of notorious abuses is sure to get torn to pieces, but an individual who pursues the even tenor of his way, may work very successfully and have the happiness to avoid such public censure . . . as would prevent his usefulness.[40]

Initially he got on well with the Anglican Bishop, and wrote in 1836 that he acted 'more like a Christian Brother than an English Bishop'.[41] McKenny's efforts to have the Methodist mission put on an equal footing with other denominations inevitably encouraged denominational rivalry, however, since the various churches individually pressed their claims for enhanced government aid. McKenny had written to London in 1836 about his contacts with the Governor:

> I do hope that in a short time I shall be able to inform you that he has placed our Society on a footing with the other religious denominations in the Colony, which will be to grant us an equal sum with that raised by us for the support of the work.[42]

Two years later, when the church bill had had its second reading in the State Legislature, he wrote in July:

> We shall now receive an allowance from Government according to the number of Persons who are regular hearers in our Chapels, and we shall have an amount equal to that raised by private subscription for Chapels and Schools.[43]

He followed this up with a letter in August, prior to the third reading of the bill, claiming that passage money and outfit grants for new missionaries would soon be made available through the government.[44] 'Not many weeks ago', he wrote, '*eight* Priests arrived to whom Lord Glenelg ordered for outfit and passage the sum of £1,200.' The bill enabling this kind of financial support to be given, became law in October, prompting McKenny to write that 'God . . . has opened the country before us in its length and breadth so that we have only to go up and possess it.'[45]

McKenny's attempts to persuade the Bishop that there was a special affinity between Methodism and the Church of England, and that the advance of the former would not be detrimental to the latter, failed to win the Bishop over. Relationships deteriorated further when the Bishop attempted to dissuade an Anglican layman from officiating at the laying of the foundation stone of a new Methodist chapel. Much to McKenny's distress, the Bishop's correspondence on the matter was published in the press. This injured the Bishop's position, but Methodism continued to grow. 'My opinion is that the Bishop will be more careful for the future', McKenny wrote.[46] In 1843, when the state of the economy was 'truly alarming' and was threatening to become even worse, McKenny drew considerable comfort from the fact that government support had by then been received for the work at Sydney, Melbourne, Paramatta, Windsor, Bathurst and Maitland. 'What anxiety and trouble it has cost me to secure this advantage . . . But my success is my reward.'[47]

McKenny was deeply convinced of the strategic importance of Protestant witness, and of Methodist witness as part of it. Writing in 1838 he claimed that the real question in Australia was whether the country would become 'a *protestant* or a *popish* Colony'.[48] He wrote that the number of priests who were being sent out was 'quite frightful'. Some months later he added that 'the Romanists are evidently organising a system to occupy, as far as they can, every part of the Colony'.[49] He then shared with the Missionary Committee at home his own assessment of the situation:

I fully admit the claims of the poor Heathen, and of places which may justly be regarded as in one sense more Missionary in their character than New South Wales; but . . . here we are in a new world, rising rapidly into immense importance . . . Our colony will form the centre of this new world, and will be the fountain of legislative and executive authority; and from this land will go forth the law of the Lord, or else the despot's mandate, which will bind men to superstition and idolatry. It will then, I trust, appear to you that the occupation of as many places as we can in this country, is closely connected with the success of the Gospel in the islands of the South Seas.

At this point it should be recognized that McKenny's dread of Roman Catholic influence, and his endeavours to outstrip it, were typical of the period. The aim of the WMMS mission in Ireland was once described as an attempt to subjugate 'Irish Popery to the faith of Christ',[50] and a statement by Coke about Ireland in 1806 expressed much the same sentiments as McKenny was to voice later about Australia. Claiming that Ireland was Methodism's most important mission field, because three million of its people were 'plunged in the deepest ignorance and super-stitition', Coke shared the hope with British Wesleyans that:

If the zeal of the missionaries, the support of the two confer-ences, and the generous assistance of the subscribers, continue, truth will prevail.[51]

McArthur expressed a similar point of view while on a visit to the United States, when he emphasized the importance of main-taining a strong evangelical witness in Ireland to meet the Roman threat. With the high rate of emigration from Ireland, how much better it was to export sound evangelical Christians to other parts of the world than Romanists!

Even with government help, McKenny argued, their re-sources in the colony were unequal to the situation, and it was wholly unrealistic to expect that the mission could soon be self-supporting. As he wrote in 1839:

The number of Emigrants who are daily coming to this Colony belonging to our Body forms a heavy tax on my time.

... They in general come with empty pockets, and poor things they must be attended to.[52]

Two and a half years later McKenny, although conscious of increasing physical weakness, was at the same time making suggestions about ways in which the work of the mission could proceed more effectively. 'I wish more fully to bring before the Committee the utter inadequacy of the present Ministerial strength of this District', he wrote.[53] The itinerant system should be extended, he suggested, with two preachers being appointed to each station, one of whom would always be on the move. Such a system of 'half circuits' had worked well in Ireland. This was a modification of the 'two by two' approach which he had already commended in Ceylon in 1824.

McKenny's last years were beset by difficulties of various kinds. The commercial life of the colony was at a low ebb, his physical strength was waning, and the aboriginal mission had fallen far short of expectations. The church's mission in other parts of Australasia was also becoming an increasing burden, with colleagues in Fiji looking to New South Wales, as the oldest mission station, for help. The start of the Maori wars in New Zealand in 1845 also heightened tension. As McKenny wrote:

> All is excitement here. The Governor is sending all the troops that can be spared. I hope they will be in time to arrest the natives in their work of destruction, but I dread the next accounts.[54]

McKenny found it increasingly difficult to maintain his position as Chairman because he came under attack from some of his missionary colleagues over stationing and other matters. He also found himself out of sympathy with a small group within the church which contained some very strong personalities. By the time the Committee in London had decided to create a new office – that of General Superintendent in Australasia – McKenny was ready to step down in favour of another person. He died in Sydney on 31 October 1847.

Though unspectacular in approach, McKenny was none the less capable of taking important initiatives, and showed impres-

sive wisdom and strength of character. His qualities and gifts
were many. He brought considerable insight to bear on several
problems, including those surrounding the aboriginal mission
in New South Wales and the threat from rigid Calvinism in
South Africa. He had a sharp eye for fresh openings and opportunities, such as the acquisition of the Colpetty site in Ceylon.
His comments on policy and strategy also merited serious consideration. He emphasized the value of missionaries occasionally
working in pairs, the vital importance of a native ministry in
Ceylon, and the strategic importance of maintaining a colonial
mission, such as the one in New South Wales, at a formative
stage in the colony's development. He had an abiding concern
for the public standing of Methodism. In South Africa this concern could look like weakness, but the appearance is misleading.
The same concern led him to take a forceful stand in New South
Wales even when it meant forfeiting the friendship of an influential Anglican Bishop. He showed courage also in challenging
what he felt to be ill-founded expectations or assumptions on the
part of the WMMS, over the financial prospects of the mission
in Ceylon, and its acquisition of the Colpetty site. Perhaps most
impressive of all was his robust faith, which prevented him from
being overwhelmed by setbacks such as he encountered early in
South Africa. This also helped to save him from bitterness when
he was misunderstood or wrongly accused; though there was at
least one occasion when his defences slipped. In 1841 he commented rather sadly:

> *Here* there is no sympathy with a man who has not robust
> health. If you cannot work like a horse, and a *strong* horse too,
> you are little worth, in the estimation of most persons here;
> who have had to *rough* it themselves, and have made property
> by *very hard labour* and plain *fare*.[55]

McKenny was wise, far-seeing and industrious. It is no exag-
geration to say that he rescued Methodism in New South Wales.
Its membership increased fivefold during his chairmanship. He
put it on a secure footing, enhanced its position in relation to
other churches, and enabled it to reach out to new areas.

– 9 –

John Barry, Controversialist

=

John Barry was born in Bandon, Co. Cork, on 18 September 1792. He died in Montreal, Canada, on 21 June 1838. Though now little remembered, he was certainly one of the most able Methodist missionaries ever to set out from Ireland.

Early Life (1792–1825)

Barry came from a French Huguenot family which settled in Bandon. They were originally known as du Barry, and are said to have been both religious and musical. Initially Anglican – indeed his parents hoped that he would have entered the Church of Ireland priesthood – Barry came under Methodist influence around 1809. In 1816, by then already an experienced local preacher, he was placed on the list of reserve for the itinerant ministry. He did not receive an appointment, however, 'owing to the distracted state of the Connexion'.[1] This was presumably a reference to the split which was developing in Ireland at that time between Wesleyan Methodists and Primitive Wesleyan Methodists. Barry became directly involved in this controversy, siding with the Wesleyans. He was considered for the new mission in Ceylon in 1816, but in the end it was decided not to send him. The high cost of the mission and his own ill-health (he contracted typhus fever), were both factors in this decision.

On 8 May 1819 he married Ann Place. She was also a descendant of a French Huguenot family, originally de la Place, which had settled in nearby Kinsale. Her father was in charge of the prison in Kinsale which held Frenchmen captured in the war with Napoleon.

Later in 1819 Barry published a forceful pamphlet on the split between Wesleyan Methodists and Primitive Wesleyan Methodists in Kinsale, arguing on the side of the Wesleyans.[2] In 1822 he is said to have been spiritually blessed during a revival in Bandon, and a year later at a meeting addressed by Adam Clarke in Cork his interest in missionary work was rekindled.

Barry was well educated, and was employed as a teacher. That he received some legal training can be deduced from the considerable knowledge he displayed of legal matters, particularly during his first period in Jamaica. With his wife and three sons he sailed for Jamaica in February 1825 as a missionary appointed by the WMMS.

Barry as World Traveller (1825–1838)

Those who assume that with the exception perhaps of Thomas Coke, the phenomenon of trans-Atlantic mobility is only a modern feature in Methodism, had better reckon with the extensive travels of John Barry.

Barry initially served under the WMMS in Jamaica from 1825 to 1830, starting in Grateful Hill, then based in Kingston, and finally moving to Spanish Town. He injured his right leg in 1829, and later feared that he might lose the use of his other leg. For a period he had to preach while kneeling on one knee, supported by a high stool specially made for the purpose. When it was suggested that an amputation might become necessary, he made a hurried return to Britain in early 1830 to seek advice and receive urgent medical attention. Although he had done so without permission from the WMMS, the Committee fully endorsed his action when they saw his condition.

After a period of convalescence spent in Kinsale and Bandon, he was able to return to Jamaica half way through 1831. He was thus in Kingston in December when an uprising took place, sparked off by the fear of some slaves that, contrary to earlier expectations, they were not after all to receive their freedom. Hundreds of people lost their lives, martial law was imposed, and planters blamed the missionaries for stirring things up and encouraging revolt. Together with another missionary who was due for furlough, he was chosen by his colleagues to return to London to acquaint the WMMS with the facts, since highly distorted accounts had received widespread publicity. Barry, of course, was not entitled to furlough, having only recently gone back to Jamaica, and his initiative was therefore strongly disapproved of by the Missionary Committee. After he had reported, they appointed him to Toronto (then known as York) rather than send him back to Jamaica.

Barry was the first regularly appointed Wesleyan preacher in Toronto since 1819, remaining there for almost a year from October 1832. He soon became involved in a controversy surrounding an ill-fated union between Wesleyan Methodists (originating in Britain) and Methodist Episcopals (originating in the United States), and it was considered wise to appoint him to Montreal. Controversy accompanied him there also, however, and for that reason he was appointed to Bermuda in 1834 by the WMMS.

Barry served in Hamilton, Bermuda, for just over two years, arriving in time to play a prominent part in the celebrations connected with the termination of slavery in August 1834. He became seriously ill again in 1836, this breakdown forcing him to return to Britain. His final months were dominated by a frantic search for health in different climates, taking him for brief spells to Guernsey, Montreal, Jamaica, Bermuda and back again to Canada. He finally died of tuberculosis in Montreal in June 1838.

In the space of only thirteen years, Barry had gone to Jamaica and to Canada on three occasions, and to Bermuda twice. He returned to Britain from Jamaica twice, without having WMMS authority to do so on either occasion. He also visited Guernsey, and on occasions felt that he should have been allowed to return to London to argue his point of view with the WMMS. One is left wondering how much farther he might have travelled if his journeys had started earlier by his being sent to Ceylon in 1816!

Barry as Preacher

By all accounts Barry was an able public speaker and eloquent preacher who made a special appeal to his more educated listeners. He possessed an uncommonly retentive memory and a facility with words, which normally meant that whilst his sermons were well prepared they were not written.

In Spanish Town, Jamaica, his preaching attracted large numbers. Congregations were doubled in 1828 as the people crowded into a church intended to seat only 300, spilling on to the piazza and into the lower hall. He wrote:

> I cannot avoid wishing that our people at home could witness the intense desire which prevails to hear the word of God. The impossibility of procuring seats, as well as the overpowering heat and crowding, prevent many from attempting to come to hear and you would be pleased to see some bringing little benches. . . . I have been frequently obliged to invite ladies into the pulpit, and request the men of the society to give up their seats to strangers.[3]

Not surprisingly, a new church was opened later in the same year. At least two published sermons by Barry survive. One was preached in Lambeth, London, in May 1832 and appeared in a short-lived periodical, the *Wesleyan Preacher*.[4] The other was delivered in Bermuda in 1834 when the slaves received their freedom. Excerpts from both sermons were printed in Montreal in 1838, along with an address delivered at his funeral. Claiming that Christ is central to the whole of Christian life – in its commencement, progress and completion – Barry expounded perfection as follows in his Lambeth sermon.

> What are we to understand by the perfection of the Christian's life? It is the loving God supremely, with all the powers and affections of the human soul – it is the bringing of every thought, temper, word, and action into perfect obedience

unto the mind and will of Christ – it is the exclusion of everything from the human mind, contrary to the will, the nature, and the law of God – it is our becoming partakers of the 'love of God shed abroad in the heart by the Holy Ghost given unto us,' as the governing principle of our thoughts, words, and actions. Religion rises as high as this; and there is no Christian believer who may not be made a partaker of the perfection of the Gospel as it has now been described.[5]

Barry as Missionary

Barry's **commitment** to overseas missions was deep and lasting. He was considered for an appointment to Asia as early as 1816, but eventually went to Jamaica in 1825. Upon leaving Jamaica in 1830, on account of lameness, he gave a donation of £30 towards the cost of a replacement, fearing that he himself might never be well enough to return. A year later, while still in Cork, he entered into correspondence with the WMMS about the possibility of a local teacher, Thomas Ilmes, going overseas. His illness caused him great unhappiness because it interrupted his own missionary service.

While in Jamaica, Barry had an eye for **fresh openings.** In 1826 he asked the WMMS to consider extending the mission to include the Maroons. These were freed or escaped slaves who had taken to the woods and mountains at the time of the British invasion (they were probably called 'Maroons' after the Spanish word for 'wild' or 'untamed'). Also, on visiting Savanna-la-Mar in 1828, Barry saw it immediately as a strategic new missionary centre, and wrote:

> The town is much larger than I expected . . . and I think the population cannot be less than two thousand. . . . Savanna-la-Mar is the key to a great number of populous estates.[6]

A little later he also asked the WMMS to send a missionary to the Santa Cruz mountains so that communication could be opened up between the eastern and western part of the island.

Barry held a **broad view of mission**, being interested in

such diverse issues as education, outreach to Jews, the removal of racial prejudice, and the ending of slavery. In 1826 he expressed the hope that a Methodist day school would be established in Kingston, to give greater strength and depth to the work. A decade later he wrote from Hamilton, Bermuda, that day schools were vital if the mission was to develop. Three day schools, which would also serve as Sunday schools, could be built if only they were given a grant of £500.

'Great numbers of Jews attend our chapel', he wrote from Kingston in 1826, adding that he had talked with several 'on the subject of Christianity', and that in his view they were 'not far from the Kingdom of God', despite their fear of offending relatives.[7] Two years later he baptized a Jewish woman. This was done without publicity so as not to upset her mother. The third church in Kingston was built on land donated by a Jew, and was completed in 1828.

He was keenly aware of the injustices brought about by **slavery**, and was greatly distressed by the **racial prejudice** he found in church circles in Bermuda. His opposition to such evils was expressed in action as well as words.

Barry as Controversialist

Barry's life can be viewed as a series of quarrels. Not one for sitting on the fence, he rarely played it safe and frequently took sides, often on behalf of the poor or against established authorities.

He became publicly involved in the dispute between Wesleyan Methodists and Primitive Wesleyan Methodists in Kinsale in 1819. Soon after his arrival in Jamaica he quarrelled with his missionary colleagues, and was accused by them of being insubordinate and having 'an unchristian spirit'.[8] This was because he had not attended a District meeting, and would not apologize. Barry's defence was that he had been informed late about the meeting, and that by the time he was told, other important matters required his attention. Fortunately the resolution of this problem cleared the way for him to become involved in a much more serious controversy, in which he was able to defend missionary colleagues in the courts after attempts had been made to prevent them from exercising their ministry.

The most famous legal case in which Barry was involved resulted from a missionary meeting in Kingston in 1829. One speaker referred to the persecution of missionaries at the hands of those intent on retaining slavery. At once a local magistrate called Beaumont, who was also editor of *The Courant* newspaper, registered a protest and accused the speaker of sedition and of incitment to rebellion. He threatened to use his power as a magistrate to close the meeting, but instead left abruptly. Barry at first played the incident down, but in the course of the ensuing public correspondence he made a claim that he had never seen the magistracy 'sunk so low', whereupon Beaumont brought a libel action against him and claimed damages of £2,000.[9] The case provided a focal point for supporters and critics of the missionaries. Barry chose to defend himself, called no witnesses and carefully cross-examined Beaumont and his witnesses. He handled the case with great skill and eloquence, and his success was greeted with great excitement. Even opponents of the mission were delighted with Beaumont's defeat, since he had previously triumphed over several others in cases of litigation.

Barry was again drawn into controversy with *The Courant* because of its coverage of the insurrection of slaves in 1832; he claimed that it had given an altogether false impression about the role of Baptist, Moravian and Methodist missionaries. Barry had no doubt that if an inquiry were held, the missionaries would be vindicated.

In Canada Barry became identified with opposition to the union between the MEC and the Wesleyan Methodists, though in correspondence with the WMMS he vehemently denied that he had taken any initiatives in Toronto to foster such opposition. A factor which made it particularly difficult for him, was the part played by some Primitive Wesleyans from Ireland. It has not been possible to unravel this fully, but it was an element which would have been little appreciated by some of the authorities concerned.[10]

He was also fiercely critical of the line taken by the *Christian Guardian* in Canada on the issue of clergy reserves. These were official government grants being offered for the first time in Canada to some of the non-Anglican churches. Barry was in favour of the grants being received, but the newspaper was against them; and in a lengthy and unrestrained correspondence he accused it of misinforming and misleading its readers, of trying to make political capital out of the issue, and of casting a slur on the integrity of those ministers who had accepted the grants. The Officers of the WMMS felt that Barry had been particularly insensitive over this issue, pointing out that, quite apart from the merits of the case, the *Christian Guardian* was the organ of the Body with which the Wesleyan Methodists were in the process of uniting![11]

The following chapter will deal with the problems posed by slavery for Methodist missions, and Barry's involvement in the controversy.

— 10 —

John Barry, Opponent of Slavery

John Barry's attitude towards slavery must be seen in the context of the position taken by other Methodists. The WMMS policy on the political involvement of missionaries is also relevant.

Wesley and Coke on Slavery

John Wesley's position on slavery is well-known, clear, and consistent – he was totally opposed to it. In 1772 he described the slave trade as 'that execrable sum of all villanies';[1] and two years later in his uncompromising pamphlet against slavery the closing appeal was directed at those engaged in the slave trade as sea captains, merchants, and planters, urging them to do away with 'all whips, all chains, all compulsion' and to treat everyone with humanity and gentleness.[2] Fearing the righteous wrath of God, they should, Wesley argued, cleanse their hands from all 'blood-guiltiness'. Wesley also preached a famous sermon against slavery in 1785 in Bristol, a city later described as that 'dark den of slave traders'.[3] He wrote to the press on several occasions, and lent his name to the efforts of the abolitionists. As is well known, his last letter was addressed to William Wilberforce, urging him not to grow weary in the struggle against slavery which Wesley described as 'the scandal of religion, of England, and of human nature'.[4]

Thomas Coke shifted his ground on slavery as a result of his direct encounter with it. It is worth considering this process in detail in view of the unique place held by Coke in Methodism's world outreach. On his first visit to America, Coke had a long discussion in March 1785 with a man in Virginia who was opposed to the strong anti-slavery rules of American Methodism (these had been defined in the Christmas Conference which met from 24 December 1784). As Coke noted, the man 'would not be persuaded'.[5] From 1 April onwards Coke began 'to venture to exhort our Societies to emancipate their slaves'. On 5 April he 'dared for the first time to bear a public testimony against slavery', when he preached at a funeral, but said nothing good about the man who had died, observing that he had been 'a violent friend of slavery'. On 7 April he helped a dying man to draw up his will with instructions for the emancipation of his eight slaves. His preaching against slavery on 10 April drove some people out of the service; one of them offered £50 to the others if they 'would give that little Doctor one hundred lashes'. After the service some people surrounded Coke, but he was left unharmed and wrote that they 'had only power to talk'.[6] On 12 April he met a man who had freed twenty-two slaves, each valued at between £30 and £40.

When his itinerary took him from Virginia into North Carolina, Coke had to change his tactics since it was not legally possible for slaves to be granted freedom there. A petition was drawn up for the law to be changed, so that those owners willing to free their slaves could do so. As Coke noted in his Journal, 'Mr. Asbury has visited the Governor, and has gained him over.'[7] On 23 April Coke addressed slaves on the importance of duty to their owners. This, he believed, would make white people more receptive to the need for a change in their status. In early May he received a deputation of local Methodists, calling for the church's rules on slavery to be repealed. When, however, he made it clear that preachers might not be appointed to minister in the churches from which they came because of this opposition 'they drew in their horns'.[8] On 13 May he stayed with a person who claimed he had read Wesley's *Thoughts on Slavery* three times, and who yet kept slaves. He was 'as kind to his Negroes as if they were White servants . . . and yet I could not beat into the head of that poor man the evil of keeping them in Slavery.'[9] On 15 May he spelt out his views on slavery to a society, and 'the principal leader raged like a lion, and desired to withdraw from the Society'. Coke took him at his word, and appointed another person in his place![10] On 26 May he went with Asbury to see General Washington. When they introduced their petition on slavery, Washington replied that although his personal sympathies were with them he felt he could not sign because of the office he held. If, however, the Assembly would consider the petition he would write a letter to make clear his personal standpoint.

In view of Coke's strong line throughout the tour, it comes as a surprise that at the Conference with which it concluded he wrote that he 'thought it prudent to suspend the minute concerning Slavery' because of opposition to it. By way of explanation, he added that the church was 'in too infantile a state to push things to extremity' on such issues.[11]

In his second tour in 1786–1787, when he visited the West Indies for the first time, Coke went back to a town in America where he had previously encountered opposition because of his line on slavery. On this occasion he had a peaceful reception, and wrote, 'I now acknowledge that however just my sentiments may be concerning Slavery, it was ill judged of me to deliver them from the pulpit.'[12]

In the third, fourth and fifth visits, between December 1788 and May 1793, in which he toured in America and in the West Indies, there are few references in his Journal to slavery. This is in sharp contrast to the first tour, in which, as we have seen, slavery was a recurring theme. That Coke modified his position considerably is illustrated by the fact that during a week's stay in Grenada in January 1793, he stated how impressed he was with the humane legislation governing the treatment of slaves.[13] John Vickers comments as follows on the change in Coke:

Slavery was so closely woven into the social and economic life of the West Indies, that an unqualified public opposition to it from the outset would certainly have alienated the majority of the Europeans, not least the upper classes on whose favour the prospects of the new mission greatly depended.[14]

Although it was Coke who was largely instrumental in persuading the British Conference in 1807 to forbid preachers marrying West Indian women in possession of slaves, it has been concluded by Vickers that 'the eternal salvation' of slaves mattered more to him than 'their temporal emancipation'. He was not prepared to jeopardize the one to effect the other.

This approach was consistent with the 'no politics' rule as it developed within Methodism. This originated with Wesley himself, and affirmed that religious concerns rather than political concerns were of paramount importance to Methodists. Involvement in politics, or in political programmes with which the leadership disagreed, would deflect the movement from its spiritual objectives. Serious problems arose, however, when, as in the case of slavery, religious and political issues were closely interwoven. In such circumstances a 'no politics' line was interpreted by some as an endorsement of an unjust *status quo*.

On one occasion Coke undoubtedly took accommodation to slavery too far when he agreed that slaves be purchased so that a coffee and cotton plantation, which had been given to the mission in St Vincent, could be developed for the benefit of Carib Indians. This was one of the points made in a bitter attack launched against him by the Irish-born William Hammett. Commenting on Coke's decision to purchase the slaves, and on his subsequent decision to free them, Hammett wrote:

Dr. C. has *printed* and *preached* against negro traffic, how consistent was he then, to give orders to purchase them upon any pretence whatever?

If it was right to purchase slaves, it was wrong for him to print and preach against it. If right to preach against it, it must be wrong to purchase. If right to purchase, why could he sport with the money of his friends in Europe, to cast so many hundreds away at one stroke, by manumitting those he bought with it? O rare superintendent, 'wisdom is thine, and it will die with thee'. . . . When from *one* to *two* thousand is thrown

away, by a man's want of judgment, or his undigested specu-
lations, it is really robbing the missionaries, robbing the poor
in Europe, and that to support a man in his extravagant
follies.[15]

Hammett, however, was himself later to be accused of purchasing slaves, settling a plantation, and becoming 'a man of the
world'.[16]

The WMMS Policy on Political Involvement and Slavery

The WMMS insisted that its missionaries should avoid all direct
involvement in politics in line with the 'no politics' rule to which
reference has been made. Thus in 1822 the task in the West
Indies was defined in official Instructions as one of encouraging
slaves to accept the *status quo*. The British slave trade had been
abolished in 1807, but many still retained the status of being
slaves. The duty of slaves was to be obedient to their owners and
to work hard, and missionaries were instructed as follows:

> Your only business is to promote the moral and religious
> improvement of the slaves to whom you may have access,
> without in the least degree, in public or private, interfering
> with their civil condition.[17]

A sermon preached by Richard Watson, the prominent
WMMS Secretary, in London in 1824 was an eloquent, per-
suasive, and passionate presentation of the Wesleyan position.
Among the points emphasized by Watson were the unjust treatment of slaves, the slaves' remarkable restraint, the shameful
record of the church in failing for so long to minister effectively
to slaves, and a firm insistence upon a gradualist and indirect
approach to the termination of slavery so that it could take place
peacefully through 'the infusion of Christian principles into the
minds of the slave population'[18] and normal legal processes.

Serious misunderstandings arose within the West Indies, however, over the interpretation of the WMMS policy, as was
highlighted particularly in what became known as the Jamaican

Resolutions. These Resolutions had been drawn up in Jamaica in 1824 by an informal group of Wesleyan missionaries who felt the need to defend the WMMS mission against false charges and threats. The missionaries had of course no authority to act on behalf of the WMMS or indeed Jamaican Methodism; and, influenced by the prohibition on political involvement, they mistakenly believed that it was inappropriate for the church as such to take a moral stand on the institution of slavery. The Resolutions appeared in the Jamaican press even before their wording had been finalized, and when they were also publicly reported in Britain they caused a storm of protest, being seen there to some degree as a defence of slavery itself. This led to a formal disavowal by the WMMS, and the transfer or recall to Britain of those who were considered to have been centrally involved. While some points in the Resolutions were beyond reproach, the Missionary Society was particularly critical on two counts: first, the unqualified statement that 'Christianity does not interfere with the civil condition of the slaves, as slavery is established by the laws of the British West Indies'; and, second, the negative reference in the Resolutions to 'emancipationists and abolitionists' in Britain who were striving for the termination of slavery.[19] In these circumstances the Committee of the WMMS felt obliged to affirm the Wesleyan position on slavery in unmistakable terms:

> Whilst they feel that all changes in such a system ought to emanate solely from the Legislature, they hold it to be the duty of every Christian government to bring the practice of slavery to an end, as soon as it can be done safely, prudently, and with a just consideration to the interests of all parties concerned; and that the degradation of men, merely on account of their colour, and the holding of human beings in interminable bondage, are wholly inconsistent with Christianity.[20]

The Committee also declared that 'the sweeping charges' made against people bracketed under the label of 'emancipationists and abolitionists' had been made in ignorance of their true principles and objects.[21]

Irish interest in the controversy centres upon James Horne, a Scotsman by birth, who had been converted in Ireland while a soldier and had then entered the Irish ministry. He was believed to have been the secretary of the informal group of missionaries which drew up the Resolutions, and was subsequently transferred from Jamaica to Bermuda. Horne, however, strongly protested against this charge and treatment, claiming that he had not even attended the meeting from which the Resolutions emerged.

Irish Responses to Slavery

Irish missionaries adhered to the official policy on slavery, avoiding direct political confrontation and encouraging obedience and industry on the part of slaves. One revealing, though extreme, example can be cited. In July 1820 Patrick Ffrench, an Irish-born missionary, wrote from the island of St Eustatius, describing a slave having his left hand cut off as a punishment for running away. 'When cut off it jumped about the road like a Bird with a broken wing.'[22] He wrote again in October describing how the slave's behaviour had improved and saying that he had now become a Methodist member. In telling of his experience, he said that 'the *Devil* took his *hand* but that Jesus Christ has taken *his heart*'.[23] These letters offered no word of criticism of the institution of slavery or of the particular slave-owner who had ordered the crude amputation of a hand, as a punishment for disobedience. In 1823 Ffrench sent a letter from St Bartholomew's about a sudden upsurge of hostility towards the mission. It was mistakenly believed, he wrote, that William Wilberforce was a Methodist, and it was therefore felt that his abolitionist activities in Britain and Ffrench's preaching in St Bartholomew's would unsettle the slaves and lead to serious disturbances. Ffrench had been quick to point out this misunderstanding to the Governor:

I assured his Excellency his information was an absolute false-hood, & that it was contrary to my principles, & to the principles of Methodism or Christianity, which binds every Minister of the Gospel to inculcate obedience to all Legal authorities under whatever Government or constitution the providence of *God* may call us to labour.[24]

This response on the part of Ffrench reveals a confusion over WMMS policy similar to that which was evident in the Jamaican Resolutions.

Complications arose in the case of those missionaries, whether from Ireland or elsewhere, who married into white West Indian families. This inevitably influenced their thinking on a range of issues, and especially on slavery, since in some instances the families owned properties on which slaves were employed. Thus John Toland was the one Irishman among five missionaries who were reported to the annual British Conference in 1811 for hold-ing slaves. As noted already, the Methodist Conference took steps against this practice in 1807.

John Rutledge was, however, the most notable Irish mis-sionary to come into this category, serving in the Bahamas from 1804 but having to resign from the itinerant work in 1814 upon marrying a local woman who had inherited slaves. Thereafter Rutledge's relationship with the WMMS and with the church in the Bahamas became extremely complicated. Although his name seldom appeared in official WMMS lists of workers after 1814, he was still regarded within the Bahamas as the most senior and experienced Methodist minister, even acting as Secretary of the District Meeting and therefore signing official correspondence with the WMMS. He was capable too of force-ful statements on behalf of slaves. Although of a mild disposition and a conservative outlook, he strongly opposed legislation introduced into the Assembly in the Bahamas in 1817 which forbade the holding of religious services between sunset and sun-rise. These of course were the only times when it would have been possible for slaves to attend worship. Writing to the WMMS he expressed himself in such forceful language as 'this persecuting law', this 'iniquitous measure', and 'an unjust oppressive law'.[25] He later wrote that 'never was there a more unreasonable un-christian measure adopted since the days of Nero'.[26] It is of interest that when he died in 1826, Rutledge left a sum of money for the work of the Irish Mission.

John Barry, Opponent of Slavery

We now revert to John Barry, whose work was considered in the previous chapter, and in particular to his position on the con-troversies about slavery.

Within months of his arrival in Jamaica in 1825 some of Barry's missionary colleagues were imprisoned for preaching at unlawful hours in unlicensed chapels. Barry himself had already experienced difficulty in obtaining a licence authorizing him to work as a Wesleyan missionary. Behind such incidents was the mistrust with which many influential white people, including some magistrates, viewed the missionaries. They saw mission-aries as posing a threat to their way of life and indeed to the economy of the colony as a whole because, in enhancing the self-respect of the slaves and providing them with education, it was believed the missionaries were throwing their weight behind the movement to give slaves their freedom. In doing this they were also undermining the very structure of a society based essentially upon the subjugation of a people. Barry revelled in such a situa-tion, appeared in court on behalf of colleagues, challenged the legality of proceedings, procured writs of habeas corpus, and moved cases from the Quarter Sessions to the Supreme Court where he was able to have them quashed.

Of all the Irish missionaries, Barry was most uncomfortable with the WMMS restrictions on political involvement. Report-ing on his response to proposed new slave legislation in Jamaica in 1828, he confided to the WMMS:

Conscious of the obvious propriety of your instruction on the subject of interfering in politics, I was unwilling to enter more largely on the question than I did, fearing such a step might not meet the approbation of the Committee.[27]

He nonetheless took some initiatives which he hoped would not be considered contrary to the Instructions. For example in November 1829 he reported that he had sent a letter to the House of Assembly prior to the second reading of a bill on slaves. He had done so not so much to impress the members of the House or even to rebut unfounded allegations against the missionaries, but more to make clear in Jamaica and in England that certain legal processes had not been observed.[28] Later in the same month Barry reported on a long conversation he had had with a lawyer on the consequences for the religious education of slaves if a certain restrictive bill was passed. In December he commented: 'If this law ultimately receive the royal assent it will destroy slave instruction at the very root.'[29] He later reported that the bill had in fact received the Governor's assent, and added: 'I trust God will remember the poor negroes in mercy.' It is all the more remarkable that Barry took such a close interest in these events since he was at the time experiencing a severe breakdown in health.

While Barry convalesced in the British Isles his *Letter addressed to the Right Hon. Sir George Murray* was published in London in 1830. This was Barry's reply, sent to the Secretary of State for the Colonies, in response to a pamphlet from Jamaica on the effects of colonial policy, which also made critical references to the work of missionaries. Barry wrote thus on the evil of slavery and the value of Christian teaching:

Slavery, by divesting the negro of character, bereaves him of those powerful incentives to action and improvement which the meanest free man possesses. Coercion is resorted to in vain to produce effects which religion alone can accomplish; punishment may for the moment excite his terror, restrain the indulgence of his appetites, and stimulate to labour: but it is the exclusive province of Christianity to communicate a controlling *principle*, so as to check permanently and effectually the impetuosity of his passions, form the moral character of the man, and elevate him to that rank in society for which his original destiny intended him, but from which a system of servitude, *excluding religious instruction*, must withhold him for ever.[30]

Wherever religion 'has been diffused', he affirmed,

industry has been promoted, moral habits formed, marriage honoured, revolting and indecent practices abolished ... guards rendered unnecessary, a spirit of insubordination and revolt suppressed.[31]

'In no case', he claimed in the letter, 'has the religious negro been engaged, however remotely, in schemes of sedition or revolt.'[32]

Under cross-examination before a parliamentary Select Committee on slavery, Barry remained uncompromisingly opposed to slavery. The points he made in response to close questioning, can be summarized as follows. First, whatever his private views, Barry accepted that as a missionary serving in Jamaica under the WMMS he was not permitted to comment on, or to interfere with, the civil condition of slaves. Second, he recognized that in his work as a missionary he was contributing, however indirectly, towards the emancipation of slaves. Third, he regarded slavery as altogether morally unacceptable, and claimed that it had led to widespread demoralization, not only among the slaves themselves, but also among white people and people of mixed race. Fourth, he affirmed that missionaries, and indeed religion itself, exerted an important restraining influence upon slaves, inculcating many virtues including loyalty and respect for authority, and thus preparing the way in a responsible manner for emancipation. Fifth, he was convinced that the danger to society would be much greater if emancipation were now withheld than if it were granted. There could be no question of reversing the movement towards emancipation. Sixth, he was sure that the Jamaican economy would not collapse after emancipation. His firm opinion was that the slaves were too intelligent, too industrious, and too astute not to be prepared to work for payment on estates where hitherto they had been forced to work without payment.

Barry was closely cross-examined on his attitude towards the Jamaican Resolutions, particularly on three matters. Did he not accept that those who had initially adopted and then rescinded the Resolutions were acting under duress from the WMMS? Why did those missionaries whose names were not attached to the Resolutions not publicly disassociate themselves from them if they were in fact against them? Did the Resolutions not take a much more positive line than Barry had done on the role of magistrates, so far as the education of slaves was concerned?

Barry's replies to the Committee were clear and forthright. It was his view that those who had changed their mind on the Resolutions did so completely voluntarily and because they now recognized their error. Also those who from the beginning had been opposed to the Resolutions did not enter the public debate, because to have done so would have been to contravene the WMMS rules on political controversy. Finally, he remained uncompromisingly critical of the record of most magistrates on their attitudes to slaves and missionaries:

> I have had more to do with the magistracy than any other missionary we have ever had on that mission; and I have, except in some few instances, seen a general indisposition to the encouragement of missions.[33]

As already stated in his evidence, he had always seen 'in the magistracy generally, a strong opposition to the instruction of the negroes'.[34]

It was fortuitous that Barry arrived in Hamilton, Bermuda, within a fortnight of the slaves being given their freedom. At a special celebratory service on 3 August 1834 he preached on the 'Claims and Duties arising out of Emancipation', taking as his text Ephesians 4: 1, 'Walk worthy of the vocation wherewith ye are called.' He set the scene in a letter to the WMMS the following day:

> The chapel was tremendously crowded. Almost all the respectable inhabitants of Hamilton were present, and the deepest

attention was paid by the people of colour within and without, for I am told there were hundreds outside. . . . I think the service will have a good effect on our cause in this island.[35]

One of the points in the sermon itself was that freedom would have been granted much earlier had it not been for the technical problem of agreeing compensation for slave owners. In eventually granting emancipation, Barry claimed that Britain had reached her finest hour:

Britain, long pre-eminent among the Nations of the World – great in power – great in wisdom – and great in arms, has rendered herself yet more glorious by an act, extending to a numerous, an oppressed, and a helpless race, the common blessing of our common nature, LIBERTY, of which they have been long and cruelly deprived, by the cupidity and injustice of man. The gift of freedom to the once degraded slave, is the most splendid achievement of Britain, and will live in the records of the Nation, when her political and military triumphs shall have been forgotten.[36]

Even in the exultation of this high point of achievement, however, Barry was not blind to the need to recognize and eliminate the prejudice which continued to lurk in the human heart. Within weeks of emancipation, he wrote of the discrimination still evident in the life of the church:

Our colored congregation in this town has greatly increased. It is high time to put down the unparalleled prejudice existing against that class, in the minds of the members of our society. It far exceeds anything I have ever known. I shall proceed prudently, but firmly, and must succeed. I think the free people of color would not be allowed to rent pews, but in a certain part of our chapels, and I am often offended at the manner in which I hear them spoken of.[37]

Five months later he expressed concern at the lack of facilities available for black people:

In none of our places of worship have we anything like the

necessary accommodation for the people of color, and in consequence they are presently compelled to remain outside. . . . The black population seldom attend in private houses which are frequented by white congregations.[38]

It is to Barry's credit that, despite enormous personal difficulties and frustrations, he remained sharply aware of the plight of those who suffered under slavery or as a result of prejudice. He dared to make plain that, in his own words, 'slavery was an object of the deepest hatred',[39] and he took risks in opposing it and in speaking on behalf of its victims.

Talented and touchy, vulnerable to personal criticism and yet vehement in his prosecution of whatever cause he considered just, John Barry frequently gave offence. As a result, too much of his time, talent and energy was dissipated in defending or explaining his attitudes and actions. This undoubtedly detracted from his usefulness. His 'unbending integrity'[40] was two-edged; it was both his strength and his weakness, causing hurt and yet also bringing crucial issues into sharp focus. Whatever his errors of judgment, particularly in terms of personal relationships, the significance of his life and work deserves much wider recognition.

— 11 —

William Butler,
Founder of Two Missions

Like Barry before him, William Butler was no stranger to sorrow and setbacks of various kinds. He was orphaned at an early age, twice widowed before he found a life partner, and, with his wife and children, given up for dead in the excesses of the Indian mutiny. Yet he was destined to play a leading part in the founding of two major MEC missions, those in India and Mexico.

Butler in Ireland (1818–1850)

Born in Dublin in 1818, Butler was brought up by his great-grandmother. He belonged to the Church of Ireland (Anglican) until his nineteenth year, describing himself at the time as moral but knowing nothing of personal religion. On becoming friendly with a woman whose husband was a judge and a former Member of Parliament, who had herself only lately experienced an evangelical awakening, Butler was introduced to Dublin Methodists. Among them he discovered personal faith. He later described his experience in these terms:

> How simple and apostolic it all appeared! The hearty singing, the extempore prayers, the experimental teaching, all de-lighted me . . . It was easy to conclude at once that these people should be my people for the rest of my life.[1]

After receiving training at Didsbury College in England he returned to Ireland, teaching for a time in a Methodist mission school in Portaferry, Co. Down, and taking services. It was at this period that he came into close contact with James Lynch, the veteran pioneer of Wesleyan Methodist missions in Ceylon and India. As Butler himself later recorded:

> I had been brought into intimate relations with Rev. James Lynch who . . . was in the last year of his ministerial service, and being feeble, I was sent to assist him. From this venerable man I heard much that was calculated to enlarge my views and deepen my interest in missionary work, especially in India.[2]

In later years, while revisiting Ireland from America, he stated at the annual Conference of the Methodist Church that 'James Lynch laid his hands on my youthful head, and from him I received the missionary spirit.'[3]

Butler entered the Methodist ministry in Ireland in 1844, and was ordained in 1848. In 1850, following the death of his first wife and his remarriage, he emigrated to the United States. Although America thus became the base for what proved to be a long and distinguished ministry, Butler never forgot Ireland, renewing his contact with it whenever possible. A few years before he died he exclaimed – 'Dear old Irish Methodism! If I have been of any use in this wide world, I owe it, under God, to her.'[4]

After the sudden death of Butler's second wife, he was joined by Clementina Rowe from Wexford who had known him in Ireland. They were married in 1854. During their time in India and Mexico, she took a special intetest in the orphanages in both places and in literature programmes. On her return to America from India she was a key figure in the setting up of the Women's Foreign Missionary Society (WFMS) in 1869. Its task was to encourage and co-ordinate the efforts of women in sending and supporting women missionaries, and in training and providing support for native women teachers and Bible readers. Her daughter, also Clementina, was for more than thirty years secretary of the New England Branch of the WFMS, and was the author of her parents' biographies.

Butler in India (1856–1864)

Although the MEC first decided to commence a mission in India in 1852, and allocated money for that purpose on an annual basis from that year, it was not until 1855 that the search for a leader was successful. The delay prompted Bishop J. M. Thoburn, who joined the India mission in 1859 and stayed for more than thirty years, to record:

> I have heard of so many men who were asked, and who for various reasons were unable to accept the post, that I incline to the opinion that no other prominent post in all the history of our Church was ever declined by so many nominees.[5]

Butler was initially interested in applying for the position, but held back in the hope that an American would come forward. When he eventually indicated his willingness to go, his offer was immediately accepted. His interest in and commitment to world mission had already been underlined by the publication of his *Compendium of Missions* (1852), and also by his preaching the annual missionary sermon at the Biblical Institute at Concord, New Hampshire.

When he set out in April 1856 his instructions were brief and to the point. The mission was to be to the native population, he was to see that the gospel was preached 'to those who have not heard', and he was to 'regard the preaching of the word to the people as the principal efficient means of their awakening and conversion'.[6]

After consultations in Britain with Lynch, and in India with church leaders and sympathetic British government officials, Butler decided to locate the mission in the province of Rohilkhand and the western half of the province of Oudh. This was one of the areas recommended for consideration by his mission authorities, and it proved a wise choice, being a distinct region, bounded on the north by the Himalayan mountains and on the west and south by the river Ganges. It was an area too in which no other missionaries were then at work.

Choosing the city of Bareilly as his base, he wrote to America

early in 1857, outlining his plans and requesting the appointment of twenty-five missionaries (eight for Lucknow; four for
Bareilly; three for Faizabad; two for Shahjahanpur; four for
Moradabad; two for Budaun; and two for Pilibhit). Not even
Butler expected all twenty-five to be appointed immediately!
Eight would do at once, he wrote, and the remainder could be
sent as soon as possible. Of the stations named by Butler, all
but two – Faizabad and Pilibhit – soon had missionaries, and
became prominent centres of Methodist activity.

Before a proper start could be made, however, tragedy struck
with the eruption of the Indian mutiny. The provinces of Oudh
and Rohilkhand became main centres of violence. The first
serious fighting took place on 10 May 1857, with many Europeans killed and Delhi itself falling the following day. Butler was
advised to take his family away from Bareilly, and on 18 May
he did so. In less than a fortnight trouble reached Bareilly itself.
Many Christians were murdered, and the first native woman to
become a member of the MEC was beheaded.

All the mission property was destroyed, and the Nawab of
Rohilkhand offered a reward of five hundred rupees for the
arrest of Butler or the delivery of his head. Indeed with Butler
and his party having to move from place to place for more than
a year, it was assumed for a time that he had been killed and
reports of his death were circulated.

The mission recommenced in 1858, receiving a great impetus
in that and the following year with the arrival of several preachers
of considerable experience and ability, including Thoburn. Butler
saw his main purpose to be the establishment of a church in India:

From the first, I have had but one desire, & that was to see in
India a reproduction of the Methodist Episcopal Church in
all its integrity as a field of action worthy of our name &
energy. I have desired this from no mere sectarian feeling, but
from a profound conviction . . . that there is no reason why
'the God of our Fathers' may not grant to the . . . Church on
this Continent a position of influence & power for good similar
to that which He has granted in 'the Western World.'[7]

Such an aim can of course be dismissed as revealing a naive and insensitive assumption that a pattern of church life which had proved itself in one culture would serve just as well in another quite alien to it. It should be noted, in Butler's defence, that he had received no guidelines suggesting that any other approach was possible. It should also be noted that at a conference held in Lahore in late 1862 and early 1863, at which the tensions arising between native Christian leaders and overseas missionaries were faced, Butler declared to fellow missionaries from various churches and missions:

> We have learned much of how careful and prudent we ought to be, especially in our intercourse with the rising Native Church in this land, so that it may take, from the very beginning, that shape and form which will be most in accordance with the will of God and most promotive of good.[8]

Butler's relationships with missionary colleagues, and with the mission authorities, were frequently strained. As founder and Superintendent of the mission Butler virtually occupied the positions of 'bishop, presiding elder, finance committee, treasurer, and corresponding secretary'.[9] With old-world ideas about prestige and authority, he was energetic, ambitious for missionary expansion, certain about the rightness of his own judgments, and impatient of restrictions imposed upon him by officials in New York. Missionary colleagues felt excluded from important decisions, and the authorities at headquarters objected to aspects of his administration, all of which led to a voluminous correspondence between New York and India. The following excerpt from a letter to Butler is not an untypical example:

> There has been in your mission . . . a feeling of uneasiness owing to the power and privileges of the Superintendent, & sensitiveness in regard to the manner of exercising them . . . The problem for you to solve therefore, is, so to execute the office of Superintendent, as not to be feeble or deficient, & yet to show deference & respect to the opinions & feelings of our younger American Brethren.[10]

Plainly Butler was not easy to work with or for, and in 1864 he resigned and returned to America. By then the initial stage of the mission had at any rate been completed.

In his final report as Superintendent he was able to list some remarkable achievements:

Nine of the most important cities have been occupied, land obtained and secured by requisite legal forms, nineteen mission houses built or purchased, ten chapels and sixteen schoolhouses erected, two large orphanages provided, and a well appointed printing establishment founded in the center of our field. Twelve congregations have been gathered and ten small Churches organised, while one thousand three hundred and twenty-two scholars, male and female, are being instructed dayly in our Christian schools; . . . and from among the converts whom God has already given us, at least four preachers and eleven exhorters are now commanding to others the salvation which they first learned from us.[11]

In 1859 there were five Methodist adherents, and only one full member. Before his death these figures had risen to over 36,000 adherents and almost 21,000 full members. New converts were being baptized at the rate of fifty per day during 1893. Statistics for numbers of workers, schools, church and other buildings, and finances indicate equally rapid progress.

Among Butler's publications, two had a direct reference to India, *The Land of the Veda* (1872) and *From Boston to Bareilly and Back* (1885).

Butler in Mexico (1873–1878)

In 1872 Butler was again invited to establish an MEC mission, this time in Mexico. He was an obvious choice as Superintendent in view of his service in India and because of his involvement as Secretary of the undenominational American and Foreign Christian Union from 1869. The major overseas thrust of this body, founded in 1849, was evangelism in what were termed 'the Papal Lands'.[12] It had become active in Mexico following the promulgation of religious freedom in the constitution of 1857, and a small though vigorous evangelical movement thus began to emerge in Mexico in the 1860s. In the decision to establish an MEC mission, care was taken to emphasize that it would be carried on in co-operation with other evangelical groups.

Butler arrived in Mexico City in February 1873, and immediately took up the task of purchasing part of a vast historic property variously known as the San Francisco Monastery, or Convent, or Cloisters, to serve as the mission's headquarters. The building had been brought to his notice by an MEC bishop who had preceded him to Mexico, and who had spent three months helping to prepare the way for the mission itself. Butler was able to finalize the deal only as a result of a chance meeting with an Irish Roman Catholic layman who knew the owner and who was attracted to Butler. As a soldier he had assisted in the British relief of Lucknow during the Indian mutiny, and he became aware that Butler had praised the courage of those taking part in this military exercise in one of his publications.

Within a year requests for preachers were received from various parts of the city and also from other places in the Republic. Butler's first annual Report indicated two English congregations already started in the cities of Mexico and Pachuca; seven Mexican congregations (three in Mexico City, and one each in Pachuca, Rio del Monte, Orizaba, and Miraflores); three Sunday schools and a day school. He was fortunate in being able to secure the services of local men who were already experienced preachers, including some who had earlier been Roman Catholics, and some gifted expatriate lay preachers who were living in Mexico.

Butler adopted a similar approach to the one which had proved so effective in India. He selected strategic centres which in turn became bases from which further initiatives were planned and launched. Puebla, Guanajuato, and Queretaro were added to the cities already named. What was totally different from India was of course the dominance of Roman Catholicism, frequently of an aggressive nature. Butler, though himself a forthright Protestant who was not at all slow to expose what he regarded as fundamental errors and weaknesses in Roman Catholicism, displayed considerable diplomatic skill in response to these ecclesiastical problems. In Puebla the property secured for the mission had been a main centre for the Inquisition in Mexico, and one task in the renovation of the premises was the distasteful one of removing human skeletons from the cells.

As in India, serious difficulties arose between Butler and the mission authorities over aspects of his administration, and he resigned and returned to the United States in 1878. His son by his second wife, John Wesley Butler, who had been born in America, continued to serve in Mexico for many years. He became minister of the first Methodist congregation in Mexico City in 1874, was District Superintendent from 1889 to 1918, and contributed to the work of the church there as an author and publisher, overseer of schools, acting President of the Mexico Institute and Mexico Theological School, and President of the Mexico annual Conference. When J. W. Butler died in 1918, there were 30,000 communicant members in Mexico. William Butler had died in the United States in 1899.

Having surveyed the main phases in William Butler's life, it is important to explore the dominant features in his view of, and approach to, mission.

Butler on the Nature of Mission and Missionary Methods

In line with the instructions received on his appointment to India, Butler was concerned to see people called to repentance and faith in Jesus Christ, and he regarded preaching as the primary means of conversion. His aim of establishing churches has to be understood in this context.

The commitment to evangelism did not of course preclude Butler, as Superintendent, attending to the temporal affairs of the missions. So long as others were able to concentrate on acquiring native languages and informing themselves about local beliefs and practices, and actually engaging in evangelism, he saw it as his task to ensure that each station was strategically located and was properly equipped to reach out into the community.

Without in any way detracting from the importance of preaching and evangelism, Butler also made it plain that he held a broad view of mission which had to be expressed in a variety of forms relevant to the diverse needs of people. In an outspoken passage in one of his books he referred to what he described as the decadence of 'Mohammedanism' and the superiority of Christianity. Christian civilization, he claimed, 'builds her reservoirs, digs her canals, or sinks her artesian wells, and so unseals the rich supplies which make famines impossible'.[13] On similar lines he wrote concerning India:

> When this land becomes Christian, and science has a chance to touch its agriculture, how the face of the earth will bloom! Their little miserable plough (made of two sticks) never yet turned up the soil to the depth of more than about five inches. Recuperative resources lie beneath which a Christian plough would bring to the surface. Heathenism is an unmitigated curse not only to the body, and soul, the heart, character, and life, but also to the very soil they till.[14]

Butler seems to have believed not only that Christian values and technological advance were interrelated, but also that such progress depended on Christian values and a Christian world-view. These and related topics continue to interest missiologists.

Butler's emphasis on printing presses, schools and orphanages, and an experiment in mulberry cultivation and the raising of silk-worms, which he reported in 1864, also illustrate a comprehensive view. Despite early discouragement and opposition, Butler was convinced of the necessity of educating Indian women and girls. Alexander Duff, the eminent Scottish Presbyterian missionary, had given an indication of the immensity of the problem when he stated in 1830 that 'you might as well try to scale a wall five hundred yards high as to attempt female education in India.'[15] It was, however, Butler's firm belief that little progress could be made in work among young men unless they had the prospect of marriage to educated young Christian women. The famine after the mutiny opened up a new educational opportunity. Butler offered initially to adopt one hundred and fifty children of each sex, and the government, in welcoming his initiative, gave financial backing to the scheme. With orphanages established, it became easier to start day and Sunday schools. Of the first group of girls, it was reckoned that eight became 'medical practitioners', five became dispensary and hospital assistants, twenty-eight became school teachers, and many were married to ministers.[16] Butler himself declared that without these 'precious girls' the mission would have had no lasting work among women, no female hospitals, no zenana visitation or girls' schools, and no Christian homes.[17]

From the beginning, the missionaries felt an urgent need for literature, especially in the vernacular languages of Rohilkhand and Oudh. In 1860 the American Mission Press (later to become the Methodist Publishing House, Lucknow) was opened. It became one of the largest publishing agencies in India. Its first major project was the printing of a hymnal in what was then called Hindustani. Similarly in Mexico a mission press was established in 1875, with Butler's son Edward in charge. An important Spanish language Christian newspaper, *El Abogado Cristiano*, was produced from 1877.

Butler's attempt to establish a model Christian village, called Wesleypore, was also a striking illustration of a broad approach to mission. The fact that the experiment itself failed and that it came to be regarded with some embarrassment, should not be allowed to detract from its significance. The background to the experiment lay in the persecution encountered by converted Sikh farmers in Moradabad and Bijnor. Butler put in a successful bid for land on offer from the government, and described his initiatives and hopes in this way:

We went to work and collected these despised and illiterate people under Brother and Sister Parker's pastoral care. A village has been built, wells dug, farms laid off and cultivated, the foundations of a church and school laid ... and the prospect is that our little town will become a sort of market town for the whole region, as we are already far in advance of them all in the way of people, tradesmen etc. . . . . No one in that community but earns his own living. What they had to borrow in order to begin to cultivate their farms they are now gratefully paying back again. Christianity may here be said to be rooting itself in the soil. A mighty influence for good ought to go out from such a center within a few years all over that region . . .[18]

This experiment did not develop as planned. Indeed Parker's biographer was to describe it as 'one of the most unfortunate enterprises in the annals of India missions'.[19] Among the factors involved in the failure were Parker's ill-health and inexperience, disagreement between Butler and Parker over management procedures, and the tensions which arose between the Parker family and another missionary family involved in the project. In addition:

It began to be apparent that the people for whose sake the village had been prepared were unwilling to come and occupy it. Sinister rumors of sickness and death at Wesleypore began to spread among the Sikhs in the North-west and the people were afraid . . . There was in fact everything to worry and discourage those who were trying to build up Wesleypore.[20]

It was a bold scheme which had much to commend it. It foundered partly because its authoritarian approach failed to take account of vital factors, including the conservatism of local people. Such failures are both painful and instructive, underlining the importance of relationships and the need for consultation.

Butler's boldness and the scale of his planning sometimes struck other people as unrealistic. When the Indian mutiny ended, Butler visited General Sir James Outram, who had become head of the government of Oudh, to present his plans and to seek support. Outram, who had earned an impressive reputation for bravery, opposed the plans in the belief that they were much too daring and dangerous. 'Do you want to provoke a second Sepoy rebellion?', he demanded of Butler. Butler's published comment was uncompromising. Here was one who, though renowned for valour in battle, was pulling back in alarm when asked to lend his support to a small group of Christian missionaries![21]

Butler's wisdom as a missionary strategist was particularly well demonstrated in his attitude towards Roman Catholicism in Mexico. In his view, much of the Protestant work already being carried on was for the most part 'political and harshly controversial', with preachers indulging in what amounted 'to little more than tirades against the Romish clergy and Church'. His own belief was that:

> Such conduct and such methods of missionary work are only calculated to irritate and disgust conscientious Romanists, and lead them to hate Protestantism, and even be willing to see it persecuted and driven away.[22]

A new strategy had to be found to promote evangelical concerns in a 'gentlemanly, Christian, and unsectarian manner'.[23] To be useful to people in Mexico the MEC mission had to avoid 'all this bitterness and theological pugnacity, and devote itself to preaching the Gospel in the spirit of the Gospel'.[24] Missionaries and native helpers must learn that they could preach the Gospel 'without abusing the Romanists', and that the best way of removing the 'darkness of superstition and sin' was simply 'to introduce the light of truth and holiness' and to sustain their teaching by an appeal to life and experience.[25] He wanted preachers to display 'tenderness for the perishing souls around them . . . till Christian love and holy living shall convince them of the excellence of our faith'.

In this connection the publications of other missions

> were harsh & controversial, without teaching how men were to be saved. They were exasperating instead of conciliatory, and, I fear leaving even their own adherents without the instruction that might save them.[26]

In Butler's opinion such an approach misrepresented evangelical religion. We could add that it did not glorify Christ either. Efforts were therefore made in Methodist publications, notably in *El Abogado Cristiano*, to communicate evangelical principles more effectively.

In many ways Butler, of all the Irish Methodist missionaries, best exemplifies what some would regard as a classical type of nineteenth-century missionary. He possessed clear vision, a driving purpose, a domineering attitude, and a determination not to be defeated by opposition, whatever its source. His achievements were enormous by any standard. One assessment of his ministry concluded:

> Contemporaries agreed, and historians confirm, that notwithstanding Butler's lack of administrative finesse, he was a wise and devoted missionary who rendered great service. His foresight and grasp of the opportunities and the needs in both India and Mexico were remarkable.[27]

Mission Yesterday and Today

=

In 1982 the World Council of Churches (WCC) published an important document entitled *Mission and Evangelism, an Ecumenical Affirmation*, the product of discussions between people from member churches of the WCC and Roman Catholics. It summarizes basic convictions held by Christians today concerning mission and evangelism. By examining the Irish Methodist missionary tradition in this light we become more sharply aware of its weaknesses, strengths and insights.

The Call to Mission

The call to mission arises from the initiatives of God himself. As stated in *Mission and Evangelism*:

> The saving ministry of the Son is understood within the action of the Holy Trinity; it was the Father who in the power of the Spirit sent Jesus Christ the Son of God incarnate, the Saviour of the whole world.[1]

Clarke and Arthur clearly shared this approach. For them, God's mission was primary and definitive, the church's mission secondary and derivative. Mission is therefore not one activity among many, an optional extra, a matter only for churches of certain traditions or for those individuals or groups within the church's membership who are enthusiasts, but is a requirement of all. According to Clarke and Arthur, all churches and Christians are called to participate in mission. It is part of their response to the life of God within them, an aspect of sharing in what God is doing in the world.

The church has one 'constitutive mark', claims *Mission and Evangelism*, 'its being apostolic, its being sent into the world'.[2] Clarke was less technical, simply stating that Methodists felt they were a missionary people. Moderately gifted Methodist missionaries showed that they too recognized this point when they referred in their letters to the 'God of missions'. Jesus' followers are sent, as he was sent (John 20.21).

The Message of Mission

The primary message of mission has always been the gospel as revealed in Jesus Christ and as expressed in the kingdom of God. It was with this message that the first missionaries went to the West Indies. Butler's instructions, as he set out for India in 1856, were along the same lines. He was to minister to the native population, sharing the gospel with them. The founding of churches was not subordinate to this enterprise, it was rather the means of enabling it to happen.

The recognition in *Mission and Evangelism* of the importance of planting local congregations, as a fundamental mission strategy, is a confirmation, if such were needed, of the wisdom of this aspect of traditional mission policy. The powerfully christological emphasis throughout the Report is reassuring to those suspicious of modern ecumenism and of the WCC in particular. It affirms that 'each person is entitled to hear the Good News',[3] and that

> at the very heart of the Church's vocation in the world is the proclamation of the kingdom of God inaugurated in Jesus the Lord, crucified and risen ... The starting point of our proclamation is Christ and Christ crucified.[4]

Mission in One World

God calls to mission in one world. Mission is one and indivisible, at home, nationally, and to the ends of the earth. This is a traditional Methodist emphasis, though it is not always acknowledged. It was Coke, the founder and promoter of Methodist overseas missions, who prompted and pioneered Methodist initiatives to those who were remote from the movement's influence in Scotland, Wales and Ireland. Thus a letter from Coke, written in Lisburn in 1809, speaks of the need for a missionary for Trinidad and Santa Cruz, and then proceeds to plead for zeal in home missions which are described as 'of infinite importance'.[5] Clarke and Arthur continued this emphasis. Clarke claimed in 1819, complacently as it now appears, that whereas Methodism had first applied itself with such success to evangelism at home, the real task then confronting it was to reach out to other parts of the world.

It is necessary to reaffirm this basis for mission in one world in the light of claims by Bernard Semmel and others, that Methodism took an increased interest in foreign missions around 1813 not primarily for reasons of the gospel but mainly because influential Wesleyan leaders believed it was politically and religiously astute to do so.[6] David Hempton and Stuart Piggin have recently examined and rejected this theory, but others have felt drawn to its conclusions even if they do not wholly accept the interpretation of events in 1813 from which it was deduced. Foremost among these is Lord Soper who has written:

(The) nineteenth-century leaders (of Methodism), unprepared to carry out the Methodist revolution in its political and social terms in England, compensated for this failure by a wholesale commitment to foreign missions. The spiritual welfare of the heathen across the seas became the prime concern of many Methodists who were unready to face the problems of the unfortunate heathen in the back streets of Leeds.[7]

What lies behind Semmel's theory is an alleged reaction within the Methodist leadership in 1813 to Tory opposition to Methodism. There was certainly a fear at the time that a parliamentary bill proposed by Lord Sidmouth, which related to the Toleration Acts, might suppress the itinerancy system within

Methodism. Had this been successful, it would have prevented the free movement of preachers. Semmel argues that a compromise was reached following conversations between Sidmouth, Coke and Clarke, with Methodism agreeing to divert much of its dynamism into non-political and remote activities overseas, having lessened its efforts at home.

In response to Semmel's thesis it is important to make the following points.[8] First, Coke and Clarke did not make any concessions to Sidmouth with regard to the itinerancy system, nor were they the only architects of Methodism's response. Second, those behind the Leeds missionary intiative in 1813 did not have to create enthusiasm for overseas missions among Methodists. It already existed, and was expressed, for example, in support of the undenominational London Missionary Society which was concerned with foreign missions. One of the aims in creating a Methodist instrument for mission was to retain scarce financial resources within Methodism. Third, those supporting the Leeds initiative, and later the formation of the WMMS, stressed continuity with previous Methodist efforts on behalf of overseas missions and the need to consolidate this work in the light of Coke's departure for Asia. Indeed, with Coke no longer directing operations, this was the first real opportunity to organize missions on a different basis. Fourth, legislative changes opened up the way for new initiatives in India. This became possible when the barrier against the promotion of Christianity in India – a feature of the terms under which the East India Company held a monopoly of trade – was removed by Castlereagh's India Bill in 1813. What had been contemplated for years, a Methodist initiative in India, could at last be attempted. The implications of the Bill were even wider. In effect it 'fixed the date of the birth of the Wesleyan Missionary Society'.[9] Fifth, those opposed to Methodism at home regarded its influence overseas with even greater suspicion since control of alien populations was more tenuous and the threat of rebellion greater. This was a factor in the hostility shown towards Methodism in the West Indies. Sixth, those who favoured Methodist overseas missions always stressed the reflex advantages at home, claiming that involvement in foreign missions revitalized home missions, providing greater resources, both financial and spiritual. It is stated in *Mission and Evangelism* that

> Christian affirmations on the worldwide missionary responsibility of the Church will be credible if they are authenticated by a serious missionary engagement at home.[10]

On this basis, credibility can certainly be accorded to those promoting Methodist overseas missions. As Clarke said at the formation of the London MMS in 1814:

> I most confidently anticipate, a revival, increase, and deepening of true religion among ourselves, by the extension of these missionary societies.[11]

Overseas missions were seen to be important not as a way of escaping domestic difficulties and challenges, but as an integral part of one mission. It was genuinely believed that rather than detracting from home missions, they would add to them.

Mission to all Realms of Life

The emphasis in *Mission and Evangelism*, based on the biblical message and especially on Jesus' teaching about the kingdom of God, on the need to relate the gospel to all areas of life, finds echoes in several of the people we have considered, including Clarke, Lynch, Barry and Arthur. Arthur's insights accorded most closely with the claim in *Mission and Evangelism* that the kingdom is a challenge to the structures of society as well as a call for individual repentance. In his words 'fearful social evils' could continue to exist in a society in which there was a considerable degree of Christian enlightenment. We have also noted his concern for racial justice in Jamaica, and for the dignity of women in India. Arthur was of the opinion that in a fundamentally uneven struggle between the powerful and powerless, the place of a Christian – if a choice has to be made – is 'beside him with whom he will share reproach not praise'. This position comes close to today's growing consensus among Christians that God has a 'preferential option for the poor'.[12]

This study has said little about Africa, due to the late entry of Irish Methodists into that continent. McKenny was the exception to this. Among those who served in South Africa towards the end of the nineteenth century was Fuller Appelbe, who exemplifies the statement in *Mission and Evangelism*, that 'the Church claims the right and duty . . . to address itself openly to issues of human concern'.[13] Appelbe resisted pressures to limit religion to private life. A close adviser to Chief Montsioa of the Baralong people, he sided with them at Mafeking in 1887, complaining that the close liaison between white settlers and the Bechuanaland Border Police was contrary to the interests of the native peoples. Seven years later he chaired a public meeting in a Methodist church in Johannesburg, at which a resolution was passed criticizing governmental action in suppressing the Malaboch people. In 1895, when the Bechuanaland territories were annexed to the Cape Colony, Appelbe lent his support to a delegation of Baralong representatives who visited London to lobby parliament. The deputation had not received total clearance from the South African authorities, and Appelbe was therefore criticized by the Missionary Committee. Of his ministry, these words from *Mission and Evangelism* are peculiarly appropriate:

> We must re-learn the . . . lesson that the Church is the mouth and voice of the poor and the oppressed in the presence of the powers that be. In our own way we must learn once again 'how to speak to the ear of the King', on the people's behalf.[24]

Inevitably those who take initiatives of this kind will, like Appelbe, have their judgment called into question and will give offence. At such times, however, there will be a special ring of truth about their witness.

Missionaries have often been accused, not always without cause, of being the handmaids of white imperialism. The contrast in some areas between the pace of political advance by the colonial power and the relatively slow response to evangelism, and the record of missionary opposition to the policies and practices of colonial governments, are a necessary corrective to this view.

Minority in Mission

It is as a religious minority that Irish Methodism makes its boldest claim with regard to mission: that, under God, its greatest strength as a movement lies in its weakness. Groups which, from a human point of view, are small, weak and un-impressive are uniquely well placed to play an important part in the life of the church and its witness to the world. So long as they are saved from selfish and destructive introversion, and abandon pretence to the trappings of power, they are free simply to be obedient to God in mission. 'Poor ourselves, we bring wealth to many; penniless, we own the world' (II Corinthians 6.10, NEB). When Methodism in Ireland has truly been itself, it has done its best work both within Ireland and beyond. Slender and struggling, it has yet been fruitful, a small lamp on a lamp-stand, a little yeast in a much larger lump. In particular Irish people have taken significant initiatives, carrying the gospel to new areas. Through emigration, especially, they have underlined the importance of family life and vital faith in forming new communities. In presenting Christ they have been faithful to the central tenets of the historic faith.

Christians in China have recently been making a similar discovery. Freed from the burden of the wrong kind of Western support, it has been easier for them to be genuinely Chinese while Christian, materially weaker yet spiritually stronger. They have become a sign of protest against an uncaring bureaucracy, a protest of the spirit, for the humble and powerless, against the claim that people live by bread alone. There are still dangers: the temptation gradually to assume the power of the powerful, or to give up protest and resign oneself to the impotence of the powerless. There is also a danger of not taking one's place within the world church through fear of corruption or persecution.

With the loss of traditional influence through the break-up of Christendom and the spread of secularism, there is a challenge here to the life-style of the church in the west. Mission, in the words of *Mission and Evangelism*, should always be 'in Christ's way', expressed through the self-emptying of the servant. It continues:

> An imperialistic crusader's spirit was foreign to him ... In all communications of the Gospel, power must be subordinate to love ... *Often the primary confessors are precisely the non-publicized, unsensational people who gather together steadfastly in small, caring communities, whose life prompts the question: 'What is the source of the meaning of your life? What is the power of your powerlessness?'* ... How often Christ is confessed in the very silence of a prison cell or a restricted but serving, waiting, praying church.[15]

Partners in Mission

Christians and churches are called to be partners in mission throughout the world. Arthur recognized this when he wrote on the threshold of the twentieth century:

> Seeing that the mission work is one and its impelling force one in every corner of the earth, why should not the cry of The Whole World for Christ! rise out of the hearts of all His followers at home and abroad ... Why should not the whole host of disciples in London cry, All England for Christ, and all the world for Christ, and those in Lakemba re-echo, All Fiji for Christ, and all the world for Christ?[16]

The WMMS had this kind of development in mind when it sought to create churches overseas which were able to assume responsibility for witness in their own areas. The encouragement of local congregations, native ministers, and sharing of the financial burdens of mission were all aspects of this. As McArthur declared to the WMMS in 1869:

It is impossible that England can send out men to all the various stations in the world. Let us, when we start a Mission, try and support that Mission for some time; but then follow the example of the Apostles, who, when they planted churches among the heathen, ordained Elders in every city, and themselves went forward to preach Christ where Christ had not been known ... We should now try and make our elder Societies self-supporting.[17]

Even more strikingly, McArthur quoted on the same occasion what John Kilner, one of the missionary secretaries, had written about progress overseas:

I mean real growth, not mere accumulation. Do you understand me? I mean increase of intelligent grasp of church relationships and obligations, spontaneous effort for general good and self-sacrifice, as contrasted with the too long tolerated dependency on foreign brains, on foreign zeal, and on foreign funds ... I feel as though we, as a Mission, had done more, if we innoculate one mind with these principles, than if a dozen converts, so called, were made to hang lovingly and lazily on the neck of the Mission in sickly infantile imbecility.

Since the founding of local and national Churches overseas has been the official policy of the WMMS, and was expressed in the formation of affiliated Methodist Conferences, it is all the more difficult to understand why partnership between Britain and Ireland did not progress towards maturity at a much quicker pace. As we have already observed, even by the end of the nineteenth century Ireland was still denied any real say in the making of WMMS policy, and the terms under which the Irish were allowed to serve overseas were far from satisfactory. In this connection, the system whereby successive British Presidents continue to chair the annual Conference of the Methodist Church in Ireland is a curious legacy from the past. If it can be justified at all, it is solely on the grounds of maintaining a unique historical tradition within world Methodism, since the British and Irish Conferences were the only ones founded, and presided over, by Wesley himself. The fact that the system prevents Irish Methodists from assuming full responsibility for their own affairs, and from being seen to do so, is, however, a telling argument against it.

Right relationships – between churches, and between missionaries, their sending bodies and the churches in which they serve – have always been a significant factor in effective mission. What *Mission and Evangelism* describes as 'the loosening of the bond of domination and dependence'[18] becomes vitally important if churches in the northern and southern hemispheres are to become effective partners in mission.

Failure in Mission

Mission sometimes fails because the aims in relation to particular aspects of the work are unattainable. One is reminded of McKenny's insistence that the hope entertained by the WMMS that Ceylon could quickly become financially self-supporting was unrealistic. At other times the situation was seriously misread overseas, as for example by McKenny in Ceylon when he assumed that Buddhism would quickly disintegrate and fade, at least locally, under attack from Christianity. Both in London and overseas there was a frequent failure to come to terms with the complexities of alien cultures and the degree to which other faiths were an integral part of their make-up. Butler's lack of respect for Islam, and an instance of cultural superiority by McKenny, are other examples of this, as was the inability of those involved in the mission among aborigines in New South Wales to make any real impact in the early 1840s. As we have also seen, Lynch's probing questions about the nature and form of Hinduism in Madras, and whether genuine worship was taking place, were quickly brushed aside by the WMMS. In general the early missionaries and the Committee in London simply did not grasp the strength or religious significance of other faiths or cultures. Neither did they understand the inevitable restrictions which result from local conditions such as linguistic and climatic differences. The policy of itinerancy which was so familiar in British and Irish Methodism, proved to be very damaging when applied to Ceylon in the early years. It imposed great strains on the health of missionaries and entailed excessive expense on account of travel and the multiplication of mission houses, chapels and schools.

Here is certainly one point at which the contrast between what we have found in our historical study and what is recommended in *Mission and Evangelism* is indeed considerable. The Report calls for a clear confession of Jesus Christ in a way that still gives respect to the followers of other faiths and takes their cultural setting seriously.

At another level, mission is more authentic when mistakes are openly acknowledged and are used as the raw material for fresh discovery. Butler's unsuccessful attempt to create a Christian model village, Wesleypore, was a cause of embarrassment and awkwardness rather than of learning and instruction. This was inevitable given Butler's style. It reflects, in the words of *Mission and Evangelism*, more the imperialistic crusader than the self-emptying servant. Butler was in the business of winning victories. Defeat came hard, and was seen in wholly negative terms. Mission, however, should be in Christ's way. He shared the hopes and sufferings of humanity, died on the cross, and was raised. The failure of bold imaginative experiments may in the end bring us closer to the mind of Christ, than the success of predictable achievement. This challenge is stated in *Mission and Evangelism*:

> Mission calls for a serving church in every land, a church which is willing to be marked with the stigmata (nailmarks) of the crucified and risen Lord. In this way the church will show that it belongs to that movement of God's love shown in Christ who went to the periphery of life. Dying outside the gates of the city (Heb. 13.12) he is the high priest offering himself for the salvation of the world. Outside the city gates the message of a self-giving, sharing love is truly proclaimed, here the Church renews its vocation to be the body of Christ in joyful fellowship with its risen Lord (I John 3.16).[19]

Receiving in Mission

Irish Methodism has benefited greatly through involvement in the world church. It has received financial support from Britain and America, but money has been the least of the benefits. It has also benefited in many other ways more difficult to define. Its horizons have been extended, its awareness of issues sharpened, and its inner life renewed. Saved from the selfishness which destroys, it has been enabled to experience a fuller and more responsible life. Editorials in the *Irish Christian Advocate* have drawn attention to this aspect of mission. In 1884 it was stated that overseas Missionary Anniversaries

> stir the spiritual pulse of our churches, they deepen our sense of obligation for home privileges, they help to counteract an ever growing tendency to selfishness, they lift our thoughts to higher altitudes of duty, and they diffuse valuable information in a most popular form concerning the condition and fortunes of our common race.[20]

Ten years later another editorial stressed the importance of overseas missions from the point of view of the church in Ireland, claiming that:

> The foreign Missionary enterprise is essential to the prosperity of the work of God at home It does not sap our strength, but acts as a spiritual tonic, preparing the churches for the more vigorous prosecution of the work at home . . . We are ever in danger of becoming contracted in our views and sympathies, and even in matters spiritual, we need to be lifted out of our insularity.[21]

Faith and Patience Repaid

Once, when complaints were made to John Wesley that he was spending too much time in Ireland, he replied, 'Have patience, and Ireland will repay you.'[22] Later, when the saintly and scholarly Thomas Walsh was converted and became a leading

Methodist preacher, it was remarked that Wesley's faith had been vindicated. This history of Ireland's involvement in world Methodism is further rich testimony to the validity of Wesley's faith and patience.

APPENDIX
Irish-born Methodist Ministers and Probationers in Canada

Notes

1. Abbreviations used in this list of Irish-born Methodist ministers in Canada are as follows:

BC	Bible Christian	PM	Primitive Methodist
MEC	Methodist Episcopal	P.Wes.	Primitive Wesleyan (in Ireland)
MNC	Methodist New Con- nexion	Wes.	Wesleyan

2. These abbreviations can be somewhat misleading, since there was at times more than one branch of Methodism in Canada with a similar name. Nonetheless, used with care and taken especially with the year in which a person entered the ministry, they will facilitate further research.

3. Laurence Coughlan is omitted because he was not a Methodist minister while in Newfoundland, and Henry Ryan because he was probably born in the United States. Others with strong Irish associations have been omitted for similar reasons.

4. In 1874 a union took place involving two Wesleyan Conferences (Canada and Eastern British America) and the Methodist New Connexion Conference. The resultant body was designated the Methodist Church of Canada. In 1884 this Church and the Methodist Episcopal, Primitive Methodist and Bible Christian Churches in Canada united to bring almost all the Methodists of the nation within a single denomination known simply as the Methodist Church. Against this background the year of entry only is indicated for those who became ministers from 1874 onwards.

5. The main sources of information in compiling this list have been biographical files in the Archives of the United Church of Canada in Toronto, which often contain extracts from Conference Minutes; and G. H. Cornish's *Cyclopaedia of Methodism in Canada* (Toronto, 1881).

Where the information in Cornish and in the Conference Minutes
diverges, the Minutes are followed.

Name	Year of entry into Canada or USA	Branch of Methodism with year of entry into ministry		Year of death
Aikens, James	1792	MEC,	1801	1823
Allen, James		Wes.,	1869	1918
Anderson, Alexander		MNC,	1835	
Argue, Thomas	c. 1848	MEC,	1861	1902
Armstrong, Alexander		MNC,	1844	
Armstrong, Andrew	1837	Wes.,	1854	1890
Armstrong, James	1837	Wes.,	1845	1875
Armstrong, John		MEC,	1828	1889
Armstrong, John B.	1834	Wes.,	1849	1920
Armstrong, Noble	1837	Wes.,	1848	
Atkinson, Thomas	c. 1825	MEC,	1852	1874
Bailey, John	1807	MEC,	1830	1863
Bailie, Robert	c. 1888		1889	1891
Bamford, Robert		MEC,	1824	
Barry, John	1833	Wes.,	1825	1838
Bartley, Thomas			1882	1919
Barton, King	1830	Wes.,	1806	1834
Baskerville, James	1846	MNC,	1850	1891
Beatty, John	1807	MEC,	1826	1864
Bell, James	1831	MNC,	1834	1879
Bell, Thomas	1842	Wes.,	1858	1900
Belton, Samuel		MEC,	1817	1861
Beynon, George	c. 1820	Wes.,	1840	1891
Bird, William		MEC,	1837	1896
Black, John	1820	MEC,	1824	1867
Blackstock, Moses		MNC,	1835	1873
Bothwell, William	1822	MNC,	1844	1882
Boyd, John H.	1851	Wes.,	1839	
Boyle, Robert		PM,	1845	1896
Bredin, John	1841	Wes.,	1842	1891
Brennan, James		MNC,	1831	1866

Name	Year of entry into Canada or USA	Branch of Methodism with year of entry into ministry		Year of death
Briggs, William	1859	Wes.,	1859	1922
Brock, James		MEC,	1830	1900
Brock, Thomas	1842	Wes.,	1858	1886
Broley, James	1837	Wes.,	1857	1890
Brown, George	1858	MNC,	1857	1907
Brown, Robert	1819	MEC,	1849	1863
Bryers, William	c. 1849	Wes.,	1853	1909
Buckley, James	1820	Wes.,	1835	1890
Burch, Thomas	1803	MEC,	1805	1849
Burns, Alexander	1847	Wes.,	1860	1900
Byers, Henry		Wes.,	1838	1890
Byrne, Alexander S.	1849	Wes.,	1848	1851
Byrne, Claudius	1849	Wes.,	1824	1876
Campbell, Alexander	1845	Wes.,	1846	1865
Campbell, Thomas	late 1820's	Wes.,	1836	1866
Campbell, Thomas	1867	Wes.,	1864	1914
Cantelon, David	1840's	BC,	1855	1872
Carson, Robert	1854	MEC,	1866	1912
Carter, Robert		MNC,	1860	
Cassidy, John		Wes.,	1856	1899
Chambers, Alexander C.		Wes.,	1868	1889
Chambers, Andrew B.	c. 1847	Wes.,	1868	1926
Clark, Andrew	c. 1840	MNC,	1854	1900
Clarke, Edward J.	1853		1878	1900
Clarke, John S.	c. 1850	Wes.,	1854	1907
Clarke, Richard	c. 1841	Wes.,	1851	1890
Clarke, Thomas R.	1853		1875	1929
Coburn, James	1871			1925
Cochran, George	c. 1834	Wes.,	1854	1901
Connor, Matthew		Wes.,	1840	
Cook, William H.		Wes.,	1870	1908
Cooney, Robert	1824	Wes.,	1831	1870
Cooper, Edward		MEC,	1810	

Name	Year of entry into Canada or USA	Branch of Methodism with year of entry into ministry		Year of death
Creighton, Kennedy	1834	MNC,	1836	1892
Creighton, William	1849	Wes.,	1850	1883
Cross, William		Wes.,	1856	1905
Culbert, Thomas	c. 1833	Wes.,	1850	1887
Cullen, Thomas	c. 1846	Wes.,	1861	1895
Darlington, Robert	1833	Wes.,	1840	1881
Davidson, John C.		MEC,	1827	
Davis, William	1854	BC,	1873	1880
Dawson, William	1864	P.Wes.		1884
Dewart, E. Hartley	c. 1834	Wes.,	1851	1903
Dickson, George N. A. F. T.	1847	Wes.,	1851	1887
Dignan, William	1839	Wes.,	1840	1864
Dixon, Trueman		MEC,	1818	
Douglas, Richardson		Wes.,	1829	
Dowler, John A.		Wes.,	1854	1902
Duke, Richard	1876	Wes.,	1869	1929
Elliott, James	1830	Wes.,	1841	1892
Ellis, John	1858		1858	1877
Ellis, William	1808	Wes.,	1808	1837
Evans, John S.	c. 1845	Wes.,	1847	1887
Farr, George		MEC,	1821	
Ferguson, George	1812	MEC,	1816	1851
Finn, Francis M.	1848	MEC,	1855	1907
Fish, Henry A.			1890	1923
Flanagan, John	c. 1827	Wes.,	1835	
Flinn, John			1843	
Gaddis, James		MNC,	1852	1892
Gardiner, James	1827	MEC,	1841	1909
Gilpin, John W.	c. 1842	PM,	1865	1905
Glass, William		Wes.,	1845	
Godfrey, Robert		Wes.,	1860	1917
Gordon, Andrew		BC,	1850	1922
Graham, James	c. 1844	Wes.,	1859	1896
Graham, Robert	1842	Wes.,	1850	1868

Name	Year of entry into Canada or USA	Branch of Methodism with year of entry into ministry		Year of death
Graham, William	c. 1847	MEC,		
			c. 1834	1872
Grandy, Thomas		MNC,	1872	1923
Gray, James		Wes.,	1846	1892
Green, Alexander T.	1821	Wes.,	1845	1910
Gundy, James	1842	MNC,	1859	1897
Gundy, John J.		Wes.,	1843	
Gundy, Joseph R.		MNC,	1859	1916
Gundy, Samuel B.	1842	MNC,	1853	1873
Gundy, William	1842	MNC,	1849	1871
Hamilton, Christopher	1845	Wes.,	1856	1904
Hamilton, Thomas	1832	MNC,	1859	1881
Hanna, Thomas	1820	Wes.,	1845	1889
Hassard, Richard	1859	PM,	1860	1909
Hetherington, John P.	1828	P.Wes.,	1827	1861
Hewitt, Robert	1880	Wes.,	1838	1892
Heyland, Edward		MEC,		
			c. 1825	1826
Heyland, Rowley		MEC,	1823	1873
Hill, Henry E.		Wes.,	1871	1903
Hill, Joseph	1831	Wes.,	1845	1897
Holmes, John	c. 1849	Wes.,	1860	1898
Holmes, Joseph W.	1862	Wes.,	1863	1918
Hughes, James	1830	Wes.,	1839	1895
Hughes, James	1847	BC,	1858	1862
Hunt, Francis	c. 1830	MNC,	1842	1893
Huston, John H.		MEC,	1827	1851
Hutchinson, James		Wes.,	1840	
Irwin, Robert F.	1892	Wes., c. 1892		1943
Irwin, William		Wes.,	1857	1879
Jackson, George	c. 1862	MNC,	1866	1919
Jackson, Thomas	c. 1850's	MNC,	1860	1915
Jeffers, Robert		MEC,	1818	1838
Jeffers, Thomas		Wes.,	1841	1871

Name	Year of entry into Canada or USA	Branch of Methodism with year of entry into ministry		Year of death
Jeffers, Wellington	c. 1850	Wes.,	1837	1896
Johnston, Edward	1817	Wes.,	1809	1858
Kerr, John L.	1852	Wes.,	1852	1898
Knowlan, James	1808	Wes.,	1806	1845
Laird, John G.		Wes.,	1848	1897
Lang, Matthew	1823	Wes.,	1823	1850
Law, John	1831	Wes.,	1833	1868
Lawerence, John	1852	MEC,	1870	1911
Lawrence, George	c. 1825	MEC,	1844	1904
Leith, Hamilton		MNC,	1860	1901
Lester, Alexander	1843	Wes.,	1861	1870
Likely, John B.	1851	Wes.,	1858	
Locke, John			1881	1935
Lowry, John	1800	Wes.,	1799	
Lynch, John		MEC,	1867	1885
McAlister, James		MNC,	1849	1902
McCann, William	c. 1854	MNC,	1864	1882
McCappin, John	1861	P.Wes.,	1857	
McClung, James	1842	Wes.,	1863	1916
McClure, William	1847	MNC,	1830	1871
McCullough, William	1834	Wes.,	1840	1879
McDonagh, William	1846	Wes.,	1852	1915
McDowell, David C.	c. 1835	Wes.,	1846	1898
McDowell, Henry	c. 1835	Wes.,	1851	1908
McDowell, Samuel	1808	Wes.,	1808	1855
McFadden, William	c. 1817	Wes.,	1832	1885
McGeary, John	1785	Wes.,	1782	
McGuire, John		MNC,	1856	1879
McMullen, Thomas	c. 1823	Wes.,	1833	1881
McMurray, John	1819	Wes.,	1833	1890
McNamara, George	1848	Wes.,	1857	1877
Mahan, John		Wes.,	1867	1917
Manley, John G.	1829	Wes.,	1834	1908
Might, Samuel		Wes.,	1859	1917

Name	Year of entry into Canada or USA	Branch of Methodism with year of entry into ministry		Year of death
Miller, George	1815	Wes.,	1817	1869
Milliken, Andrew	c. 1850	Wes.,	1856	1891
Milliken, Robert	1882		1889	1946
Mills, John	c. 1848	Wes.,	1851	1907
Mitchel, James		MEC,	1806	1859
Montgomery, Hugh		Wes.,	1835	
Morrow, Edward		Wes.,	1862	1918
Morton, William	c. 1821	Wes.,	1842	1891
Neelands, John		Wes.,	1840	1864
Norris, James		MEC,	1827	1884
Norton, William		Wes.,	1855	1901
O'Hara, James		MNC,	1861	1920
Patchell, Thomas H.		Wes.,	1871	
Pattyson, William M.	1840	Wes.,	1846	1890
Pearson, Marmaduke L.	1850	Wes.,	1862	1915
Phillips, Robert		Wes.,	1868	1902
Poole, George		MEC,	1827	1853
Poole, Jacob		MEC,	1823	1884
Poole, William H.	1831	Wes.,	1846	1896
Potts, John	1855	Wes.,	1857	1907
Ragan, John	1783	Wes.,	1789	1797
Reid, Henry	1840	Wes.,	1846	1882
Reid, Thomas	1831	MNC,	1846	1892
Remmington, John	1804	Wes.,	1802	1838
Rennie, Thomas		MNC,	1870	1916
Richey, Matthew	1820	Wes.,	1821	1883
Robinson, Richard	1825	P.Wes.,	1816	1854
Robinson, Robert	1844	Wes.,	1844	1890
Rollins, William	1864	BC,	1874	1928
Rolston, David D.	c. 1847	MNC,	1846	1914
Rutledge, William L.	c. 1857	Wes.,	1870	1927
Ryan, David	c. 1846	Wes.,	1859	1915
Sadler, Mitchell	1825		1884	1905
Sanderson, John	1831	MNC,	1835	1880

Name	Year of entry into Canada or USA	Branch of Methodism with year of entry into ministry		Year of death
Sanderson, William	1831		c. 1865	1915
Scott, James	1843	MNC,	1852	1886
Scott, James		Wes.,	1872	
Scott, John	1851	Wes.,	1857	1875
Seymour, James	1858	MNC,	1830	1881
Seymour, James C.	1857	MNC,	1857	1902
Shannon, William	1850	Wes.,	1855	1897
Shaw, William H.	1849	MEC,	1858	1912
Sherlock, Benjamin	c. 1850	Wes.,	1858	1909
Shortt, William K.	1869	Wes.,	1872	1923
Smiley, John	1846	Wes.,	1865	1896
Somerville, William W.	1872		1880	1917
Sparling, Philip	1848	MEC,	1866	1896
Stevenson, John C.	1870	Wes.,	1870	1928
Stewart, John	1850	Wes.,	1862	1898
Stoney, Edmund	1818	MEC,	1823	1862
Taylor, Andrew	1835	Wes.,	1796	1841
Tuke, Michael	c. 1808	MEC,	1821	1870
Turner, James	1870	Wes.,	1870	1916
Visser, A. Herman			1880	1915
Walker, John	1830	MNC,	1854	1898
Washington, George	1848	PM,	1819	1887
Webster, Thomas	c. 1812	MEC,	1838	1900
White, James	1842	MNC,	1859	1893
Williams, David	1852	Wes.,	1867	1882
Willoughby, William	1821	Wes.,	1836	1890
Wilson, James	1816	MEC,	1817	1851
Wilson, John V.	1826	Wes.,	1854	1900
Wilson, Samuel	1831	Wes.,	1857	1911

BIBLIOGRAPHY AND SOURCES

This book is largely based on previously unpublished material, or on publications out of print and difficult to obtain. These can be consulted at Methodist archival collections in London (School of Oriental and African Studies); Belfast (Irish Branch of the Wesley Historical Society, Aldersgate House); and Toronto (United Church of Canada); or at the British Library.

In references to collections of Archives the following abbreviations are used:

MMSA   The Overseas Division of the Methodist Church (Methodist Missionary Society), held in London

UMCA   The United Methodist Church (USA), held at Madison, N.J.

IWHSA   The Irish Branch of the Wesley Historical Society, Belfast

When a reference relates to MMSA material, the number given in brackets at the end refers to the box number in the archival collection at the School of Oriental and African Studies, London.

An extensive list of material, published and unpublished, is contained in the author's thesis, 'The Irish Factor in World Methodism in the Eighteenth and Nineteenth Centuries' (Queen's University, Belfast, 1981).

The most recent general account of Methodist missions is that by N. A. Birtwhistle in the first chapter of R. Davies, A. R. George, G. Rupp (edd.), *A History of the Methodist Church in Great Britain*, Epworth Press, London 1983, iii, pp. 1–116.

NOTES

Preface

1. R. Davies, A. R. George, G. Rupp (edd.), *A History of the Methodist Church in Great Britain*, London 1983, iii, p. 29.
2. Quoted in W. J. Townsend, H. B. Workman, G. Eayrs (edd.), *A New History of Methodism*, London 1909, ii, p. 35. Arthur was here applying to Methodism in Ireland what had been said of Joseph – see Genesis 49.22.
3. *Irish Christian Advocate*, 23 October 1891.
4. *Minutes of Conference*, 1898, Pastoral Address.
5. N. W. Taggart, 'The Irish Factor in World Methodism in the Eighteenth and Nineteenth Centuries' (Ph.D. thesis, Queen's University, Belfast, 1981).

1. The Irish and Methodism's World Outreach

1. A. Clarke, *Memoirs of the Wesley Family*, New York 1848, p. 168.
2. M. Edwards, *Family Circle*, London 1949, p. 29.
3. J. Telford (ed.), *The Letters of John Wesley*, London 1931, i, p. 188.
4. Telford (ed.), op. cit. i, p. 190.
5. N. Curnock (ed.), *The Journal of John Wesley*, London 1909, i, p. 418.
6. G. G. Findlay and W. W. Holdsworth, *The History of the Wesleyan Methodist Missionary Society*, London 1921, i, p. 31.
7. *Irish Evangelist*, April 1866, pp. 47f.
8. A. Stevens, *History of the Methodist Episcopal Church*, New York 1865, i, p. 48.
9. This is quoted in the chapter on Canada, p. 68.
10. R. Carwardine, *Transatlantic Revivalism*, Connecticut and London 1978, pp. 33f.
11. S. Gregg, *The History of Methodism within the Bounds of the Erie Conference*, New York 1865, i, p. 211.
12. C. Elliott, *Slavery Contrary to the Spirit of Christianity*, New York, n.d., p. 2.
13. *Christian Guardian*, 29 November 1865.
14. *Irish Christian Advocate*, 21 March 1902, p. 142.
15. Ibid., 3 April 1903, p. 161.
16. IWHSA MSS, Hibernian Auxiliary Minute Book, 11 January 1888.
17. *Irish Christian Advocate*, 8 March 1895.
18. MMSA MSS, W. A. Darby, 26 May 1838 (660).

19. *Irish Evangelist*, March 1868, article entitled 'One Methodist Conference for the United Kingdom'.
20. MMSA MSS, J. Wiggins, 23 March 1821 (74).
21. *Irish Christian Advocate*, 1 April 1898. Webster worked in India from 1887.
22. Ibid., 31 May 1895.
23. Ibid., 17 May 1895.

2. The Missionary Society – Helping or Hindering Mission?

1. *Proceedings of the Wesley Historical Society*, xxx, June 1955, p. 28.
2. T. Coke, *Address to the Pious and Benevolent*, quoted in J. Vickers, *Thomas Coke, Apostle of Methodism*, London and Nashville 1969, p. 138.
3. *Missionary Notices*, 3rd series vii, 25 June 1860, pp. 134f.
4. *Occasional Papers* of the Ladies Auxiliary of the WMMS, MMSA, i (1859–1867), p. 538; ii (1868–1874), pp. 363f.
5. *Missionary Notices*, xiv (new series vi), June and July 1848, p. 103.
6. Ibid., February 1896, p. 18.
7. MMSA MSS, Bunting, Taylor, Watson to Irish Conference, 1 July 1819 (22).
8. *Irish Christian Advocate*, 19 November 1954.
9. MMSA MSS, Kilner to McKee, 30 October 1882 (38).
10. MMSA MSS, Missionary Committee, 25 October 1816, p. 9 (546).
11. W. Reilly, *An Answer to Several Charges*, Cork 1822, p. 7.
12. Ibid. p. 12.
13. MMSA MSS, Morley to Doolittle, 1 September 1824 (24).
14. MMSA MSS, R. Huston, 30 May 1842; Huston with Pilcher to Hoole, 30 November 1859 (76).
15. *Irish Christian Advocate*, 29 April 1898.
16. Ibid., W. Lumley, 1 July 1898.
17. MMSA MSS, Hartley to Nicholas, 30 August 1900 (38).
18. A. McCrea (ed.), *Irish Methodism in the Twentieth Century*, Belfast 1931, p. 101; F. Jeffery, *Irish Methodism*, Belfast 1964, pp. 61f.
19. MMSA MSS, P. Ffrench, 18 June 1828 (75).
20. MMSA MSS, Minutes of Antigua District Meeting, 31 January 1825.
21. *Irish Evangelist*, March 1868, p. 29.
22. Palestine was the country under consideration. See *Irish Christian Advocate*, 31 May 1895.
23. Ibid., 21 September 1906, p. 446.
24. Ibid., 28 October 1898.

3. Emigration – Losses and Gains

1. *Irish Evangelist*, July 1867, p. 74.
2. G. O'Tuothaigh, *Ireland before the Famine*, Dublin 1972, p. 141.
3. D. Fitzpatrick, *Irish Emigration 1801–1921*, Dublin 1984, p. 3.
4. J. Lee, *The Modernisation of Irish Society*, Dublin 1973, p. 6.
5. Fitzpatrick, op. cit., p. 1.

6. Curnock (ed.), *The Journal of John Wesley*, v, p. 131.

7. Minutes of Conference, 1818.

8. (*a*) The figures in the Table relate to membership. A distinction is made within Methodism between those people who, by defined procedures, become 'members' and those who are regarded as 'adherents'. The total Methodist community, as revealed for example in public census returns, is much larger than the figure for membership. The former includes both members and adherents. (*b*) The figures refer to Wesleyan Methodists only in the period before 1878. Thereafter they are combined figures for both Wesleyans and Primitive Wesleyans.

9. *Missionary Notices*, xiii (new series v), June and July 1847, p. 126.

10. Minutes of Conference, 1886, Pastoral Address. This illustrates what Fitzpatrick has pointed out concerning Irish emigration in the second half of the nineteenth century. There was a significant concentration in the narrow age-band of those who had just entered the employment market and were about to enter the marriage market. Another feature was the even balance between the sexes (Fitzpatrick, op. cit., p. 8).

11. WMMS Annual Report, 1870, p. 106.

12. W. F. Adams, *Ireland and Irish Emigration to the New World*, New Haven, Conn. 1932, pp. 129ff.

13. O'Tuothaigh, op. cit., pp. 16f.

14. Adams, op. cit., p. 2.

15. These two paragraphs are based on material contained in Fitzpatrick, op. cit., especially pp. 21, 29, 31f.

16. *Missionary Notices*, xiii (new series v), June and July 1847, p. 126.

17. WMMS Annual Report, 1863, p. 163.

18. *Irish Evangelist*, 1 February 1872, p. 20.

19. D. Hempton, *Methodism and Politics in British Society 1750–1850*, London 1984, pp. 116ff., 179ff.

20. Ibid., p. 37.

21. W. Crook, *Ireland and the Centenary of American Methodism*, London 1866, p. 31.

22. Minutes of Conference, 1827, Address to British Conference.

23. Ibid., 1841, Reply by British Conference.

24. J. Ker, *The Clarke Memorial Church, Portrush*, Glasgow 1887, p. 28.

25. *Irish Christian Advocate*, 24 April 1885, p. 202.

26. Ibid., 17 July 1885, p. 589.

27. MMSA MSS, 16 August 1839 (516).

28. *Irish Christian Advocate*, 31 August 1883, p. 564.

29. Ibid., 8 January 1886, p. 16.

30. Ibid., 5 May 1887, p. 207.

31. Findlay and Holdsworth, *The History of the Wesleyan Methodist Missionary Society*, iii, p. 94.

4. *The Laity, Primary Agents of Mission*

1. *Missionary Notices*, 3rd series iii, February 1856, pp. 17f.

2. F. Baker in A. Godbold (ed.), *Forever Beginning 1766–1966*, Lake

Junaluska, 1967, p. 172. The exception was Captain Thomas Webb.

3. *Methodist History*, iv, no. 2, January 1966, p. 7.

4. A. Stevens, *A Compendious History of American Methodism*, London 1885, p. 37.

5. K. A. Gottry, *200th Anniversary of the Cambridge–Ashgrove ME Church*, Cambridge, N.Y. (?1970), p. 7.

6. *Methodist History*, xvi, no. 2, January 1978, pp. 104ff.

7. McCrea (ed.), *Irish Methodism in the Twentieth Century*, p. 100.

8. *Historical Studies – Australia and New Zealand*, no. 40, Melbourne 1963, pp. 431ff.

9. MMSA MSS, E. Eagar, 20 June 1812 (514).

10. J. S. Udy, *Living Stones*, Sydney 1974, p. 167.

11. T. McCullagh, *Sir William McArthur*, London 1891, p. 105.

12. Ibid., p. 106.

13. Ibid., p. 103.

14. Ibid., p. 132.

15. Ibid., p. 179.

16. *Missionary Notices*, 4th series viii, June and July 1876, p. 148.

17. McCullagh, op. cit., p. 332.

18. Ibid., p. 357.

19. MMSA MSS, Emfundesweni Circuit Report, 1881 (343).

20. MMSA, WW Minute Book, 9 October 1894 (1105).

21. A. M. Wood, *A Corner of Cathay*, MMSA, MMS Library, G 533, p. 5.

22. A. M. Wood, *Woman's Call to Woman*, MMSA, MMS Library, G 532, p. 4.

23. A. M. Wood, *A Corner of Cathay*, p. 13.

24. Ibid., p. 23.

25. Ibid., p. 9.

26. Ibid., p. 16.

27. A. M. Wood, *Woman's Call to Woman*, p. 1.

5. *Canadian Case Study*

1. W. Crook, *Ireland and the Centenary of American Methodism*, p. 190.

2. *The Journal* of the Canadian Church Historical Society, ii, no. 3, May 1955.

3. *The Canada Year Book, 1912*, Ottawa 1913, pp. 23, 28f.

4. *Christian Guardian*, 26 June 1872.

5. Townsend, Workman and Eayrs (edd.), *A New History of Methodism*, ii, p. 201.

6. These details on Dawson are compiled from several sources. See F. C. Stephenson, *One Hundred Years of Canadian Methodist Missions*, Toronto 1925, pp. 26f.; Findlay and Holdsworth, *History of the Wesleyan Methodist Missionary Society*, i, pp. 310f.; T. W. Smith, *History of the Methodist Church of Eastern British America*, Halifax, N.S., 1877–1890, i, pp. 412f.

7. MMSA MSS, 29 June 1819 (74).

8. J. Carroll, *Case and his Cotemporaries*, Toronto 1867–1877, ii, pp. 322f.

9. Ibid., ii, pp. 365f.

10. Ibid., iii, p. 38.

11. Ibid., iii, p. 274.

12. Ibid., iii, p. 351.

13. Smith, op. cit., ii, pp. 255ff.

14. See Appendix, pp. 194-201.

15. *Christian Guardian*, 28 November 1866.

16. *Irish Christian Advocate*, 15 May 1885.

17. These figures are based on material in G. H. Cornish, *Cyclopaedia of Methodism in Canada*, Toronto 1881. A more detailed examination of the complicated divisions within Canadian Methodism is here inappropriate.

18. J. D. Hoover, 'The Primitive Methodist Church in Canada 1829–1884' (University of Western Ontario, London, Ontario 1970), p. 69.

19. *Irish Christian Advocate*, 19 December 1884, p. 599.

20. Ibid., 20 February 1885, p. 88.

21. J. Woodsworth, *Thirty Years in the Canadian North-West*, Toronto 1917, pp. 220f.

22. P. O'Flaherty, *The Rock Observed*, Toronto 1979, p. 27.

23. W. Wilson, *Newfoundland and its Missionaries*, Cambridge, Mass. 1866, p. 180.

24. MMSA MSS, J. Remmington, 16 July 1805 (91).

25. MMSA MSS, S. McDowell, 9 July 1813 (91).

26. MMSA MSS, W. Ellis, 18 January 1815 (91).

27. MMSA MSS, Ellis, September 1824 (94). The Newfoundland Wesleyans used Wesley's *Sunday Service* until c. 1850.

28. MMSA MSS, Ellis, 26 November 1826 (95).

29. MMSA MSS, Ellis, June 1827 (95).

30. MMSA MSS, Ellis, 12 August 1834 (98).

31. Ibid.

32. MMSA MSS, Ellis, 27 May 1837 (100).

33. Findlay and Holdsworth, op. cit., ii, p. 251.

34. A. Sutherland, *Methodism in Canada*, London 1903, pp. 111f.

35. MMSA MSS, E. Johnston and R. L. Lusher, 19 November 1817 (91).

36. MMSA MSS, Johnston, 27 April 1818 (91).

37. MMSA MSS, Johnston, 28 September 1818 (91).

38. MMSA MSS, Taylor to Johnston, 14 December 1818, pp. 406f. (545).

39. MMSA MSS, General Committee, 27 January 1819, pp. 197–202 (546).

40. MMSA MSS, 29 September 1819 (46).

41. MMSA MSS, Johnston, 24 August 1830 (75).

6. *Adam Clarke and William Arthur – the Theology of Mission*

1. M. Edwards, *Adam Clarke*, London 1942, pp. 44f.

2. Ibid., p. 45.

3. T. B. Stephenson, *William Arthur*, London 1907, p. 54.

4. *Missionary Notices*, ii, March 1819, p. 32.

5. A. Clarke, *A Short Account of the Introduction of the Gospel into the British Isles*, London 1815, p. 31.

6. G. G. Findlay and M. G. Findlay, *Wesley's World Parish*, London 1913, p. 30.

7. This claim, repeated in N. B. Harmon (ed.), *The Encyclopedia of World Methodism*, Nashville 1974, i, p. 517, was denied in 1983 by the Keeper of Egyptian Antiquities at the British Museum, in correspondence with the author.

8. W. Arthur, *A Mission to the Mysore*, ed. H. Haigh, London 1902, pp. 202ff.

9. *Missionary Notices*, ix (new series i), November 1840, p. 387.

10. Ibid., ii, March 1819, p. 35.

11. A. Clarke, *Principles of the Christian Religion*, London 1820, p. 60.

12. Ibid., p. 61.

13. Ibid., p. 60.

14. Ibid., p. 61.

15. A. Clarke, *Clavis Biblica*, London 1820, p. 49.

16. Ibid., p. 50.

17. *Missionary Notices*, ii, March 1819, p. 126.

18. Arthur, *A Mission to the Mysore*, p. vii.

19. Ibid., p. 153.

20. Ibid., p. 34.

21. Ibid., p. 156.

22. Ibid., p. 200.

23. Ibid., p. 193.

24. Ibid., pp. 387, 404f., 407, 413.

25. Ibid., p. 77.

26. Ibid., p. 413.

27. Ibid., p. 245.

28. Ibid., p. 94.

29. Ibid., p. 231.

30. Ibid., p. 217.

31. *Missionary Notices*, ix (new series i), November 1840, p. 386. We shall find that James Lynch commented on idol worship less negatively than Arthur.

32. Clarke, *Clavis Biblica*, p. 50.

33. A. Clarke, *Christian Missions* in *Miscellaneous Works*, London 1837, xiii, p. 75.

34. Clarke, *A Short Account* etc., p. 22.

35. *Missionary Notices*, ii, March 1819, p. 32. In the manuscript edition of the letter the words 'missionary people' are in capitals and are underlined twice – MMSA MSS (628).

36. *Missionary Notices*, iii, March 1821, pp. 33f.

37. The title of a paper read by Arthur in London on 16 October 1888.

38. W. Arthur, *The Tongue of Fire*, London 1885, p. 86.

39. MMSA MSS, A. Clarke, 1 January 1819 (628).

40. *Missionary Notices*, February 1896, p. 19.

41. See above, p. 94.

42. Arthur, *The Tongue of Fire*, p. 96.

43. *Missionary Notices*, ii, April 1820, p. 253.

44. Article by Clarke entitled 'The Necessity and Existence of Missions', *Miscellaneous Works*, xiii, pp. 51ff. (here p. 74).
45. Arthur, *The Tongue of Fire*, pp. 278f.
46. Ibid., p. 125.
47. W. Arthur, *Women's Work in India*, London 1882, p. 75.
48. Clarke to Lewis, 13 January 1825, *Miscellaneous Works*, xiii, pp. 230f.
49. Clarke to Wears, 1826, ibid., p. 260.
50. Clarke to Wears, 6 August 1826, ibid., p. 304.
51. Ibid., pp. 390f.
52. Arthur, *The Tongue of Fire*, p. 133.
53. Ibid., p. 131.
54. Ibid., p. 130. But note his rejection of *individualism* here and on p. 98.
55. Ibid., p. 132.
56. W. Arthur, *The Outbreak in Jamaica*, London 1865, pp. 5f.
57. Ibid., p. 14.
58. Arthur, *A Mission to the Mysore*, p. 263.
59. Ibid., pp. 262f.
60. Arthur, *Women's Work in India*, p. 90. How revealing that the reference is to the effect of a man, rather than a woman, embracing Christianity!
61. Ibid., pp. 75f.

7. *James Lynch – Reluctant Leader*

1. D. Hempton, *Methodism and Politics*, p. 96.
2. MMSA MSS, J. Lynch, 7 October 1815 (443).
3. We have already noted the influence of these missionaries on Susannah Wesley (p. 3 above).
4. MMSA MSS, Lynch, 12 May 1817; 7 October 1817 (432).
5. MMSA MSS, Lynch, 16 June 1829 (75).
6. MMSA MSS, Lynch, 5 September 1816 (443).
7. MMSA MSS, Lynch, 6 December 1816 (443).
8. MMSA MSS, Lynch, 15 November 1815 (443).
9. MMSA MSS, Lynch, 13 March 1818 (432).
10. Ibid.
11. MMSA MSS, Lynch, 23 June 1820 (432).
12. MMSA MSS, Taylor to Lynch, 9 October 1821 (24).
13. MMSA MSS, Lynch, 13 March 1818 (432).
14. MMSA MSS, Taylor to Lynch, 28 October 1818, p. 350 (545).
15. MMSA MSS, Lynch, 9 September 1814 (443).
16. MMSA MSS, Lynch, 29 September 1820 (432).
17. MMSA MSS, Lynch, 19 October 1820 (432).
18. MMSA MSS, Lynch, 5 February 1816, item 51 (443). This important letter survives only in part, and is torn.
19. See p. 99.
20. MMSA MSS, Lynch, 18 June 1816 (22).
21. MMSA MSS, Buckley to Lynch, 23 August 1816 (545).
22. MMSA MSS, Marsden and Watson to Lynch, 29 October 1816 (545).
23. *Missionary Notices*, vi, June 1830, p. 283.

24. MMSA MSS, Lynch, 2 May 1820 (432).
25. MMSA MSS, Lynch, 6 June 1815 (443).
26. MMSA MSS, Lynch, 25 August 1816 (443).
27. MMSA MSS, Lynch, 6 September 1816 (443).
28. MMSA MSS, Lynch, 14 September 1816 (443).
29. MMSA MSS, Lynch, 17 February 1817 (432).
30. MMSA MSS, to Lynch, 22 March 1819 (22).
31. MMSA MSS, to Lynch, 22 May 1821 (24).
32. MMSA MSS, General Committee Minutes, 7 June 1821, p. 282 (546).
33. MMSA MSS, Lynch, 26 May 1821 (432).
34. MMSA MSS, Lynch, 20 June 1821 (432).
35. MMSA MSS, Lynch, 15 July 1822 (432).
36. MMSA MSS, Lynch, 2 August 1822 (432).
37. MMSA MSS, General Committee Minutes, 18 December 1822, p. 4 (547).
38. MMSA MSS, Lynch, 6 June 1815 (443).
39. MMSA MSS, Lynch, 15 November 1815 (443).
40. MMSA MSS, to Lynch, 30 March 1816, p. 189 (545).
41. MMSA MSS, Taylor to Lynch, 22 March 1819 (22).
42. MMSA MSS, Lynch, 6 September 1821 (432).
43. MMSA MSS, Lynch, 1 September 1823 (432).
44. MMSA MSS, Minutes of South Ceylon District, 22 January 1822 (457).
45. Ibid.
46. Correspondence between Lynch and his brother and nephew in America appears in MMSA MSS, box 628. The reference to slavery is in a letter from Millersburgh, 28 July 1837.
47. I Corinthians 1.26–28, RSV.

8. *John McKenny, Pioneer on Three Continents*

1. MMSA MSS, J. McKenny, 31 January 1837 (516).
2. L. A. Hewson, *An Introduction to South African Methodists*, Cape Town 1950, p. 1.
3. MMSA MSS, McKenny, 23 September 1814 (299).
4. MMSA MSS, McKenny, September 1814 (299).
5. MMSA MSS, McKenny, 3 December 1814 (299).
6. MMSA MSS, McKenny, 22 May 1815 (299).
7. MMSA MSS, McKenny, 3 March 1816 (299).
8. MMSA MSS, McKenny, 2 October 1816 (443).
9. Hewson, op. cit., p. 2.
10. MMSA MSS, McKenny, 11 June 1816; 2 October 1816 (443).
11. MMSA MSS, McKenny, 28 May 1817 (443).
12. MMSA MSS, McKenny, 8 December 1821 (444).
13. MMSA MSS, McKenny, 10 January 1831 (447).
14. MMSA, *Minutes of Several Conversations between the Wesleyan Missionaries*, Colombo 1820, p. 132.
15. MMSA MSS, McKenny, 26 September 1831 (447).

16. MMSA MSS, McKenny, 31 January 1832 (447).

17. MMSA MSS, McKenny, 31 July 1834 (447).

18. MMSA, *Minutes of Several Conversations between the Wesleyan Missionaries*, p. 18.

19. *Missionary Notices*, ii, November 1819, p. 166.

20. Ibid, v, January 1828, pp. 385f.

21. MMSA MSS, McKenny, 26 September 1831 (447).

22. MMSA MSS, McKenny, 14 October 1816 (443).

23. MMSA MSS, McKenny, 17 November 1817 (443).

24. MMSA MSS, McKenny, 15 April 1818 (443).

25. MMSA MSS, McKenny, 12 June 1824 (445).

26. *Missionary Notices*, iv, March 1825, pp. 417f.

27. MMSA MSS, McKenny, 29 July 1830 (447).

28. MMSA MSS, McKenny, 5 February 1830 (447).

29. MMSA MSS, McKenny, 28 October 1824 (445).

30. MMSA MSS, Lynch, 29 September 1820 (432).

31. MMSA MSS, McKenny, 29 December 1834 (447).

32. MMSA MSS, McKenny, 28 February 1834 (447).

33. MMSA MSS, General Committee, 9 March 1831 (548).

34. MMSA MSS, Jones and Edwards to Erskine, 15 March 1831 (24).

35. *The Journal of Religious History*, Sydney 1973, p. 236.

36. MMSA MSS, Beecham to McKenny, 9 October 1835 (24).

37. MMSA MSS, McKenny, 2 March 1841 (516).

38. MMSA MSS, McKenny, 1 March 1842 (516).

39. MMSA MSS, McKenny, 30 March 1842 (516).

40. MMSA MSS, McKenny, 21 July 1836 (515).

41. Ibid.

42. Ibid.

43. MMSA MSS, McKenny, 20 July 1838 (516).

44. MMSA MSS, McKenny, 18 August 1838 (516).

45. MMSA MSS, McKenny, 11 October 1838 (516).

46. MMSA MSS, McKenny, 14 February 1839 (516).

47. MMSA MSS, McKenny, 3 May 1843 (517).

48. MMSA MSS, McKenny, 11 October 1838 (516).

49. *Missionary Notices*, ix (new series i), February 1840, p. 240. The author is not named, but it is unlikely that it was anyone other than McKenny.

50. C. H. Crookshank, *History of Methodism in Ireland*, London 1886, ii, p. 167.

51. MMSA MSS, Dr Coke's draft on Irish Missions for the Report of 1806, quoted in Hempton, *Methodism and Politics*, p. 121.

52. MMSA MSS, McKenny, 13 April 1839 (516).

53. MMSA MSS, McKenny, 31 December 1841 (516).

54. MMSA MSS, McKenny, 9 April 1845 (517).

55. MMSA MSS, McKenny, 31 December 1841 (516).

9. *John Barry, Controversialist*

1. *Irish Christian Advocate*, 26 October 1888, p. 518.

2. J. Barry, *A Statement of the Proceedings which have lately Agitated the Methodist Society in Kinsale*, Cork 1819.

3. P. Samuel, *The Wesleyan Methodist Missions in Jamaica and Honduras*, London 1850, p. 121.

4. *Wesleyan Preacher*, London 1832, ii, pp. 98–107.

5. Ibid., p. 101.

6. Samuel, op. cit., p. 302.

7. MMSA MSS, Barry, 4 September 1826 (123).

8. MMSA MSS, Barry, 21 April 1826 (123).

9. Samuel, op. cit., p. 57.

10. MMSA MSS, Barry, 12 January 1833 (98). The union proved to be profoundly disappointing and came to an end in 1840 with bitter recriminations.

11. MMSA MSS, Beecham to Barry, 2 April 1835 (24).

10. *John Barry, Opponent of Slavery*

1. M. Edwards, *John Wesley and the Eighteenth Century*, London 1955, p. 114.

2. *The Works of John Wesley*, third edition, London 1830, xi, pp. 78f.

3. M. Edwards, op. cit., p. 120.

4. J. Telford (ed.), *The Letters of John Wesley*, viii, p. 265.

5. T. Coke, *Extracts of the Journals of Five Visits to America*, London 1793, p. 33.

6. Ibid., p. 35.

7. Ibid., p. 37.

8. Ibid., p. 39.

9. Ibid., p. 40.

10. Ibid., p. 41.

11. Ibid., p. 46.

12. Ibid., p. 69.

13. Ibid., p. 174.

14. J. Vickers, *Thomas Coke – Apostle of Methodism*, p. 170. Coke frequently favoured 'the upper classes'.

15. W. Hammett, *An Impartial Statement of the Known Inconsistencies of the Rev. Dr. Coke*, Charleston 1792, p. 15.

16. See *Methodist History*, x, no. 1, October 1971, p. 41.

17. WMMS *Annual Report*, 1822, p. xii ('Instructions to Missionaries').

18. R. Watson, *The Religious Instruction of the Slaves in the West India Colonies*, London 1824, p. 15.

19. P. Duncan, *A Narrative of the Wesleyan Mission to Jamaica*, London 1849, p. 164.

20. Ibid.

21. Ibid., p. 165.

22. MMSA MSS, Ffrench, 29 July 1820 (115).

23. MMSA MSS, Ffrench, 16 October 1820 (116).

24. MMSA MSS, Ffrench, 26 May 1823 (119).

25. MMSA MSS, Rutledge, 3 January 1817 (113).

26. MMSA MSS, Rutledge, 18 June 1817 (113).

27. MMSA MSS, Barry, 19 April 1828 (126).

28. MMSA MSS, Barry, 14 November 1829 (128).

29. MMSA MSS, Barry, 27 November 1829 (128). The writing of the letter was completed in December.

30. J. Barry, *Letter addressed to the Right Hon. Sir George Murray*, London 1830, p. 25.

31. Ibid., pp. 26f.

32. Ibid., p. 28.

33. *Reports from Committees* (HMSO, 16), Slavery: West India Colonies, xx, 1831–1832, p. 99.

34. Ibid., p. 91.

35. *Missionary Notices*, vii, November 1834, p. 565.

36. R. L. Lusher, *The Last Journey: A Funeral Address* etc., Montreal 1838, p. 35.

37. MMSA MSS, Barry, 22 August 1834 (135).

38. MMSA MSS, Barry, 22 January 1835 (136).

39. Lusher, op. cit., p. 38.

40. Ibid., p. 30.

11. *William Butler, Founder of Two Missions*

1. C. Butler, *William Butler, The Founder of Two Missions*, New York 1902, p. 24.

2. W. Butler, *From Boston to Bareilly and Back*, New York 1885, p. 61.

3. Findlay and Holdsworth, *History of the Wesleyan Methodist Missionary Society*, v, p. 178.

4. *Irish Christian Advocate*, 4 September 1896.

5. W. C. Barclay, *History of Methodist Missions*, New York 1950, iii, p. 450.

6. Ibid., p. 451.

7. Ibid., p. 473.

8. *Report of the Punjab Missionary Conference*, Lodiana 1863, p. 337.

9. N. B. Harmon (ed.), *The Encyclopedia of World Methodism*, i, p. 365.

10. Barclay, op. cit., iii, p. 454.

11. Ibid., p. 473.

12. Ibid., p. 828.

13. W. Butler, op. cit., p. 104.

14. Ibid., p. 283.

15. Ibid., p. 228.

16. Ibid., p. 337.

17. Ibid., p. 341.

18. 44th *Annual Report* of the Missionary Society of the MEC, New York 1863, pp. 20ff.

19. J. H. Messmore, *The Life of Edwin Wallace Parker*, New York 1903, p. 70.

20. Ibid., pp. 75f.

21. W. Butler, op. cit., pp. 167f.

22. Barclay, op. cit., iii, p. 834.

23. 57th *Annual Report* of the Missionary Society of the MEC, New York 1876, p. 143.

24. Barclay, op. cit., iii, p. 834.

25. 57th *Annual Report*, 1876, p. 141.

26. UMCA MSS, Butler to Mission Board, 14 April 1877 (Butler folder).

27. N. B. Harmon (ed.), *Encyclopedia*, i, p. 366.

12. *Mission Yesterday and Today*

1. *Mission and Evangelism: an Ecumenical Affirmation*, WCC, Geneva 1982, reissued BCC, London n.d. [1983]; cit. from p. 6. (Pages 5-29 first appeared in the *International Review of Mission*, LXXI, 1982, pp. 427-51.)

2. Ibid., p. 7.

3. Ibid., p. 10.

4. Ibid., p. 8.

5. MMSA MSS, T. Coke, 31 July 1809 (74).

6. B. Semmel, *The Methodist Revolution*, London 1974. The evidence on which Semmel argues his case is, however, partial and is capable of other interpretations.

7. *Books and Bookmen*, July 1974, p. 14. For a discussion of Semmel's theory see Hempton, *Methodism and Politics*, p. 97; and S. Piggin, 'Halévy Revisited: The Origins of the Wesleyan Methodist Missionary Society etc.' in *The Journal of Imperial and Commonwealth History*, ix, no. 1, October 1980, pp. 17f.

8. Semmel is aware of some of these points, but does not give adequate weight to them.

9. Findlay and Holdsworth, *History*, i, p. 97.

10. *Mission and Evangelism*, p. 21.

11. A. Clarke, *A Short Account of the Introduction of the Gospel into the British Isles*, London 1815, p. 34.

12. *Mission and Evangelism*, p. 19.

13. Ibid., p. 13.

14. Ibid.

15. Ibid., pp. 17f.

16. W. Arthur, *The Twentieth Century in the View of Mission Work and Workers*, London 1899, p. 2.

17. *Missionary Notices*, 4th series i, 25 May 1869, p. 83.

18. *Mission and Evangelism*, p. 23.

19. Ibid., p. 18.

20. *Irish Christian Advocate*, 4 April 1884, pp. 158f.

21. Ibid., 27 April 1894.

22. H. Moore, *Life of the Rev. John Wesley*, 1824-1825, ii, p. 133n.

INDEX

Aborigines, 25, 57, 61, 139f., 144f., 190
Abyssinia, 1
Adam's Cove, 78
Adams, William Forbes, 40, 205
Africa, 6, 33, 63, 130, 186
Agriculture, 176–8, 191
Aikens, Mr, 71
Albany, 53f.
America, xii, 3, 5–7, 10–12, 20, 24, 36–9, 41f., 45f., 51–4, 60, 68, 71, 76, 84, 88, 126f., 155f., 169f., 173, 192, 212
An Address to the Pious and Benevolent, etc., 20, 204
Anglicans, 9, 24, 29, 67f., 76, 78, 82, 128, 141, 146, 168
An Answer to several Charges, etc., 27f.
Anti-Roman Catholic sentiment, 43, 47, 80, 142–4, 179f.
Antigua, 19f., 204
Antrim, 87
Appelbe, R. Fuller, 186
Ardara, 49
Armagh, 73
Arthur, William, x, 12f., 17, 23f., 30, 61, 87–103, 110, 181, 183–5, 188, 203, 207–9, 214
Asbury, Francis, 11f., 76
Ashburton, 49
Ashgrove, 53
Ashton, Thomas, 53f.
Asia, 1, 20, 63, 104, 127, 150, 184
Ault, William, 119
Australasia, 37, 41, 144
Australia, 6, 24, 46, 54–9, 137, 143
Avard, Joseph, 70

Badulla, 63
Bahamas, 11, 161
Baker, Frank, 51f., 205
Ballingrane, 37, 69
Baltimore, xii

Banbridge, 51
Bandon, 146f.
Bangalore, 63
Baptists, 82, 136, 152
Baralong, 186
Barclay, W. C., 213
Bareilly, 170f., 173, 213
Barry, John, ix–x, 15, 146–53, 154, 162–7, 168, 185, 195, 211–13
Bathurst, 142
Batticaloa, 63
Baugh, G., 63
Beauchamp, A. M., 23, 63
Beauchamp, Charlotte E., 23, 63f.
Beaumont, Mr, 152
Bechuanaland, 186
Beecham, John, 139, 211f.
Belfast, 23, 45, 49, 60, 88f.
Bellamont, Earl of, 69f.
Benefits (of missionary involvement), 33f., 184f., 192
Bermuda, 8, 79, 148, 151, 160, 165
Best of Causes, The, 97
Bible, 94f., 97, 112
Bible Christians, 194ff.
Bijnor, 177
Bird Island Cove, 78
Birtwhistle, Allen, 19, 23, 202
Black, John, 72, 195
Black, William, 76f., 80
Blackhead, 76, 78
Black People, 60f., 101f., 129, 140, 166f.
Blackstock, Moses, 71, 195
Blanshards, 121
Boardman, Richard, 24
Böhler, Peter, 3
Bollen, J. D., 139
Bombay, 105, 123
Bonavista, 78
Booth, Robin, 33
Boston, 173, 213
Brahmanism, 92f., 110, 112

Briggs, William, 81, 196
British and Foreign Bible Society, 90
Brookeborough, 84
Brown, David, 49
Buckley, James, 209
Budaun, 171
Buddhism, 24, 90, 98, 114f., 134f., 190
Bunting, Jabez, 10, 43, 204
Bunting Dale, 140
Burin, 78
Burke's *Landed Gentry of Ireland*, 55
Butler, Clementina, 169
Butler, Edward, 177
Butler, John W., 175
Butler, William, 8, 60, 126, 168–80, 182, 190f., 213f.

Calcutta, 63, 107
Calvinism, 2, 4, 5, 10, 105f., 130, 145
Camden Valley, 53f., 69
Canada, x, 12, 15, 36–8, 41, 47f., 60, 67–86, 146, 148, 194–201
Canton, 64f.
Cape Colony, ix, 8, 128–31, 186
Cape Town, 15, 128f., 131f.
Carbonear, 7
Carey, William, xii
Carib, *see* Indians (Carib)
Caribbean, x, 15, 32
Carroll, John, 71f., 206
Cartwright, Richard, 56
Carwardine, Richard, xv, 7, 203
Case and his Cotemporaries, 71f., 206
Caste, 102, 112f.
Caughey, James, 9f.
Cavan (Canada), 71f.
Cavan (Ireland), 71, 73
Ceylon, 8, 15, 21, 23, 63, 88, 90, 92, 94, 105–7, 113, 115, 117, 120, 123–5, 127f., 130–7, 145–7, 169, 191, 210
Charleston, 11
China, 1, 33, 61, 64–6, 187
Christian Endeavour, 33
Christian Guardian, 13, 48, 68, 81, 153, 203, 206
Christmas Conference, xii, 155
Church Missionary Society (CMS), 13
Church of England, 78, 142

Church of Ireland, 15, 128, 146, 168
Clare, 73
Clarke, Adam, 17, 21, 30, 70, 87–103, 114–16, 124, 131, 147, 181, 183–5, 203, 205, 207–9, 214
Clavis Biblica, 94, 208
Clough, Benjamin, 120
Cloughjordan, 32, 77
Cochran, George, 81, 196
Coke, Thomas, xii, 5, 8, 11, 14f., 17, 19–21, 25, 70, 96, 104f., 118f., 123, 127, 131, 143, 147, 154–7, 183f., 204, 211f., 214
Cole, Lee, 26–7
Coleraine, 128
Colombo, 120, 136
Colpetty, 136f., 145
Communication, problems in, 120f., 123–6, 130, 138
Compendium of Missions, 170
Conception Bay, 76
Concord, 170
Congregational Church, 11
Connecticut, 80
Cooper, J. I., 67
Cork, 15, 33, 40, 55f., 146f., 150
Cornish, G. H., 194f., 207
Cornwallis, Lord, 69
Coughlan, Laurence, 7f., 53, 67, 69, 76, 79, 194
Courant, The, 192
Crook, William, 43, 67, 205f.
Crookshank, C. H., 48, 55, 211
Cultural differences, 65f., 140, 172, 190f.
Cultural superiority, 133, 190
Curnock, Nehemiah, 203, 205
Cyclopaedia of Methodism in Canada, 194f., 207

Darby, William A., 15f., 203
Davies, Rupert, 202f.
Dawson, Thomas, 69f., 206
Deale, Alfred, 18
Delaware, 126
Delhi, 171
Denmark, 106
Dewart, Edward Hartley, 68, 81, 197
Dissident, 10–12
Donegal, 9, 59, 104, 126
Doolittle, Thomas W., 204

Down, 77, 169
Dromgoole, Edward, 8
Dromore, 77
Drumsna, 53
Dublin, 9, 11, 18, 20–3, 27f., 30, 45, 60, 70, 72, 75, 83, 87, 168
Duff, Alexander, 176
Dufferin and Clandeboy, Lord, 42f.
Duncan, Peter, 212
Dutch, 129, 133

Eagar, Edward, 55–9, 206
Eagar, Richard, 5
Earnest Appeal to Men of Reason and Religion, 19
East India Company, 1, 184
Eayrs, G., 203, 206
Education, 15, 62f., 81, 88, 102, 107–9, 135f., 151–63, 165, 176f.; see also Schools
Edwards, Maldwyn, 203, 207, 212
Edwards, Thomas, 211
El Abogado Cristiano, 177, 180
Elliott, Charles, 9, 203
Elliott, James, 80f., 197
Ellis, William, 77–9, 207
Elliston, 78
Embury, Philip, xi, 8, 10, 52–4, 60, 69
Emfundesweni, 63, 206
Emigration, x, 17, 35, 36–49, 67, 73, 127, 187, 205
Empire Loyalists, 47, 54
Enniskillen, 84
Enquiry into the Obligations of Christians, etc., xii
Erskine, George, 8, 131, 137–9, 211
Evangelism, 54, 88, 175f., 183, 187

Failure, 17f., 22, 140, 178, 190f.
Faizabad, 171
Far East, 90
Ferguson, George, 80, 197
Fermanagh, 73f.
Ffrench, Patrick, 32, 160f., 204, 212
Fiji, 61, 144, 188
Finance, problems of, 26–30, 119–23, 131f., 145f., 190
Finance, support for missions, 12–14, 20f., 26–30, 33, 107, 116, 120, 139, 142, 177, 184, 188
Findlay, G. G., 203, 205–8, 213f.
Findlay, M. G., 208

Fintona, 48
Fitzpatrick, David, 36, 204f.
Fletcher, John W., 106
Foreign Languages, 2, 4, 25f., 89f., 93, 106f., 127, 140, 175, 177, 190
France, 24, 146f.
Frederick County, 53
Freshman, Charles, 81
From Boston to Bareilly and Back, 173, 213

Galle, 105, 121, 135f.
Galway, 40, 73
Gambia, The, 15, 61
General Committee, see under Wesleyan Methodist Missionary Society
George, A. R., 202f.
Georgetown, 106
Georgia, 2–4
Germany, 3, 37, 52
Gibraltar, 8
Gilbert, Nathaniel, 19
Glenelg, Lord, 142
Godbold, A., 205
Gold Coast, 61
Gottry, Kenneth A., 20
Grateful Hill, 147
Gregg, Samuel, 203
Grenada, 156
Griffith, Walter, 89
Guanajuato, 174
Gubbi, 92
Guernsey, 20, 70, 148

Halifax, 77
Hamilton, 148, 151, 165
Hammett, William, 8, 10f., 20, 157f., 212
Harbour Grace, 76, 79
Harbour of Trinity, 77
Hare, Robert, 48
Hare, John J., 48
Harmon, N. B., 208, 213f.
Hartley, 204
Harvard, William, 106, 120
Heathen, xii, 3, 16, 20, 22–4, 29, 91, 94, 108, 110, 116, 133f., 139, 143, 176, 183, 189
Heck, Barbara, xi, 8, 10, 52–4, 60, 69
Hempton, David, 43, 105, 183, 205, 209, 211, 214

Herrnhut, 3
Hewson, L. A., 210
Hibernian Auxiliary, 13f., 18, 22, 30f., 33, 203
Hindostan, 1
Hinduism, 1, 92–4, 102, 109–13, 190
History of Methodism in Ireland, 48, 55, 211
History of the Methodist Church in Great Britain, ix, 202f.
Hoey, Isobel, 63
Holdsworth, W. W., 203, 205–7, 213f.
Holy Communion, 112f.
Honduras, 212
Hong Kong, 8
Hoole, Elijah, 204
Hoover, J. D., 74, 207
Horne, James, 160
Huguenots, 146
Hunter River, 48
Huston, John, 204
Huston, R., 72

Idolatry, 92–4, 109f., 112, 132, 208
Ilmes, Thomas, 150
Immigration, 49, 67, 70f.
Imperialism, 186
India, 1, 3, 6, 23, 33, 60, 63f., 87–9, 92, 94f., 102, 105–7, 113f., 118, 121f., 126f., 168f., 170–3, 174–8, 180, 182, 185, 204
Indians (American), 2, 3
Indians (Canadian), 78
Indians (Carib), 157f.
Industrial Mission, 99f., 115–18, 176f.
Instructions to Missionaries, 158, 163, 212
Iowa, 9
Irish Christian Advocate, 18, 28, 33, 46, 49, 192, 203–5, 207, 211, 213f.
Irish Evangelist, 16, 32, 36, 42f., 46, 203–5
Irish 'Firsts', 7f., 47f., 52–5, 69f., 76, 80, 106, 128, 170
Irish Methodism in the Twentieth Century, 31, 204, 206
Irish Mission, 13–15, 25–30, 33, 162, 211
Islam, 24, 91, 95, 116, 136, 176, 190

Is the Bible to lie under a Ban in India?, 94
Italy, 89
Itinerancy, 8, 52, 114, 146, 183f., 190f.

Jackson, Andrew, 8f.
Jaffna, 105f., 120
Jamaica, x, 8, 10f., 15f., 101, 147f., 150f., 159f., 162, 164, 185, 212
Jamaica Resolutions, 158–61, 165
Janes, E., 5–7
Japan, 81
Jeffers, Wellington, 81, 198
Jeffery, Frederick, 31, 204
Jersey, 20, 88
Jews, 24, 81, 91, 151
Johannesburg, 186
Johnson, Sir Alex, 114
Johnston, Edward, 81–5, 199, 207
Johnston, Thomas, 15
John Street Church, 53f.
Jones, David, 211
Juvenile Missionary Association, 21f.
Juvenile Offerings, 14

Kanarese, 90
Karachi, 51
Kean (Keene), Arthur, 27
Ker, John, 46, 205
Kerry, 55, 73
Killarney, 55
Kilner, John, 189, 204
Kingsbury, Mr, 47
Kingston (Canada), 81
Kingston (Jamaica), 151f.
Kinsale, 146f., 151, 212
Koran, 95

Labrador, 78
Ladies' Committee for the Amelioration, etc., 22, 89
Lahore, 172
Laity, 4, 5, 7, 10, 39, 46, 48f., 50–66, 69, 74–7, 79, 105, 117, 142, 174
Lakemba, 188
Land of the Veda, The, 173
Languages, *see* Foreign Languages
Lanktree, Matthew, 15
Ledsam (Lidsam), Jeremiah, 47f.
Lee, J., 36, 204

Leigh, Samuel, 55
Leitrim, 53
Lewis, John, 209
Limerick, 37, 49, 52, 69f.
Lindsay, Robert, 15
Lisburn, 183
Literature, 62, 81, 173, 175–7, 179f.
Londonderry, 40, 59, 87
London Missionary Society (LMS), 184
Louth, 15, 73
Lowe, Charlotte, 63
Lower Canada, 69
Lucknow, 171, 174, 177
Lumley, W., 204
Lusher, R. L., 207, 213
Lutherans, 52, 82
Lynch, Hugh, 104, 126f., 210
Lynch, James, 8, 92, 104–27, 131, 137, 169, 185, 190, 208–11
Lynch, Samuel, 104, 126f., 132, 210

MacDade, S. H., 49
Macquarie, Governor, 58f.
Madras, 8, 63, 105–7, 110, 114f., 118, 120–22, 124f., 190
Mafeking, 186
Magistracy, criticisms of, 152, 162, 165
Maitland, 47f., 142
Malaboch, 186
Manitoba, 71
Manual of Laws and Discipline, 47
Maori wars, 144
Maroons, 150
Marsden, George, 209
Maryland, 1, 52f.
Mayo, 15, 74
McArthur, Alexander, 61
McArthur, Sir William, 30, 59–63, 73, 143, 188f., 206
McBride, Sergeant-Major, 51
McCaine, Alexander, 10–12
McCarty, James, 69
McClure, William, 12, 199
McCrea, Alexander, 31, 204, 206
McCullagh, T., 206
McDade, S. H., 49
McDowell, Samuel, 77, 199, 207
McGeary, John, 76f., 79, 199
McKeag, Hugh, 13
McKee, T. A., 204

McKenny, John, ix–x, 8, 47f., 116, 125, 128–45, 186, 190, 210f.
McLachlan, Noel, 55–9
McMillen, Dr, 14
McMullen, James, 8
Meath, 73
Medical missions, 33, 64, 66, 177
Melbourne, 142
Melbourne, Professor A. C. V., 58f.
Membership, 38, 173, 205
Messmore, J. H., 213
Methodism, as a Missionary Movement, see under Missionary Movement
Methodist Episcopal Church (MEC), xii, 5–12, 45f., 53, 71, 74, 80–2, 104, 126, 148, 152f., 168, 170f., 173f., 179, 194ff., 214
Methodist Missionary Society (MMS), see under Wesleyan Methodist Missionary Society
Methodist New Connexion, 12, 74, 194ff.
Methodist Protestant Church, 11
Methodist Women's Association (MWA), 23
Mexico, 8, 60, 126f., 168, 173–5, 177, 179f.
Millersburgh, 210
Minority, Methodism as a, x–xi, 187f.
Miraflores, 174
Miramichi, 72
Missionary Committee, see Wesleyan Methodist Missionary Society
Mission and Evangelism, xv, 181f., 185f., 188, 190f., 214
Missionary Movement, Methodism as a, ix, 1, 4, 17, 95, 182, 208
Missionary Notices, 21, 23, 204–9, 211, 213f.
Missionary Secretaries, see Wesleyan Methodist Missionary Society
Missionary Strategy, see under Strategy
Mohammedanism, see Islam
Monaghan, 69, 85
Montreal, 146, 148f.
Montsioa, Chief, 186
Moore, H., 214
Moradabad, 171, 177

Moravians, 3, 152
Morley, George, 204
Morrows, 71
Mount Allison, 72
Muff, 104
Murray, Rt. Hon. Sir George, 163, 213
Muslims, *see* Islam
Mysore, 87f., 90, 110

Native Ministry, 108, 113, 115, 137, 145, 173, 179, 188
Neal, Major George, 69
Necessity and Existence of Missions, 94
Negroes, 4, 19, 60, 155, 163–5
Neill, John E., 55
Nero, 162
Newfoundland, 8, 15, 20, 67, 69, 75–80, 207
Newry, 107
Newstead, Robert, 134
New Brunswick, 72, 75
New England, 169
New Hampshire, 54, 170
New South Wales, 23, 37, 47, 49, 56–9, 61, 128, 137–45
New World, 5, 41, 126
New York, 6, 45, 52–4, 60, 81, 172
New Zealand, 24, 37, 48f., 55, 144
Nicholas, Dr, 204
North America, 6, 8, 24, 46, 49, 62, 68, 79
North Carolina, 155
Northern Ireland, 9
Nova Scotia, 6, 15, 20, 69, 75f.

Oglethorpe, General, 2
Ohio, 126
O'Kelly, James, 10–11
O'Flaherty, P., 207
O'Tuathaigh, G., 36, 39f., 204f.
Ontario, 34, 68, 74
Orizaba, 174
Ottawa, 72
Oudh, 170f., 177
Ouseley, Gideon, 48, 81
Outram, General Sir James, 178f.

Pachuca, 174
Pakistan, 51
Palatine Community, 37, 47, 52, 54, 69, 71

Palestine, 204
Paramatta, 142
Parker, E. W., 177f., 213
Partnership, 20–3, 188f.
Philadelphia, 45, 49
Piggin, Stuart, 183, 214
Pilcher, J., 204
Pilibhit, 171
Pilmoor, Joseph, 24
Place, Ann, 146
Plan of the Society for the Establishment of Missions, xii, 19f.
Plütschau, H., 3, 106
Point Pedro, 63
Politics, 61f., 82f., 154, 157–67
Polynesians, 61
Pondo, 63
Portadown, 15, 23
Portaferry, 169
Port de Grave, 78
Port Hope, 72
Portrush, 205
Portuguese, 133
Potts, John, 75, 81, 200
Preaching, 80f., 88, 94, 98, 111, 130, 149f., 155, 170, 175
Presbyterians, 10, 67f., 71, 74, 76, 82, 176
Primitive Methodists (Canada), 74, 194ff., 207
Primitive Wesleyans, 12, 147, 151f., 194ff.
Prince Edward Island, 70
Principles of the Christian Religion, 90f., 97, 208
Publishing, *see* Literature
Puebla, 174
Punjab, 213

Quakers, 82
Quebec, 20, 81
Queretaro, 174

Race, 65, 101f., 108, 113–15, 151, 166, 185
Rathkeale, 37
Reilly, William, 27f., 204
Relationships, between Ireland and the WMMS, 17, 25, 32–4, 189f.
Relationships, between Missionaries and the Missionary Society, 118–26, 131f., 136–8, 161, 172, 189f.

Relationships, Overseas, 76–7, 81f., 140–2, 151f., 161, 167, 172, 178, 189f.
Remmington, John, 77, 80, 207
Republican Methodist Church, 11
Rhine valley, 37
Richey, Matthew, 80, 200
Richmond (Canada), 72
Rideau, 72
Rio del Monte, 174
Robinson, James, 48
Rohilkhand, 170f., 177
Roman Catholicism, 1, 8f., 11f., 17, 24, 40, 43, 47, 60, 63, 67–9, 80, 93, 104, 109f., 127, 142–4, 174f., 179f., 181
Roscommon, 40, 73
Rosetta Stone, 90
Ross, John, 8
Rowe, Clementina, 169
Royapettah, 106
Ruckle, 71
Rupp, Gordon, 202f.
Rutledge, John, 161f., 212f.
Ryan, Henry, 80, 194
Ryland, William, 8f.

St Bartholomew's, 160
St Eustatius, 160
St John's, 79–80
St Kitts, 8, 10
St Lawrence, 69
St Vincent, 157
Sackville, 72
Sam's Creek, 53
Samuel, P., 212
Santa Cruz, 150, 183
Savanna-la-Mar, 150
Schools, 25, 28, 87f., 94, 97, 107–9, 117, 135f., 151, 173f., 176f., 191; see also Education
Schumacher, E. F., x
Semmel, Bernard, 183–5, 214
Shahjahanpur, 171
Shastras, 93, 95
Sherlock, Benjamin, 73f., 201
Shetland Islands, 88, 99f., 116
Shillington, Barbara, 48
Sidmouth, Lord, 183f.
Sierra Leone, 61
Sikhs, 177f.
Singhalese, 105, 125, 132f., 136f.

Slavery, 4, 8f., 19, 100f., 118, 126, 133, 147–9, 151–3, 154–67, 210
Sligo, 8, 33, 53, 73
Smith, T. W., 72, 206f.
Smith's Creek, 71
Social Influence, 4, 5, 61f., 99–103, 115–18
Society for Promoting Female Education, etc., 102
Society for the Propagation of the Gospel (SPG), 67, 69
Soldiers, 8, 51, 69, 72, 128f., 133, 136, 160, 174
Somerset, Lord Charles, 129
Soper, Lord, 183
South Africa, 8, 23f., 63, 100, 107, 116, 131, 145, 186, 210
South Carolina, 4, 11
South Monaghan, 71
South Seas, 57
Spanish Town, 147, 149
Spurgeon, Charles H., 62
Stephenson, F. C., 206
Stephenson, John, 8
Stephenson, T. B., 207
Stevens, Abel, 6, 203, 206
Strategy, Missionary, 49, 107, 135–7, 140, 144f., 174, 179f., 182, 189
Strawbridge, Robert, 8, 10f., 52f., 60
Stretton, John, 79f.
Sunday Service, 207
Summerfield, John, 6
Surinam, 1
Sutherland, A., 207
Sweet, William W., 53
Switzer, 71
Sydney, 48, 55, 57, 142
Sydney Gazette, 56

Taggart, Norman W., 203
Tamil, 105–8, 125f.
Tandragee, 53
Taylor, J., 204, 207, 209f.
Teasey, Liz., 63
Telford, John, 203, 212
Thames (Canada), 72
Thoburn, James M., 170f.
Thomey, Arthur, 79f.
Thoughts on Slavery, 155f.
Toland, John, 161
Tonga, 128

Tongue of Fire, The, 97, 208f.
Toronto, 7, 15, 48, 68, 148, 152, 194
Townsend, W. J., 203, 206
Tranquebar, 3, 106
Trincomalee, 115
Trinidad, 183
Tuffey, Commissary, 69
Tweedy, Robert, 72
Tyrone, 73, 81

Udy, James S., 59, 206
United Church of Canada, 76
United States of America, 6, 8, 10, 12, 36f., 40, 42, 46, 48, 53, 60, 68, 75, 85, 104, 126f., 143, 148, 169, 175
Upper Canada, 69, 80, 82, 107

Vandieman's Land (*sic*), 137
Vickers, John, 156f., 204, 212
Victoria, 49
Virginia, 155

Walsh, Thomas, 192f.
Washington, 8
Washington, George, 69, 156
Waterford, 73, 79
Watson, Richard, 118, 122, 158, 204, 209, 212
Waugh, Thomas, 39, 42
Wears, William, 209
Webb, Thomas, 206
Webster, Ebenezer, 16, 204
Wesley, Charles, 2–4
Wesley, John, ix, 1–5, 19f., 37, 52, 69, 76, 79f., 82, 87, 106, 154f., 189f., 192f., 207, 212, 214
Wesley, Samuel, 1f.
Wesley, Susanna, 2f., 209
Wesley Methodist Church (Canada), 74, 148, 152, 194ff.
Wesley Methodist Missionary Society (WMMS), 12–18, 19–35,
39, 42, 46, 48f., 51, 56, 58f., 62, 78, 83–5, 87, 89, 95, 106f., 111–13, 115–25, 130–2, 136–40, 143–5, 147f., 150, 152f., 158–65, 184–6, 188–90, 203ff.
Wesley Preacher, The, 149
Wesleypore, 177f., 191
Wesleyville, 72
West Indies, xii, 6, 11, 19–21, 32, 51, 101f., 118, 133, 156f., 159, 161, 182, 184
Wexford, 169
Whitham, F. E., 75
Wiggins, John, 16, 204
Wilberforce, William, 154, 160
Wilson, William, 207
Windsor (New South Wales), 55f., 142
Wollongong, 48
Women's Foreign Missionary Society (WFMS), 169
Women Missionaries, *see under* Beauchamp, Butler, C., Lowe, Teasey and Wood
Women, supporting Missions, *see under* Heck, Ladies' Committee etc., Methodist Women's Association, and WFMS
Women's Work in India, 102
Wood, Annie M., 63–6, 206
Wood, Connie, 64
Wood, Fanny, 64, 66
Woodsworth, James, 75, 207
Workman, H. B., 203, 206
World Council of Churches (WCC), xv, 181f.

York (later Toronto), 148
Youghal, 63

Zend Avesta, 95
Ziegenbalg, B., 3, 106